THE EPIC OF THE PATRIARCH
The Jacob Cycle and the Narrative
Traditions of Canaan and Israel

HARVARD SEMITIC MUSEUM

HARVARD SEMITIC MONOGRAPHS

edited by
Frank Moore Cross

Number 42
THE EPIC OF THE PATRIARCH
The Jacob Cycle and the Narrative
Traditions of Canaan and Israel
by
Ronald S. Hendel

Ronald S. Hendel

THE EPIC OF THE PATRIARCH
The Jacob Cycle and the Narrative Traditions of Canaan and Israel

Scholars Press
Atlanta, Georgia

THE EPIC OF THE PATRIARCH
The Jacob Cycle and the Narrative
Traditions of Canaan and Israel

by
Ronald S. Hendel

The figure on the cover is a West Semitic lyre player from a wall
painting in an Egyptian tomb (Beni Hasan), early nineteenth
century B.C.E.

Library of Congress Cataloging in Publication Data

Hendel, Ronald S.
  The epic of the patriarch.

  (Harvard Semitic monographs ; 42)
  Revision of the author's thesis (Ph. D.--Harvard
University, 1985)
  Bibliography: p.
  Includes index.
  1. Jacob (Biblical patriarch) 2. Bible. O.T.
Genesis--Criticism, interpretation, etc. 3. Narration
in the Bible. 4. Ugaritic literature--Relation to the
Old Testament. 5. Heroes in the Bible. I. Title.
II. Series: Harvard Semitic monographs ; no. 42.
BS580.J3H46 1987   222'.11066   87-23409
ISBN 1-55540-184-8

Printed in the United States of America
on acid-free paper

You by the cavern over the black stairs,
Rung bone and blade, the verticals of Adam,
And, manned by midnight, Jacob to the stars.

Dylan Thomas

Contents

Preface

Jacob, if he ever existed, would no doubt be perplexed at the ways that his stories are scrutinized nowadays, much as Moses was confused by the discussions in Rabbi Akiba's academy, according to the Talmudic legend. Nonetheless, biblical criticism goes on, each generation approaching the text with new questions and new concerns.

This book is a revision of a Ph.D. thesis submitted to the Department of Near Eastern Languages and Civilizations at Harvard University in 1985. I wish to thank my thesis advisor, Frank M. Cross, and the other members of my thesis committee, Paul D. Hanson and Michael D. Coogan, for their advice, criticisms, and encouragement. I also wish to thank my other teachers for ideas and comments that directly or indirectly affected the shape of my work, especially William L. Moran, Thomas O. Lambdin, Gregory Nagy, and Albert B. Lord. The following were kind enough to read the work and offer helpful suggestions: JoAnn Hackett, Susan Niditch, and Lloyd Barré. My thanks also to Eugene Lovering for his assistance in the preparation of the final manuscript.

In 1985 part two of this work was awarded the Mitchell Dahood Memorial Prize in Biblical Hebrew and Northwest Semitic, under the title "Parallel Themes in the Ugaritic Epic Poems and the Hebrew Bible." I wish to express my appreciation to the Society of Biblical Literature and Doubleday for sponsoring this award.

And finally, my thanks to Ann Hendel, who doesn't have to read this book.

Ronald S. Hendel
July, 1987

Abbreviations

AB	Anchor Bible
AHw	W. von Soden, *Akkadisches Handwörterbuch*
AnBib	Analecta biblica
ANEP	J. B. Pritchard (ed.), *Ancient Near East in Pictures*
ANET	J. B. Pritchard (ed.), *Ancient Near Eastern Texts*
AnOr	Analecta orientalia
AOAT	Alter Orient und Altes Testament
AOS	American Oriental Series
BA	*Biblical Archaeologist*
BASOR	*Bulletin of the American Schools of Oriental Research*
BDB	Brown-Driver-Briggs, *Hebrew and English Lexicon of the Old Testament*
Bib	*Biblica*
BKAT	Biblischer Kommentar: Altes Testament
BZAW	Beihefte zur ZAW
CTA	A. Herdner, *Corpus des tablettes en cunéiforme alphabétiques*
CBQ	*Catholic Biblical Quarterly*
CBQMS	Catholic Biblical Quarterly - Monograph Series
DN	Divine name
ErIsr	Eretz Israel
ExpTim	*Expository Times*
Gilg.	SB Gilgamesh Epic, Tablets I-XII
Gilg. Har.	OB Gilgamesh Epic, Harmal fragments
Gilg. Me.	OB Gilgamesh Epic, Meissner fragment
Gilg. P.	OB Gilgamesh Epic, Pennsylvania tablet
Gilg. Y.	OB Gilgamesh Epic, Yale tablet
HKAT	Handkommentar zum Alten Testament
HR	*History of Religions*
HSM	Harvard Semitic Monographs
HTR	*Harvard Theological Review*
ICC	International Critical Commentary

IDBSup	Supplementary volume to G. Buttrick (ed.), *Interpreter's Dictionary of the Bible*
IEJ	*Israel Exploration Journal*
JANES	*Journal of the Ancient Near Eastern Society of Columbia University*
JAOS	*Journal of the American Oriental Society*
JBL	*Journal of Biblical Literature*
JCS	*Journal of Cuneiform Studies*
JNES	*Journal of Near Eastern Studies*
JPOS	*Journal of the Palestine Oriental Society*
JSOTSup	Journal for the Study of the Old Testament - Supplement Series
JTS	*Journal of Theological Studies*
KAI	Donner-Röllig, *Kanaanäische und aramäische Inschriften*
KB	Koehler-Baumgartner, *Lexicon in Veteris Testamenti Libros*
LSJ	Liddell-Scott-Jones, *Greek-English Lexicon*
OB	Old Babylonian
OTL	Old Testament Library
OTS	*Oudtestamentische Studien*
PE	Eusebius, *Praeparatio evangelica*
RB	*Revue biblique*
RS	Ras Shamra
SB	Standard Babylonian
SBL	Society of Biblical Literature
TDOT	G. Botterweck and H. Ringgren (eds.), *Theological Dictionary of the Old Testament*
UF	*Ugarit-Forschungen*
VT	*Vetus Testamentum*
VTSup	Vetus Testamentum, Supplements
ZA	*Zeitschrift für Assyriologie*
ZAW	*Zeitschrift für die alttestamentliche Wissenschaft*
ZDMG	*Zeitschrift der deutschen morgenländischen Gesellschaft*
ZDPV	*Zeitschrift des deutschen Palästina-Vereins*

Introduction

In recent years the study of biblical narrative has experienced a metamorphosis. The great historical and theological questions posed by the eighteenth and nineteenth century biblical scholars have been altered by the influences of anthropology, literary criticism, and related disciplines. The result is a congeries of approaches, with the consequence that some researchers are turning their backs on the achievements of the past, while others are denying the potential of new methods and new questions. The bifurcation of old and new is unfortunate: interpretation is a total, comprehensive task or it is nothing at all.

One of the old words of biblical studies, "exegesis," still appears to indicate the essence of the task. The Greek noun *exēgēsis* comes from the verb *exēgeisthai*, meaning "to lead the way, to go first." An *exēgētēs* is "one who leads on, an advisor" or "an expounder or interpreter" of oracles, dreams, omens, and sacred customs.[1] To our modern sensibility the image of an advisor to a group or to a governor does not conflict with the image of an advisor to a reader of a text. The task of "leading the way" in difficult terrain is common, whether the terrain be geographical, political, or textual. The terrain may be difficult, and mistakes may be made, but the task of advising goes on.

The biblical text is difficult territory. Problems abound from basic matters of scribal inaccuracies in the process of transmission to more complex matters concerning the intention(s) of the author(s) of a text. How do we even define the biblical text, when it appears that the sources and authorship are often plural? How do we define the author of a text, when it appears that the literary composer is often mediating the oral tradition of the culture, and when it seems that editors have altered the original shape of the composed text? From whose standpoint do we interpret the text: that of the literary composer? the ancient

[1]See the references in *LSJ*, 593.

Israelite audience? the modern reader? the Rabbis or Church Fathers?

There are no set answers to any of these questions; one's choice of stance is an individual choice, perhaps even an "ethical" choice.[2] The stance that I have chosen is generally that of the narrative, cultic, and cultural traditions presumed by the original audience of the written text, in short, the world-view of ancient Israel. Such a stance has its inherent methodological problems, but I find it unavoidable in order to grasp what is individual and compelling in an ancient narrative. Other interpretations are possible, but I believe that it is only fair to begin with the culture presupposed by the text, and to let the timeless qualities of a text arise from the place of its origins.

The sage of Ecclesiastes asked: מִי יוֹדֵעַ פֵּשֶׁר דָּבָר "Who knows the interpretation of a matter?" (8:1) The question is rhetorical, for no one possesses a definitive interpretation. At least one Israelite author knew this; perhaps all of them did. It would be ungrateful, at the very least, to pretend that any of the interpretations offered in this study are definitive. All I can hope for is to offer advice, to present a series of possible interpretations of the Jacob story and related texts.

[2]See the discussion of E. D. Hirsch, Jr., *The Aims of Interpretation* (Chicago: University of Chicago, 1976) 74-92.

Part I

A History of Interpretation

A comprehensive presentation of the history of the interpretation of the Jacob cycle is far beyond the scope of the present work. A simple catalogue of the relevant literature in a recent commentary takes up over thirty pages.[1] In spite of the massive bulk of past studies, the resurgence of interest in the patriarchal narratives has generated two full-length reviews of scholarship, one in German and one in English.[2] Since these admirable treatments already exist, I will take the liberty of merely stressing the highlights of the history of interpretation, as a backdrop to the following chapters. As in all aspects of humanistic scholarship, the past is scattered with works of brilliance and works of idiosyncrasy. Since these two traits are often (perhaps usually) mixed, I will attempt to exercise the hindsight of the observer and indicate what of past works is a genuine contribution and what, in retrospect, is merely talk. If some of my judgments seem unduly harsh, it should be kept in mind that my joining issue with these thinkers is a testimony to the continuing importance of their work and thoughts.

HERDER

Johann Gottfried von Herder (1744-1803) was a prolific German critic and philosopher whose lifelong interest in folk poetry and the Bible left an indelible impression on biblical scholarship.[3]

---

[1]C. Westermann, *Genesis 12-36* (BKAT I/2; Neukirchen-Vluyn: Neukirchener, 1981) 91-115, 128-138, 495-496.

[2]H. Weidmann, *Die Patriarchen und ihre Religion im Licht der Forschung seit Julius Wellhausen* (Göttingen: Vandenhoeck & Ruprecht, 1968); W. McKane, *Studies in the Patriarchal Narratives* (Edinburgh: Handsel, 1979).

[3]For Herder's influence on biblical scholarship, see H.-J. Kraus, *Geschichte der historisch-kritischen Erforschung des Alten Testaments* (3rd ed.; Neukirchen-Vluyn: Neukirchener, 1982) 114-132; H. W. Frei, *The Eclipse of Biblical Narrative:*

1

Herder was a man of many interests and moods; the historian Peter Gay describes him as "the thinker who preached a sentimental religion of humanity in which historicism, poetry, piety, primitivism, and rationalism were strangely woven together and touched with genius."[4] Herder regarded himself an enemy of the proud rationalism of the Enlightenment and devoted much of his work to the exploration of folk cultures and folk literatures as a corrective to the Eurocentric attitudes of the *philosophes*. He initiated the first collections of German folk songs and inspired the work of Goethe, the Grimms, and others in preserving and transforming local folk literatures.

His interest in biblical narrative followed the same impulse. The roots of the Genesis stories in folk narrative were all too clear to Herder. Against the traditional doctrine of the church, Herder declared:

> In human fashion must one read the Bible, for it is a book written by humans for humans: human is the language, human the external means by which it was written and preserved; human finally is the sense with which it may be grasped, every aid that illumines it, as well as the aim and use to which it is to be applied.[5]

Of the biblical narratives, Herder wrote:

> Therefore, the stories which we have of Paradise, of the Patriarchs, and of the oldest fortunes of our race are shepherds' stories: they contain that which a shepherd might know and preserve in his sphere of life, as much as was adopted to his forms of thought and mode of living.[6]

A Study in Eighteenth and Nineteenth Century Hermeneutics (New Haven: Yale University, 1974) 183-201; and T. Willi, *Herders Beitrag zum Verstehen des Alten Testaments* (Tübingen: Mohr, 1971). See also R. T. Clark, Jr., *Herder: His Life and Thought* (Berkeley: University of California, 1955); and I. Berlin, *Vico and Herder: Two Studies in the History of Ideas* (New York: Viking, 1976) 143-216.

[4]P. Gay, *The Enlightenment: An Interpretation. The Rise of Modern Paganism* (New York: Norton, 1977) 351.

[5]Herder, *Briefe, das Studium der Theologie betreffend*, in *Sämmtliche Werke*, ed. B. Suphan (Berlin: Weidmann, 1877-1913) vol. 10, p. 7.

[6]Herder, *Vom Geist der ebraischen Poesie*, I (Leipzig: Barth, 1825) 36. ET: *The Spirit of Hebrew Poetry*, trans. J. Marsh (Burlington: Smith, 1833).

Herder's emphasis on the "forms of thought and mode of living" (*Denkart und Lebensweise*) of the people of biblical Israel represented a significant advance in the interpretation of biblical narrative. The frame of reference for interpretation was no longer to be the doctrines of religion or the norms of modern culture, rather the goal was to think historically into the life setting of the original tellers of the tales. The stories were conditioned by their original cultural circumstances; thus we must carry ourselves back and look at the stories through their eyes.

Herder invented a word for this process: *Einfühlung*, feeling one's way into the spirit of something; we would call it sympathetic understanding or empathy. Herder wrote:

> In order to judge a nation, one must live in their time, in their country, must experience their modes of thinking and feeling, must see how they lived, how they were educated, what scenes they saw, what were the objects of their passions, the character of their atmosphere, their skies, the structure of their organs, their dances, and their music.[7]

Herder regarded the patriarchal stories as "shepherds' stories" (*Hirtensagen*).[8] The tales are touched with the beauty and poetry of a childlike, simple people. Indeed, Herder felt that the purity of the stories was best appreciated when heard "under the open sky, and if possible, at dawn . . . because it was itself the dawn of the illumination of the world, while our race was yet in its infancy."[9] Herder's sentimental primitivism is of a piece with his interpretive framework: the stories are beautiful because they are simple, primitive, and untouched by "so-called culture."[10]

Herder's contribution to the interpretation of the Jacob narrative was twofold. First, he contributed the essential strategy of comprehending the cultural setting of a story as a prelude to understanding the story itself. This strategy was never emphasized as vigorously before and has often been neglected since. The second part of his contribution was less fortunate. The

[7]Ibid., 4-5.
[8]Ibid., 36.
[9]Ibid., 27.
[10]See Berlin, *Vico and Herder*, 180.

companion to Herder's cultural emphasis was his primitivism. Herder's advocacy of the simplicity and purity of the original biblical narratives has had a powerful influence on subsequent biblical scholarship. In spite of the thorough critique of primitivism in other branches of the humanities,[11] primitivism still remains a presupposition in certain circles of biblical scholarship.[12] Especially among many biblical "form critics," the two sides of Herder's interpretive approach, the cultural insight and the sentimental primitivism, have simply remained together, the explanatory power of the former tending to overcome the inadequacy of the latter. It is difficult to fault Herder for his primitivism, but it is essential to understand it as a symptom of his own cultural bias, and not to import it into modern interpretive strategies.

WELLHAUSEN

Julius Wellhausen (1844-1918), the greatest biblical scholar of the nineteenth century, formulated the classical account of the "documentary hypothesis," the analysis of the source documents of the Pentateuch.[13] The existence of different source documents in the Pentateuch had been known since the mid-eighteenth century,[14] but it was not until Wellhausen's *Prolegomena zur*

---

[11]E.g., E. E. Evans-Pritchard, *Theories of Primitive Religion* (Oxford: Clarendon, 1965); C. Lévi-Strauss, *The Savage Mind* (Chicago: University of Chicago, 1966); D. Sperber, "Is Symbolic Thought Prerational?" in *Between Belief and Transgression: Structuralist Essays in Religion, History, and Myth*, eds. M. Izard and P. Smith, trans. J. Leavitt (Chicago: University of Chicago, 1982) 245-264.

[12]For a critique of primitivism in biblical form criticism, see S. M. Warner, "Primitive Saga Men" *VT* 29 (1979) 325-335; see also the critical remarks of M. Douglas, *Purity and Danger* (London: Routledge & Kegan Paul, 1966) 25-27, 45; and J. W. Rogerson, *Anthropology and the Old Testament* (Sheffield: JSOT Press, 1984) 46-65..

[13]On Wellhausen's work, see Kraus, *Geschichte*, 255-274; L. Perlitt, *Vatke und Wellhausen* (BZAW 94; Berlin: Töpelmann, 1965) 153-243; J. W. Rogerson, *Old Testament Criticism in the Nineteenth Century: England and Germany* (Philadelphia: Fortress, 1985) 257-272; and the articles by R. Smend, D. A. Knight, J. H. Hayes, P. D. Miller, Jr., L. H. Silberman, and B. S. Childs in *Semeia* 25 (1982).

[14]Kraus, *Geschichte*, 95-97.

Geschichte Israels, first published in 1878,[15] that the nature and extent of the sources was finally placed on a stable, historical footing.   Although significant aspects of Wellhausen's presentation have been superseded, the basic identification and sequence of the documents has remained secure.[16] J (the Yahwist) is the oldest source, followed by E (the Elohist), both from the period of the early monarchy. D (the Deuteronomistic source) is next in the sequence, and the last source, dating from around the period of the Babylonian Exile, is P (the Priestly source).

The history of the biblical traditions was, for Wellhausen, equivalent to the history of the biblical documents. The oldest document, J, composed in the era of the monarchy, projects an idealized view of Israelite prehistory from the point of view of the literary composer: "this later age is here unintentionally projected, in its inner and outward characteristics, into extreme antiquity, and is reflected there like a radiant mirage."[17]

Although he shared Herder's aesthetic bent and his primitivism,[18] Wellhausen interposed the literary document between the oral origin of the stories and the final Pentateuchal work, thus setting a limit to the investigation of the early development of the stories. For Wellhausen and his followers, the era prior to the monarchy was *ein vielsagendes Vakuum*, "a many-storied vacuum."[19] It will be seen that this is an excessively cautious view, though such caution is not to be rejected simply as nihilism. What was methodological caution for Wellhausen, however, all too easily became dogma for his followers.

---

[15]The title of the first edition, *Geschichte Israels, I* (Berlin: Reimer, 1878), was changed to *Prolegomena zur Geschichte Israels* for the second edition (Berlin: Reimer, 1883) and later editions. ET: *Prolegomena to the History of Ancient Israel*, trans. J. S. Black and A. Menzies (Edinburgh: Black, 1885).

[16]For recent controversies in source criticism, see especially the contributions by R. Rendtorff, R. N. Whybray, J. Van Seters, N. E. Wagner, G. E. Coats, H. H. Schmid, R. E. Clements, and G. J. Wenham in *JSOT* 2 (1977) 2-60; see also D. A. Knight, "The Pentateuch," in *The Hebrew Bible and Its Modern Interpreters*, eds. D. A. Knight and G. M. Tucker (Chico, CA: Scholars, 1985) 263-296..

[17]Wellhausen, *Prolegomena* (3rd ed.; 1886) 331.

[18]See Kraus, *Geschichte*, 270.

[19]Wellhausen, *Israelitische und Jüdische Geschichte* (5th ed.; Berlin: Reimer, 1904) 11.

GUNKEL

It was Hermann Gunkel (1862-1932) who first proposed a rigorous method for going beyond the source documents into the shadowy prehistory of biblical narrative.[20] He regarded the primary task of source criticism to have been basically accomplished with the work of Wellhausen, and he set himself to what he regarded as the next task, "an attempt to construct a history of Israelite literature."[21] Gunkel considered his debts to Herder and to Wellhausen to be profound, and he acknowledged his predecessors eloquently: "We walk in the paths of Herder and Wellhausen when we consider for special study the form of the creations of the Old Testament "[22]

Gunkel's method for constructing a history of biblical literature consisted of isolating the literary types (*Gattungen*) embedded in the text and inquiring into their individual history and development. For example, he isolated the major types of narrative as follows:

> Narrative is generally found in prose form, and we can distinguish various types of narrative: stories about the gods, i.e., myths, and primitive folktales, both found in Israel only in fragments, the popular story, the longer novella, the religious legend, and lastly, the historical narrative in the stricter sense.[23]

Following from Herder's emphasis on the cultural setting of a story, Gunkel stated his attitude toward understanding the literary type once isolated:

[20]On Gunkel's work, see Kraus, *Geschichte*, 341-367; W. Klatt, *Hermann Gunkel* (Göttingen: Vandenhoeck & Ruprecht, 1969); P. Gibert, *Une Théorie de la légende: Hermann Gunkel et les légendes de la bible* (Paris: Flammarion, 1979); D. A. Knight, *Rediscovering the Traditions of Israel* (Missoula: Scholars, 1975) 71-83. See also the critical remarks of Warner, "Primitive Saga Men."

[21]Gunkel, "Die Grundprobleme der israelitischen Literaturgeschichte," *Reden und Aufsätze* (Göttingen: Vandenhoeck & Ruprecht, 1913) 30. ET: "Fundamental Problems of Hebrew Literary History," in *What Remains of the Old Testament and Other Essays*, trans. A. K. Dallas (London: Allen & Unwin, 1928).

[22]Gunkel, "Ziele und Methoden der Erklärung des Alten Testamentes," *Reden und Aufsätze*, 22.

[23]Gunkel, "Grundprobleme," 31.

> To understand the literary type one must in each case make
> the whole situation clear and ask, who is speaking? Who
> are the listeners? What is the general mood of the
> situation? What effect is aimed at?[24]

Gunkel's emphasis on performance and audience was essential
to his approach; it formed the basis for both the strength and the
weakness of his method. The strength was that he brought the
narratives into a human focus, grounded in the actual lives of the
tellers and listeners. The weakness was the strictly hypothetical
nature of his specific conclusions. One can see, first of all, that his
dissection of literary types was somewhat haphazard - what
distinguishes a "story" (*Sage*) from a "legend" (*Legende*) after
all?[25] His further subdivisions carried this arbitrariness even
further; he divided the *Sagen* into the following categories:
historical, ethnographic, aetiological, etymological, ceremonial,
geological, and mixed.[26] By these categories he indicated the
origin of the story as a response to various types of questions:
where did this custom or religious rite or geological formation or
word come from?

To his credit, Gunkel admitted that many *Sagen* had a mixed
origin, and that often "the motifs of the story that are intelligible
to us were added later, and . . . the story itself is much older."[27]
Nonetheless, his categories are arbitrary and, indeed, not all that
useful, even in his own analyses.

Another serious weakness of Gunkel's hypothetical
reconstructions of the history of the literary types was his specific
criterion for isolating the "unit" (*Einheit*) of a narrative. In
keeping with the primitivism of Herder, Gunkel regarded the
original biblical narratives as the product of a simple, childlike
folk, who told stories in short, pristine units. He wrote:

[24]Ibid., 33.

[25]For a discussion of the difficulties in making generic distinctions in folk
narrative, see D. Ben-Amos, "Analytical Categories and Ethnic Genres," in *Folklore
Genres*, ed. Ben-Amos (Austin: University of Texas, 1976) 215-242.

[26]Gunkel, *Genesis übersetzt und erklärt* (HKAT; Göttingen: Vandenhoeck &
Ruprecht, 1901) xi-xvii. All citations will be from the first edition of Gunkel's
Genesis unless otherwise noted. ET of introduction: *The Legends of Genesis*, trans. W.
H. Carruth (New York: Schocken, 1964).

[27]Gunkel, *Genesis*, xvi.

> The oldest Hebrew folksong is contained in only one or
> perhaps two long lines; the people of that period were not
> able to understand more![28]

The production of longer units and the amalgamation of units into
longer story cycles (*Sagenkränze*) were products of a later, more
developed level of culture:

> Just as we see the growth of our children's minds in the
> gradually increasing amount of material that they can
> absorb at one time, so we see in the growth of the literary
> units in Israel a feature of the history of civilization.[29]

The extent of Gunkel's primitivism is not surprising for a
scholar of his day; what is surprising is the extent to which this
Herderian legacy still forms the basis for modern treatments of the
"unit" of biblical narrative.[30] Short and pristine is synonymous
with early, even though few now would consciously assert that the
early Israelites were childlike primitives.

Gunkel's view of the growth of the Jacob cycle has formed the
basis for most subsequent treatments. There is a symmetry to his
reconstruction that has a certain appeal: it is simple and
comprehensive at the same time.   Unfortunately, the
presuppositions are rather too simplistic to sustain his structure.
Gunkel posited four strata to the Jacob cycle:

1. Narratives about Jacob and Esau.
2. Narratives about Jacob and Laban.
3. Narratives of cult places that Jacob founded.
4. Narratives about Jacob's children.[31]

The narratives about Jacob and Esau are, in Gunkel's view, the
oldest stratum.[32] Yet even this stratum is composed of two parts,

[28]Gunkel, "Grundprobleme," 34.

[29]Ibid., 34.

[30]See the critical remarks of Warner, "Primitive Saga Men," 328-330; J. A.
Wilcoxen, "Narrative," in *Old Testament Form Criticism*, ed. J. H. Hayes (San
Antonio: Trinity University, 1974) 64-65; and below, p. 28.

[31]Gunkel, *Genesis*, 266-268.

[32]Ibid., 266.

an earlier and a later. The earliest part tells how Jacob acquired Esau's birthright and his father's blessing. This section depicts the roguish Jacob and his stupid brother. The later part of this stratum, telling of Jacob's reunion with Esau, was added by storytellers as a continuation of a good tale, but Jacob is now a somewhat weak figure and Esau is rather noble. Gunkel remarked that "here too the sequel is inferior in imaginative power and freshness to the first part."[33] The sequel is specifically localized in sites east of the Jordan, while the original was only loosely located somewhere in the south of Canaan. These inconsistencies are indications of secondary growth, according to Gunkel.

The narratives about Jacob and Laban are the second major stratum of the Jacob story.[34] They also depict the roguish Jacob and this time his foil is his equally roguish father-in-law. The individual stories of this cycle have been woven together and, in time, they were incorporated as a whole into the Jacob-Esau narrative. The Jacob-Esau narrative forms a frame (*Rahmen*) for the Jacob-Laban narrative, and the journeys of Jacob to and from Laban's home in Haran are the artful transitions from one story cycle to the next. The original tone of the Jacob-Esau-Laban story cycle was humorous, then it was gradually revised toward a more lofty and religious tone.[35]

The third stratum, narratives of cult places, was the next addition to the cycle.[36] Brief stories of Jacob's association with the cult places at Bethel, Mahanaim, Penuel, and Shechem were amalgamated into the cycle, attached at segments of Jacob's journeys. Gunkel attributes this stratum to the joining of local traditions which occurred at pilgrimage festivals, when local groups would come together, or perhaps at the hand of travelling storytellers, who would weave local traditions into a connected whole.[37] The founders of the various cult places were originally

---

[33]Gunkel, "Jakob," *Preussische Jahrbücher* 176 (1919) 352; ET: "Jacob," in *What Remains of the Old Testament and Other Essays*, trans. A. K. Dallas (London: Allen and Unwin, 1928) 151-186.

[34]Gunkel, *Genesis*, 292.

[35]Ibid., 266.

[36]Ibid., 266-267.

[37]Ibid., xliii-xliv.

different figures; they only became identified with Jacob at a period when he was looked on as a national ancestor.[38] This explains, for Gunkel, why the religious Jacob stories were grafted onto the secular Jacob stories. It also explains the inconsistencies of character in the various stories:

> According to one story, Jacob is a giant who fights with God himself; according to another he is very clever but cowardly; these appear to be totally different characters; probably a third figure is the Jacob to whom the God of Bethel reveals himself.[39]

The last stratum is the stories of Jacob's children, their birth and their later fortunes.[40] These stories, according to Gunkel, were tribal legends and were attached to Jacob only after the latter had come to be seen as the ancestor of the twelve tribes. The original Jacob story predated this era, since the ancestral eponym "Israel" appears to be a late addition to the cycle, "Jacob" being the primary name. Also, nowhere does Jacob himself represent a tribe, thus the origin of his story is at a remove from the origin of the tales of the twelve tribes. In general, the tales of Jacob's children are secondary and somewhat tangential to the movement of the basic narration.

The growth and amalgamation of these four strata from the individual units to the final whole must have taken quite a while, according to Gunkel, yet even the latest stratum shows signs of antiquity and obscurity which indicates an ancient date of origin. "The beginnings of the process reach in any case back to the oldest period, unreachable by us; the whole was already rather finished in a very ancient era."[41]

The identification of Jacob with Israel and Esau with Edom is a late addition, probably stemming from the early monarchic period after David had conquered Edom. Originally Jacob and Esau were unconnected with the nations of Israel and Edom; this is shown by their main characteristics: "in the story Jacob is afraid of his

[38]Gunkel, "Jakob," 348-349.
[39]Gunkel, *Genesis*, xliv.
[40]Ibid., 267.
[41]Ibid., 267.

brother, in history Israel conquered Edom in war; in the story Esau is dumb, in history he is famous for his wisdom."[42]

Gunkel's reconstruction of the growth of the Jacob cycle remained constant throughout his works, but on one major point his views changed sharply. In the first edition of his Genesis commentary (1901) he regarded the patriarchal stories as belonging to the same category as stories from Mesopotamia, Egypt, and Greece.[43] In fact, some of his remarks on the origin of the patriarchal narratives have a prescient ring:

> The cult stories of Genesis, one can assume with great certainty, originally were connected with the places of which they treat. It is therefore probable that most of the patriarchal stories were already known in Canaan before Israel. Above all, however, the religion of Genesis suggests a non-Israelite origin for most of the stories: two of our sources (E and P) avoid calling the God of the Patriarchs "Yahweh;" one may see in this a last relic of the feeling that these narratives really have nothing to do with "Yahweh," the God of Israel.[44]

Gunkel conjectured, therefore, that "the patriarchal stories are essentially Canaanite."[45]

By the time of the third edition of the Genesis commentary (1910), Gunkel had come under the influence of Wilhelm Wundt's theory that folktales are the original form of folk narrative, and sagas and myths are secondary developments.[46] Hugo Gressmann, a close friend of Gunkel, had applied Wundt's theory to the patriarchal stories in an article that appeared in 1910 (but which Gunkel had earlier seen in draft form),[47] and Gunkel enthusiastically adopted the new theory. Accordingly, in this

---

[42]Gunkel, *Genesis* (3rd ed.; 1910) xx; see also *Genesis*, 287. On the wisdom of the Edomites, see Jer 49:7, Bar 3:22-23, and the book of Job.

[43]Gunkel, *Genesis*, xl-xliii.

[44]Ibid., xlii.

[45]Ibid., xlii.

[46]On this phase of Gunkel's work, see Klatt, *Gunkel*, 129-138; J. W. Rogerson, *Myth in Old Testament Interpretation* (New York: de Gruyter, 1974) 57-65; McKane, *Studies in the Patriarchal Narratives*, 43-53.

[47]Gressmann, "Sage und Geschichte in den Patriarchenerzählungen" *ZAW* 30 (1910) 1-34.

phase of his work, Gunkel abandoned the theory of Canaanite
origins of the patriarchal narratives and argued instead that they
were originally simple folktales, told by shepherds in the steppes
to the south and east of Canaanite civilization.[48]   The original
kernel of the story was still the Jacob-Esau narrative, but this
kernel is now understood as a simple folktale of the shepherd
versus the hunter in which the smart shepherd wins: "the clever,
weak one defeats the strong, stupid one."[49]   Jacob and Esau are
generic figures, the one the type of the shepherd, the other the
type of the hunter, and only later does ethnographic and
historical coloring enter the tale. In the Jacob-Laban cycle, Jacob
outwits the older shepherd, his clever father-in-law; here again
Jacob is "in sum, a true folktale figure."[50]

Gunkel's "folktale" phase has not been taken up by other
scholars, and rightly so.   The argument over which comes first,
myth, legend, or folktale, has been long viewed as irrelevant,[51]
and it seems an odd detriment in Gunkel's work. His earlier views
on the international character of Israelite narrative, and
particularly the Canaanite roots of patriarchal narrative, have
proven much more productive, and are especially impressive when
reckoned with the fact that Gunkel formed his opinions nearly
three decades before the discovery of the Canaanite mythic and
epic texts from the ancient city of Ugarit, which predate the
biblical texts by several centuries.

The basic edifice of Gunkel's theories constitutes a monument to
his learning, insight, and imagination.   It is commonly
acknowledged that his Genesis commentary has yet to be
superseded. It is perhaps inevitable that, in the exuberance of his
investigations, he entertained certain faulty presuppositions: he
projected a sentimental primitivism onto early Israelite society,
and he dissected the stories into imaginary "units" (*Einheiten*)

---

[48]Gunkel, *Genesis* (3rd ed.) lix-lxi.

[49]Gunkel, "Jakob," 360.

[50]Ibid., 356.

[51]See S. Thompson, "Myths and Folktales" in *Myth: A Symposium*, ed. T. A.
Sebeok (Bloomington: Indiana University, 1958) 169- 180; and G. S. Kirk, *Myth: Its
Meaning and Functions in Ancient and Other Cultures* (Berkeley: University of
California, 1970) 31-41.

and then recombined them according to an improvised method. At one point he borrowed a metaphor from geology and stated his determination to "first remove the top layer in order to expose the layers below."[52] But, sitting in his study, prior to the era of fieldwork in societies with living oral traditions, Gunkel could not have known that geological strata and stories are wholly different. Stories, unlike stones, do not exist in fixed form in an oral folk tradition. Oral tradition is fluid and multiform; stories change with each telling and with each generation.[53] While archaic features may be preserved, the story itself does not accumulate like sedimentary deposits; it changes incessantly, more like the sea than stone.

NOTH

Although many of the criticisms levelled against Gunkel's method apply equally well to the work of Martin Noth (1902-1968), the massive impact of the latter on biblical scholarship necessitates an equal (albeit cursory) treatment. The work in question is Noth's *Überlieferungsgeschichte des Pentateuch*,[54] widely regarded as a classic of modern biblical scholarship. Indeed, its impact is such that it has become, in certain circles, more a proof-text than a work of speculative thought. Yet even the English translator of the work is willing to admit the centrality of "creative imagination" in Noth's elaborate system.[55]

[52]Gunkel, "Jakob," 344.

[53]For recent work on oral tradition, see especially A. B. Lord, *The Singer of Tales* (Cambridge: Harvard University, 1960); idem, "Perspectives on Recent Work on Oral Literature" *Forum for Modern Language Studies* 10 (1974) 187-210; and J. M. Foley, *Oral-Formulaic Theory and Research: An Introduction and Annotated Bibliography* (New York: Garland, 1984). For recent work in the biblical field, see especially R. C. Culley, "Oral Tradition and the OT: Some Recent Discussion" *Semeia* 5 (1976) 1-33; idem, *Studies in the Structure of Hebrew Narrative* (Philadelphia: Fortress, 1976) 1-68; and H. N. Wallace, "The Yahwistic Source and Its Oral Antecedents," in *The Eden Narrative* (HSM 32; Atlanta: Scholars, 1985) 29-64; and below.

[54]Stuttgart: Kohlhammer, 1948; ET: *A History of Pentateuchal Traditions*, trans. B. W. Anderson (Englewood Cliffs, NJ: Prentice-Hall, 1972).

[55]B. W. Anderson, "Martin Noth's Traditio-Historical Approach in the Context of Twentieth-Century Biblical Research," in Noth, *Pentateuchal Traditions*, xxvi.

Without dwelling on the inconsistencies and perplexities of Noth's general method,[56] much of which he borrowed or adapted from Gunkel, I will instead sketch his reconstruction of the history of the Jacob cycle, stressing where he diverged from Gunkel.

Rather than deriving the patriarchal stories from Canaanite legends or local shepherds' folktales, Noth relied on the theory of Albrecht Alt that the patriarchal stories had their origin in the cult sites where the "God of Abraham," the "God of Isaac," and the "God of Jacob" were worshipped.[57] According to Alt, as the early Israelites migrated from the desert to the arable land of Canaan, they brought their "God of the Father" cult with them, as well as the names of the cultic founders, Abraham, Isaac, Jacob, etc. Traditions then accumulated around the new Palestinian cult sites, and the patriarchs, who in the first instance were merely the eponyms of cult founders, became the characters of a narrative tradition.

Accordingly, Noth reversed the historical sequence of Gunkel's narrative strata. His sequence, in order of antiquity, is:

1. Narratives of Jacob at the cult sites of Shechem and Bethel.
2. Narratives of Jacob-Esau and Jacob-Laban.
3. Narratives of the birth of the Israelite tribal ancestors.
4. Additional local legends: Penuel, Sukkot, etc.[58]

Noth's determination of the oldest stratum followed Alt's idea of the cultic origins of the traditions of the patriarchs. Jacob's association with Shechem (Gen 33:18-20) was regarded by Noth as the oldest unit of the Jacob tradition, arising in the early settlement period.[59] Because Shechem was "the place where the

[56]See especially R. Polzin, "Martin Noth's *A History of Pentateuchal Traditions*" *BASOR* 221 (1976) 113-120.

[57]A. Alt, "Der Gott der Väter," *Kleine Schriften zur Geschichte des Volkes Israel*, (Munich: Beck, 1953 [1929]) I.1-78; ET: "The God of the Fathers," in *Essays on Old Testament History and Religion*, trans. R. A. Wilson (Garden City, NY: Doubleday, 1966) 1-100. For modifications of Alt's views, see F. M. Cross, *Canaanite Myth and Hebrew Epic: Essays in the History of the Religion of Israel* (Cambridge: Harvard University, 1973) 1-75.

[58]Noth, *Pentateuch*, 86-111.

[59]Ibid., 86-95.

Israelite tribes established their central covenantal cult,"[60] the patriarch associated with this site was in a position "to be first to become a figure of interest to all Israel and to enter into the Pentateuchal traditions with their all-Israel orientation, and thereby to become the 'patriarch.'"[61] The other early cult site that was associated with Jacob was Bethel. Noth explained the journey from Shechem to Bethel in Genesis 35 by the notion, again first proposed by Alt,[62] that the narrative represented a historical pilgrimage from Shechem to Bethel. This pilgrimage was itself a reminiscence of the transfer of certain cultic acts from Shechem to Bethel which "resulted from historical events unknown to us."[63] The density of speculation and conjectural history in Noth's hypothesis is remarkable; these and other reconstructions add up to a detailed "just-so story," alluring in its sheer accumulation of hypothetical data.

The second stratum of Noth's sequence is the Jacob-Esau-Laban cycle.[64] Noth basically agreed with Gunkel that the Jacob-Esau cycle and the Jacob-Laban cycle developed independently, only later being combined into a composite cycle, but Noth diverged sharply on a number of specific issues. Most interesting is Noth's emphasis on the East Jordanian nature of this stratum of narrative. The Jacob-Laban cycle is localized in Haran, well east of the Jordan. The Jacob-Esau cycle occurs mainly west of the Jordan, though Noth dispenses with this datum by regarding its localization as secondary. According to Noth, the origins and significance of the East Jordan Jacob tradition are evident from the traditions of Jacob's burial:

> That such a tradition must have existed and that it was of some significance is evident solely from the fact, remarkable in the present context of the Pentateuchal narrative, that the old Pentateuchal sources contain

[60]Ibid., 89.

[61]Ibid., 89.

[62]Alt, "Die Wallfahrt von Sichem nach Bethel," *Kleine Schriften* [1938], I.79-88.

[63]Noth, *Pentateuch*, 87.

[64]Ibid., 95-109.

statements according to which Jacob must have been buried originally in East Jordan.[65]

Noth admitted that other traditions of Jacob's burial west of the Jordan existed, but he regarded these traditions as secondary and late.[66]   Noth's high regard for burial traditions as primary and ancient data is evident in his treatment of the Moses burial tradition as well.[67]   In any case, the trace of a burial tradition is Noth's keystone for the East Jordan Jacob tradition.

Noth remarked that:

> The East Jordan Jacob has a folk originality and a vitality
> rooted in the land . . . his character is clearly and distinctly
> different from the Jacob of Shechem and Bethel.[68]

Since the cultic narratives of Shechem and Bethel were necessarily older according to his view, Noth conjectured that the tradition of Jacob was brought to the East Jordan area by its earliest settlers, Israelites from the hill country of central Palestine, where the stories of Jacob were current.   Because of the changed circumstances of the East Jordanian settlers, their Jacob became more "worldly" than the Jacob of West Jordan.   The "worldliness" of the East Jordan Jacob was itself an important datum for Noth, according to his presuppositions:

> Here it is obvious that we have a later kind of narrative,
> distinct from the older sacral style of tersely composed
> narratives concerning God's revelations and promises to the
> "patriarchs."[69]

Noth here aligned his developmental sequence: *sacred -->
worldly*, with Gunkel's sequence: *terse --> discursive*.   Simple and sacred is primary, worldly and prolix is secondary.   A history of culture is implicit in Noth's sequence of the history of tradition, although he contradicted himself in other applications of these

[65]Ibid., 96.
[66]Ibid., 96, 111.
[67]Ibid., 186-191.
[68]Ibid., 98.
[69]Ibid., 99.

principles.[70]

The starting point of the Jacob-Laban cycle, which Noth saw as contemporary with the Jacob-Esau cycle, was the treaty between Jacob and Laban at Mt. Gilead.[71] Noth did not state why this should be so, but it is clear that he preferred historical-sounding events, such as burials and treaties, as the starting points of traditions. On the treaty between Jacob and Laban, which Noth regarded as an early tribal agreement between Israelites and Arameans, he stated: "We are dealing here, as far as we know, with the first historical contact between Israelites and Arameans."[72] Again, Noth does not tell us why this should be so, but he spins out an elaborate tale of the early relations of the Israelites and Arameans which generated various episodes of the Jacob-Laban cycle.[73]

Noth's analysis of the Jacob-Esau cycle differs little from Gunkel's, except for the fact that he regarded its localization west of the Jordan as secondary, following the later amalgamation of the East Jordan Jacob tradition with the West Jordan Jacob tradition. The "worldly" character of the Jacob-Esau cycle certified it as East Jordanian in origin:

> The subject matter of the Jacob-Esau cycle stems from a time when in "Gilead" the hunter, who had been there first and was therefore "older," was on the verge of being displaced by the "younger" herdsman. . . . Of course, the story in its transmitted form already presupposes the transition from herding to agriculture.[74]

The circular nature of Noth's argument is evident.

The Jacob-Esau cycle was combined with the Jacob-Laban cycle, as in Gunkel's theory, and finaly amalgamated with the West Jordan Jacob traditions attached to Shechem and Bethel. The last two strata of traditions enter at this time: the "late passage" of the birth of the tribal ancestors whose father was the West

[70]See Polzin, "Martin Noth."
[71]Noth, *Pentateuch*, 100-101.
[72]Ibid., 101.
[73]Ibid., 101-103.
[74]Ibid., 107.

Jordanian Jacob,[75] and the journeys which took Jacob to Mahanaim, Penuel, and Sukkot, attracting to Jacob the traditions localized there.[76]   The final point of the Jacob narrative was the harmonizing of the burial traditions, one in East Jordan belonging to the East Jordan Jacob, and one in West Jordan belonging to the West Jordan Jacob:

> the two corresponding grave traditions were harmonized in favor of the West Jordan grave site, so that the East Jordan grave site by the "threshing-floor of the bramble" was demoted to the scene of mourning alone.[77]

Noth's massive system is ingenious and learned, but its flaws are only too evident in retrospect. His sequence from sacred story to worldly story is extremely arbitrary, as is his continuance of Gunkel's sequence of simple preceding complex. Indeed, Noth claimed to have superseded Gunkel in the truth of his method, but the claim sounds hollow. Noth stated:

> [Gunkel's] view rests on a one-sided preference for a history of *material*, considered in the light of a particular scheme of development, in which the origin is simply a "tale of rivalry." But this fails to consider that only a particular *form* of tradition can be primary, around which all sorts of narrative materials later crystallized.[78]

Noth argued against the primacy of the *theme* of rivalry in favor of the *form* of cultic narrative. The arbitrariness of either claim is striking to us today, for whom the quest for ultimate origins is either irrelevant or unreachable. Noth, like Gunkel, liked to speak in terms of geological metaphors, as for example, "narrative elements which are preserved only fragmentarily or stand out like erratic blocks (*wie erratische Blöcke dastehenden*)."[79] But, as is the case with Gunkel, Noth's rhetoric and his reconstruction are rendered suspect by recent work on the

[75]Ibid., 109-110.
[76]Ibid., 110-111.
[77]Ibid., 111.
[78]Ibid., 111 n. 299.
[79]Ibid., 112 n. 299.

formation and transmission of oral narrative.[80] According to a recent book devoted to the "history of tradition" school of which Noth is the most important figure, a consequence of recent studies of oral literature appears to be "that traditio-historical research becomes basically invalid."[81]

ALBRIGHT

Noth's antithesis on the American scene was the prolific scholar William F. Albright (1891-1971). Noth believed that detailed traditio-historical analysis of biblical narrative was the primary task of the investigator, other tasks coming after. Albright insisted, with equal tenacity, that the accumulation and interpretation of extra-biblical data were the only empirical means whereby the biblical accounts could be evaluated.[82] The choice of methods, of course, prejudged the type of results that the two men reached. Nor was the choice a particularly conscious one. Hans Frei has discussed the bifurcation of methods in English and German biblical scholarship reaching back to the early eighteenth century:

> The relation between historical criticism and hermeneutics has remained an unresolved issue ever since its inception in the eighteenth century. . . . Unlike the English discussion of the fact issue, which had by this time become completely mired in the external evidence question, the German scholars' procedure was . . . almost exclusively internal, i.e. literary-historical.[83]

The eighteenth century antithesis of "external evidence" versus "literary-history," practiced by the English and the Germans respectively, has been neatly replicated in the work of Albright and Noth and their colleagues in the twentieth century.

[80] See above, n. 53.

[81] Knight, *Rediscovering the Traditions of Israel*, 391. Knight is referring specifically to the work of A. B. Lord.

[82] See the discussion of Knight, *Rediscovering the Traditions of Israel*, 193-213.

[83] Frei, *Eclipse of Biblical Narrative*, 56.

Albright's work did not, however, merely repeat the work of
his eighteenth century counterparts. The last century has seen an
explosion in the amount of data recovered from archaeological
excavations pertaining to the ancient world. Albright's role in the
midst of this explosion was that of an archaeologist, historian,
epigraphist, Assyriologist, Egyptologist, biblicist, and occasionally classicist and philosopher of history. The title of Albright's
book, *From the Stone Age to Christianity*, aptly describes the
range of his work. Of course, virtually all the fields which
Albright practiced were in their infancy; since his day each field
has become more specialized and thus less accessible to the general
scholar. Albright's errors were those of a grand synthesizer:
textual and archaeological data intertwine in ways that are no
longer acceptable but which are nonetheless understandable in
retrospect.

Albright believed that the mass of extra-biblical data in
general supported the picture of the biblical patriarchs as
historical figures: "We can hardly . . . be surprised to find archaeological discoveries confirming Israelite tradition almost always,
as far as they go."[84]   And again: "there is no reason to doubt the
general accuracy of the biographical details and the sketches of
personality which make the Patriarchs come alive with a
vividness unknown to a single extrabiblical character in the whole
vast literature of the ancient Near East."[85]

Of course "vividness" is not a quality that necessarily pertains
to historicity, nor is the statement that "there is no reason to
doubt" this historicity particularly reassuring. In Albright's
rhetoric, as with many other scholars, such a statement of
confidence generally conceals a noticeable lack of supporting
evidence.

Albright's argument for the essential historicity of the
patriarchal accounts was based on six primary assertions:

1. Oral tradition is historically trustworthy.

[84]Albright, *From the Stone Age to Christianity: Monotheism and the Historical Process* (Garden City, NY: Doubleday, 1957) 76.

[85]Albright, *The Biblical Period from Abraham to Ezra: An Historical Survey* (New York: Harper & Row, 1963) 5.

2. The patriarchal movements from Mesopotamia to Palestine correspond to the early migrations of the Amorites.

3. The Mari texts corroborate the place names and personal names of the patriarchal accounts.

4. The Nuzi texts corroborate the social and legal practices of the patriarchal accounts.

5. The population element known as the ʿApiru in the early texts corresponds to the early Hebrews.

6. The mythic material in Genesis 1-11 corresponds most closely to old Mesopotamian lore which was carried to Palestine by the patriarchal Hebrews.[86]

Detailed refutations and/or modifications of Albright's assertions have been made by a number of scholars,[87] and there is no need to repeat their results here. A few remarks might be in order, however, concerning some of Albright's statements.

Albright misrepresented the relationship between history and oral tradition. Although he astutely cited the Homeric epics of Greece and the Arthurian cycle of England as parallels to the biblical traditions,[88] he emphasized the "fundamental historicity" of these narrative traditions and states, misleadingly, that "the burden of proof is increasingly on those scholars who deny the basic historicity of the Iliad" and other traditions.[89] But the scholarly work he cited, especially that of the brilliant classicist Martin Nilsson, did not assert the "fundamental historicity" of these traditions, rather they record the cultural, historical, and religious items that are preserved in the narrative tradition *along with* themes, plots, and characters

[86] Albright, *Stone Age to Christianity*, 236-241; *Biblical Period*, 2-5; *Yahweh and the Gods of Canaan: A Historical Analysis of Two Contrasting Faiths* (New York: Doubleday, 1968) 53-109.

[87] See M. Weippert, "Abraham der Hebräer? Bemerkungen zu W. F. Albrights Deutung der Vater Israels" *Bib* 52 (1971) 407-432; T. L. Thompson, *The Historicity of the Patriarchal Narratives: The Quest for the Historical Abraham* (New York: de Gruyter, 1974); J. Van Seters, *Abraham in History and Tradition* (New Haven: Yale University, 1975); R. de Vaux, *The Early History of Israel*, trans. D. Smith (Philadelphia: Westminster, 1978) 161- 287; W. G. Dever, "The Patriarchal Traditions" in *Israelite and Judaean History*, eds. J. H. Hayes and J. M. Miller (Philadelphia: Westminster, 1977) 70-120.

[88] Albright, *Stone Age to Christianity*, 73-75.

[89] Ibid., 74.

that are traditional rather than historical. Nilsson wrote acutely on this subject:

> There are certainly historical facts underlying heroic myths to a certain extent, but mythology can never be converted into history, and we can never attain a knowledge of these historical facts if there is not an independent historical tradition as there is, e.g., in the case of the Nibelungenlied. . . . For Greek myths no historical tradition exists which can serve as a control.   There is only archaeology, and control by archaeology does not suffice for proving historical events but serves at most to present the cultural milieu.[90]

Similar remarks could be made about the relation between history and tradition in the Arthurian cycle, and, had Albright perceived it, in the patriarchal cycle as well.

Albright's fervor in proclaiming the essential historicity of the patriarchal cycles also clouded some of his other assertions. The migrations of the early Amorites are a problematic topic,[91] as is the history of the ancient use of the term ʿApiru.[92] The use of the Mari and Nuzi texts to substantiate the patriarchal accounts is a case study in the overinterpretation and distortion of data in order to prove a point.[93]   Finally, the Mesopotamian influence on the narratives of Genesis 1-11 signifies nothing more than that Mesopotamian lore was well known in the West Semitic area, a

---

[90]M. P. Nilsson, *The Mycenaean Origin of Greek Mythology* (Berkeley: University of California, 1932) 31.

[91]On the problem of the Amorite "migrations," see Dever, "Patriarchal Traditions," 84, 86; idem, "The Beginning of the Middle Bronze Age in Syria-Palestine" in *Magnalia Dei: Essays on the Bible and Archaeology in Memory of G. Ernest Wright*, eds. F. M. Cross, et al. (Garden City, NY: Doubleday, 1976) 3-38; idem, "New Vistas on the EB IV (MB I) Horizon in Syria-Palestine" *BASOR* 237 (1980) 35-64, and references.

[92]On the problem of the ʿApiru, see recently H. Cazelles, "The Hebrews," in *Peoples of Old Testament Times*, ed. D. J. Wiseman (Oxford: Clarendon, 1973) 1-28; M. Weippert, *The Settlement of the Israelite Tribes in Palestine*, trans. J. D. Martin (London: SCM, 1971) 63-102; and O. Loretz, *Habiru-Hebräer* (Berlin: de Gruyter, 1984).   The classic treatments remain J. Bottéro, *Le problème des Ḫabiru* (Paris: Imprimerie Nationale, 1954); and M. Greenberg, *The Ḫab/piru* (AOS 39; New Haven: American Oriental Society, 1955).

[93]On the misuse of the Mari and Nuzi texts, see Thompson, *Historicity of the Patriarchal Narratives*, 52-66, 196-297; Van Seters, *Abraham in History and Tradition*, 65-103.

point that no one would dispute. A fragment of the Gilgamesh epic has been found at Middle Bronze Age Megiddo; the myth of Adapa and the epic "King of Battle" are known from the Amarna archives; a fragment of the Babylonian deluge myth is known from Late Bronze Age Ugarit; and more.[94] Mesopotamian lore is present in the West Semitic area from the early second millennium on.

In 1961, Albright presented a new version of his theory of the historicity of the patriarchs. He claimed to have discovered, by means of a careful investigation into trade routes and caravans of the early second millennium, that Abraham was after all the leader of a donkey caravan. After a rather forced interpretation of several biblical passages, Albright concluded:

> These and other data which we have presented are meaningless unless we take them at their face value and recognize in the hoary figure of "Abram the Hebrew" a caravaneer of high repute in his time, the chief traditional representative of the original donkey caravaneers of the 19th century B.C., when this profession reached the climax of its history.[95]

This thesis has also been subject to careful scrutiny and emphatic rejection.[96] It might be appropriate simply to agree with F. M. Cross's understated remark: "We need not accept all the conclusions of Albright's *tour de force*."[97]

[94]For references, see Weippert, "Abraham der Hebräer?" 427-431; J. H. Tigay, *The Evolution of the Gilgamesh Epic* (Philadelphia: University of Pennsylvania, 1982) 119 n. 35.

[95]Albright, "Abram the Hebrew: A New Archaeological Interpretation" *BASOR* 163 (1961) 52.

[96]Weippert, "Abraham der Hebräer?"; and Thompson, *Historicity of the Patriarchal Narratives*, 172-186.

[97]Cross, *Canaanite Myth and Hebrew Epic*, 9 n. 20.

CRITIQUE AND PROSPECTS

The decade of the 1970's saw a reaction against the views of Albright and his followers, on the one hand, and Gunkel's and Noth's followers, on the other. The debate over the "external evidence" question versus the "literary-historical" question has been joined in several recent discussions. The two works which most thoroughly criticize the "external evidence" approach are T. L. Thompson's *The Historicity of the Patriarchal Narratives*[98] and J. Van Seters's *Abraham in History and Tradition*.[99] Van Seters's work extends also to a critique of the "literary-historical" approach, as does F. M. Cross's *Canaanite Myth and Hebrew Epic*.[100] While none of these works specifically addresses the Jacob cycle in detail, they nonetheless have important implications for the study of the Jacob cycle.[101]

The bulk of Thompson's book and the first half of Van Seters's consist of thorough examinations of the data adduced by Albright and others (Cyrus Gordon, E. A. Speiser, Nelson Glueck, G. Ernest Wright, John Bright, et al.) to support the argument of the "fundamental historicity" of the patriarchal narratives. The criticisms, several of which I have mentioned above, are sound, and the result is a thorough discrediting of the attempt to isolate a particular "patriarchal age" in the second millennium B.C.E. As Thompson states: "the methods used . . . are wholly inadequate."[102]

[98]New York: de Gruyter, 1974.

[99]New Haven: Yale University, 1975.

[100]Cambridge: Harvard University, 1973.

[101]The most important recent treatment of the Jacob cycle is A. de Pury, *Promesse divine et légende cultuelle dans le cycle de Jacob. Genèse 28 et les traditions patriarcales*, 2 vols. (Paris: Gabalda, 1975). The most significant aspects of de Pury's study are his thorough critique of the prevailing view that the individual story is the primary "unit" of the Jacob cycle, and his extensive argument that the cycle of stories, based on the traditional pattern of the flight, adventures, and return of the hero, is the primary basis of the Jacob tradition (473-517). "En d'autres termes, l'unité de base est le cycle lui-même, non les épisodes" (608). Cf. the remarks of Westermann, *Genesis 12-36*, 496-497.

[102]Thompson, *Historicity*, 320.

Historical reconstructions which would appear extremely hypothetical or even totally untenable on their own merits and within their own field of discipline, achieve, nevertheless, the appearance of plausibility when they are interpreted in the light of similar reconstructions of possibly related materials, which reconstructions themselves first appear plausible in the projection of the total synthesis. It is on the basis of such mutual affirmation and harmonization that the chain of evidence has been constructed, a chain which in the scholarly literature has proved far stronger than its very strongest link.[103]

Thompson chooses to fall back upon a more cautious position, what I would call a minimalist position, that of Wellhausen's "notorious remark:"

Certainly there is no historical knowledge to be gained about the patriarchs, only about the time when the stories about them arose among the Israelite people.[104]

Thompson suggests that this time is the era of the Yahwistic composition, and that "the stories were taken up into the Yahwistic tradition directly from the contemporary Canaanite/Israelite milieu."[105] Beyond this era we cannot go.

Van Seters reaches a different conclusion after his similar critique of attempts to reconstruct a "patriarchal age" in the second millennium. He concludes that "the tradition as it stands reflects only a rather late date of composition."[106] He operates in a rather contradictory fashion by pointing to early- or mid-first millennium data as the "closest" extrabiblical parallels, thus opting for a late date for the formation of the patriarchal narratives. Yet his "parallels" are often just as suspect as those cited by his predecessors.[107] Thompson's caution, that one should be wary of comparing narratives with other *types* of data - legal,

[103]Ibid., 317.
[104]Ibid., 7.
[105]Ibid., 326.
[106]Van Seters, *Abraham*, 122.
[107]See especially the reviews by J. J. M. Roberts, *JBL* 96 (1977) 109-113; and H. Cazelles, *VT* 28 (1978) 241-155.

social, etc. - for purposes of dating, is more cogent than the method followed by Van Seters. Van Seters's method for asserting first millennium origins for the patriarchal traditions is as faulty as the method he criticizes for locating the patriarchal age in the second millennium.

Van Seters, however, goes a step farther. In the second part of his book he questions the necessity of positing an oral tradition, as do Gunkel, Noth, and others, to account for the formation of the patriarchal narratives. He concludes that:

> The degree to which the stories reflect any oral tradition may be explained entirely by the use of folkloristic forms and motifs that were accessible to Israelite culture throughout its history and not primarily by the deposit of a preliterate period.[108]

> It appears to me at the present time that one can say little about any oral tradition.[109]

It seems that Van Seters's goal in his criticism of oral tradition is simply to buttress his claims for the first millennium origin of the patriarchal traditions, and not to discern the real differences between oral tradition and written composition. Although many of his criticisms of Gunkel, Noth, Westermann, and others are valid, his understanding of the nature of oral tradition is suspect. He relies almost exclusively on the antiquated work of Axel Olrik, whose "epic laws," published in 1909, remain interesting though simplistic.[110] Furthermore, Van Seters's "points of comparison," which distinguish between oral and written composition, are faulty. He states that "a combination of genres [such as tales and songs] is a literary phenomenon."[111] This is simply untrue. Many oral traditional compositions from a number of cultures incorporate a combination of genres. Myths, laments, catalogues, songs of praise and blame, and more are found in the Homeric epics, whose

---

[108]Van Seters, *Abraham*, 309.

[109]Ibid., 312.

[110]See the comments of Warner, "Primitive Saga Men," 330-335; Culley, *Studies in the Structure of Hebrew Narrative*, 28-30.

[111]Van Seters, *Abraham*, 163.

oral origins have been convincingly demonstrated.[112] Oral narratives from African cultures and from Native American cultures often contain a variety of genres: aphorisms, incantations, songs, genealogies, prayers, etc.[113]

Van Seters states that "oral tradition does not assume knowledge of various aspects of the story, so the 'blind motif' does not exist."[114] Precisely the opposite is true. The relationship between the performer and the audience in an oral tradition is such that *both* are operating within the tradition. The audience already knows the stories, and it is the performer's duty to *retell* the tales with sufficient artistry to entertain his audience. The performer selects from the traditional stock of tales and weaves a version which is both continuous with previous performances and unique in itself.[115] Both the performer and the audience already know the essential story, but since each telling is a fresh re-creation of the story, themes and motifs may often be narrated inconsistently, thus the common appearance of a "blind motif." Albert Lord has noted this tendency in oral traditions:

> In the traditional song . . . there is a pull in two directions: one is toward the song being sung and the other is toward the previous uses of the same theme. The result is that characteristic of oral poetry which literary scholars have found hardest to understand and to accept, namely an occasional inconsistency, the famous nod of a Homer.[116]

Thus, as a whole, Van Seters's treatment is flawed. His critical remarks are sound, but his alternatives lack conviction. Nonetheless, the necessity of formulating a sound methodology for an appraisal of the nature and origins of the patriarchal

---

[112]On the various genres in the Homeric epics, see G. Nagy, *The Best of the Achaeans: Concepts of the Hero in Archaic Greek Poetry* (Baltimore: Johns Hopkins University, 1979) 6 and passim

[113]See, e.g., D. P. Biebuyck, "The African Heroic Epic," in *Heroic Epic and Saga*, ed. F. J. Oinas (Bloomington: Indiana University, 1978) 353-358; K. Kroeber, "An Introduction to the Art of Traditional American Indian Narration" in *Traditional Literatures of the American Indian*, ed. K. Kroeber (Lincoln: University of Nebraska, 1981) 9-11, 23 n. 7.

[114]Van Seters, *Abraham*, 163.

[115]Lord, *Singer of Tales*, 94-123.

[116]Ibid., 94.

narratives has been made clear by the work of Thompson and Van Seters.

F. M. Cross, among others, has of late urged a more stringent attention to the possibility of oral origins for the early narrative traditions of the Pentateuch.[117] He has cited in particular recent research into the oral origins of the Homeric epics of ancient Greece as a useful model for the investigation of biblical narrative. He regards such researches, especially the work of Milman Parry and Albert Lord on the nature of South Slavic oral tradition and its bearing for Homeric studies, as of primary importance. "Among other things, they sharply undercut theoretical conceptions of oral transmission presently ruling certain circles of both Old and New Testament studies."[118] Findings such as the essential fluidity and multiformity of oral narrative tradition and the variable length of oral compositions directly contradict the presuppositions of Gunkel and Noth, as I have indicated above. Rather than regarding short "units" as being prior to longer "complexes" of narrative, it appears that it is more accurate to regard the whole range of narrative cycles as being the primary "given" of a narrative tradition, the task of the performer being that of selection and elaboration from the existing stock of traditional lore.[119] Thus, for example, the Iliad, long as it is, was a selection of events from the existing narrative tradition concerning the Trojan War. The story of the Odyssey was another selection, also narrated at length.[120]

Cross's most important contribution to the question of the nature and origin of the Pentateuchal materials centers on his comparison of Canaanite and Israelite lore. It appears that several of the mythic and epic texts found at the site of ancient Ugarit, written down sometime prior to 1365 B.C.E. by the scribe Ilimilku, are amenable to the same type of oral-compositional analysis that

---

[117]See also the works discussed by Culley, "Oral Tradition and the Old Testament," 1-33.

[118]Cross, *Canaanite Myth*, 112 n.3.

[119]Lord, *Singer of Tales* 94-123; see also de Pury, *Promesse divine*, 473-517.

[120]Lord, *Singer of Tales* 141-197.

Parry and Lord applied to the Homeric epics.[121] A similar degree
of density of formulaic epithets and expressions, of repetition of
compositional "themes" or "type-scenes,"[122] and of repetition of
story patterns appears to typify the Ugaritic narratives and the
Homeric epics. Cross observes:

> There can be no doubt that this poetic cycle [Baal and Anat]
> was orally composed. It is marked by oral formulae, by
> characteristic repetitions, and by fixed pairs of synonyms (a
> type of formula) in traditional thought rhyme
> (*parallelismus membrorum*) which marks Semitic oral
> literature as well as much of the oral literature throughout
> the world. Moreover, their repertoire of traditional
> formulae overlaps broadly with that of the earliest
> Hebrew poetry, a circumstance impossible to explain unless
> a common tradition of oral literature embraced Israel in the
> south and Ugarit in the north.[123]

The nature of the textual evidence indicates that Cross's
position is essentially correct. The Ugaritic compositions show the
earmarks of oral composition. The density of formulaic expressions
at least indicates this. The fact of the broad overlap between the
formulaic expressions in Ugaritic poetry and the formulae of
Hebrew poetry clearly indicates an oral milieu embracing both,
even if the preserved body of Hebrew poetry is often a step
removed from direct oral composition.[124] The formulaic
conventions of Hebrew poetry can only have had their origins in
oral composition, since the formulae are continuous with the

[121]See R. E. Whitaker, "A Formulaic Analysis of Ugaritic Poetry"
(dissertation, Harvard University, 1970); idem, "Ugaritic Formulae," in *Ras
Shamra Parallels*, vol. III, ed. S. Rummel (AnOr 51; Rome: Biblical Institute, 1981)
207-219.

[122]On the importance of traditional "themes" or "type-scenes" as building-
blocks of oral traditional narrative, see especially Lord, "Perspectives on Recent
Work on Oral Literature," 205-209. The work of biblical literary critics on "type-
scenes" (e.g., R. Alter,*The Art of Biblical Narrative* [New York: Basic, 1981] 47-62; J.
Williams, "The Beautiful and the Barren: Conventions in Biblical Type-Scenes"
JSOT 17 [1980] 107-119) needs to be nuanced by attention to the oral traditional roots
of this phenomenon.

[123]Cross, *Canaanite Myth*, 112.

[124]See P. B. Yoder, "A-B Pairs and Oral Composition in Hebrew Poetry" *VT* 21
(1971) 470-489; R. C. Culley, *Oral Formulaic Language in the Biblical Psalms*
(Toronto: University of Toronto, 1967) 112-119.

Canaanite poetry of a different time and geography, as well as a different linguistic dialect and system of writing. In addition, there is a steadily decreasing density of formulaic expressions as the transition is made from early Hebrew poetry to "classical" Hebrew poetry,[125] also indicating that the earliest Hebrew poetry had its roots in oral tradition.

Beyond the question of oral formulae, Cross has also demonstrated several instances of a continuity of narrative pattern. Perhaps the best example is his discussion of Exod 15:1-18, "The Song of the Sea," in which Cross has noted a continuity of pattern with a segment of the Ugaritic Baal cycle in which Baal does battle with the god Sea (*Yamm*).[126] Cross notes that in the biblical tradition:

> a familiar mythic pattern may be discerned. The Divine Warrior [Yahweh] marched forth in wrath to win a crucial victory - at the sea, or in a variant tradition by cleaving through Sea - and then led a triumphal procession to his mountain, where he appeared in glory, constructed his sanctuary, and established his kingdom. A similar if not identical pattern of themes is found in the mythic cycle of Baʿl in Late Bronze Age Canaan (Ugarit), and in the classic Akkadian cosmogony known as *Enūma eliš*.[127]

The continuity of the mythic pattern in Israel, Canaan, and Mesopotamia indicates a widespread diffusion of narrative traditions, and therefore argues for the oral traditional origin of its biblical manifestation. Certain shared locutions and formulae indicate a close continuity between the Canaanite and Israelite versions of this narrative complex.[128]

---

[125]On the corpus of early Hebrew poetry, see F. M. Cross and D. N. Freedman, *Studies in Ancient Yahwistic Poetry* (Missoula: Scholars, 1975); Albright, *Yahweh and the Gods of Canaan*, 1-28; and D. A. Robertson, *Linguistic Evidence in Dating Early Hebrew Poetry* (Missoula, MT: Scholars, 1972).

[126]Cross, *Canaanite Myth*, 112-144.

[127]Cross, "The Epic Traditions of Early Israel: Epic Narrative and the Reconstruction of Early Israelite Institutions" in *The Poet and the Historian: Essays in Literary and Historical Biblical Criticism*, ed. R. E. Friedman (Chico: Scholars, 1983) 13.

[128]Cross, *Canaanite Myth*, 112-144.

Based on these and other results, Cross has formulated a theory of the oral origins of much of the early Pentateuchal traditions:

> We are inclined to reconstruct a long and rich poetic epic of the era of the league, underlying JE, and to take the prose epic variants (with their surviving poetic fragments) . . . as truncated and secondary derivatives. In any case, we possess long, poetic epics from old Canaan, from ancient Mesopotamia, and Homeric Greece, and to find the same phenomenon in Israel would not be suprising. [129]

> No doubt the Epic cycle was originally composed orally and was utilized in the cult of covenant-renewal festivals of the league, taking on variant forms at different sanctuaries and in different times.[130]

While several scholars have been critical of Cross's proposals,[131] I submit that they present at least a plausible scenario for the investigation of the Pentateuchal traditions. If the proposals of Thompson, Van Seters, and Cross are arrayed against each other, it seems that a wide range of possibilities is presently available for investigation into the nature of the Jacob cycle. The narrative can be regarded as a free composition of the Yahwist who is consciously joining together bits of contemporary Canaanite/Israelite traditions; it can be regarded as a late literary composition with little or nothing drawn from oral tradition; or it can be regarded as a variant literary form of an older, fully elaborated epic cycle with roots in the traditional forms of West Semitic oral narrative.

[129]Ibid., 124 n. 38.

[130]Ibid., 293.

[131]See the critical remarks of C. Conroy, "Hebrew Epic: Historical Notes and Critical Reflections" *Bib* 61 (1980) 1-30; S. Talmon, "Did There Exist a Biblical National Epic?" in *Proceedings of the Seventh World Congress of Jewish Studies: Studies in the Bible and the Ancient Near East* (Jerusalem: Magnes, 1981) 41-61; and see Cross, "Epic Traditions," 13-19. Many of the objections concerning the use of the term "epic" to apply to biblical narratives can be obviated by the adoption of the definition given by the folklorist R. M. Dorson ("Introduction," in *Heroic Epic and Saga: An Introduction to the World's Great Folk Epics* [Bloomington: Indiana University, 1978] 4): "a traditional narrative . . . honoring the heroes of a people." Dorson notes that traditional epics can be composed in poetry or in prose (p. 4).

The differences among these scenarios are crucial in reaching an understanding and appreciation of the Jacob cycle. The bulk of the following chapters will tend to support the view of a full and complex oral tradition underlying the final Pentateuchal compositions. My lines of comparison of narrative material will be primarily within the Canaanite and Israelite sphere, but I hope to indicate that the range of significances in the Jacob cycle is not confined to its most specific cultural sphere, the ancient Levant, but extends on the one hand to the era of prehistory, and on the other hand to modern times.

Part II

The Jacob Cycle and Canaanite Epic

Hans-Georg Gadamer has described the act of interpretation as a "fusion of horizons" between the world of the text and the world of the interpreter. One questions the text just as one questions a conversational partner, and gradually an adequate understanding unfolds.[1] The text, however, is a silent partner in this exchange: it has already spoken before the interpretation begins. The questioner, therefore, must be circumspect in the choice and in the pace of questions, and must take into account what the text may or may not disclose.

The questions asked of the relationship between the Jacob cycle and the Canaanite epics from Ugarit have tended to center on matters of history. Researchers have generally made use of the texts to reconstruct various scenarios for the political, the cultic, or the economic history of Syro-Palestine, rarely pausing to ask whether these narratives are appropriate sources for the reconstruction of such histories. The question poses itself: are these matters the central concerns of these narratives? If, as it seems, they are not, then perhaps the questioning of these texts has been misplaced, and a different set of questions ought to be asked instead. This is not to say that a historian ought not to use whatever data may be available for a particular research; it is rather to say that if *only* historical questions are asked of the texts, then one has not interrogated the texts fully, and a large part of their meaning has been shunted aside or avoided. The fusion of horizons that is possible, it seems, has barely begun.

In this section of the study, I will compare the Jacob cycle with the Canaanite epics from Ugarit in order to show how their interplay reveals certain key aspects of the texts and of the narrative traditions from which they stem. The questions posed

[1]H.-G. Gadamer, *Truth and Method,* trans. G. Barden and J. Cumming (New York: Sheed and Ward, 1975) 258-341.

will be directed to the texts as narrative, specifically as reflections of traditional narrative, and not to the texts as the remains of history. In the first part I will ask how the shared episodes and events in the two bodies of text relate to the question of multiformity in an oral epic tradition. The episodes of main concern will be the birth stories and the story of the revelation at Bethel. In the second part I will inquire into the relationship between story and cult in the encounter between Aqhat and Anat and in Jacob's deception of Isaac. In the third part I will investigate a shared style of literary composition in the narrative roles of Pughat in the Aqhat epic and Rachel in the Jacob epic.

The intended results of these questionings will be a broader perspective on the nature of the Jacob cycle in the context of ancient West Semitic narrative. In the following section of the study the scope will be drawn in to the specifically Israelite sphere, so as to allow both the general and the specific features of the Jacob cycle to come into view. The horizons of a story differ according to the questions asked, so it seems appropriate to fashion a series of different questions, posed from slightly different perspectives, in order to get the most out of the interpretive encounter.

1. The Forms of Tradition

In his now classic work of 1960, *The Singer of Tales*, A. B. Lord described in detail the form and manner of composition of the South Slavic oral epics which he and his teacher, Milman Parry, had collected beginning in the 1930's.[2] Parry had conceived the idea, developed first in his doctoral dissertation, that the Homeric poems were traditional epics shaped by the formulaic techniques of oral singers of tales.[3] To test his idea, Parry ventured out of the academy to the villages of Yugoslavia where, with Lord, he investigated the actual workings of a living tradition of oral narrative. The results of their research, presented in full form by Lord, demonstrate the applicability of the South Slavic model to the Homeric traditions, and have proven fruitful in the study of other narrative traditions, both living and ancient.[4]

Lord's description of the oral-formulaic technique of traditional "singers of tales" has proven useful in the study of biblical and Ugaritic narrative, as demonstrated in the works of Whallon, Gevirtz, Culley, Yoder, Cross, Whitaker, and others.[5] The ensemble of shared compositional techniques available to the Ugaritic and biblical traditions include: the formulaic paired terms used in the traditional parallelism of West Semitic poetry; relatively fixed descriptions of such traditional themes as journeys, feasts, fear, mourning, etc.; and basic story patterns such as the battle of the Warrior God with the Sea, or the pattern of the birth, adventures, and triumph of the hero.

The workings of Ugaritic poetry have been greatly illuminated by the oral-formulaic model of oral epic composition, suggesting that the extant Ugaritic texts may be the direct outcome of an oral

---

[2]A. B. Lord, *The Singer of Tales* (Cambridge: Harvard University, 1960).

[3]See A. Parry, ed., *The Making of Homeric Verse. The Collected Papers of Milman Parry* (Oxford: Clarendon, 1971).

[4]See Foley, *Oral-Formulaic Theory and Research: An Introduction and Annotated Bibliography* (New York: Garland, 1984).

[5]For discussion and references, see R. C. Culley, "Oral Traditions and the OT: Some Recent Discussion" *Semeia* 5 (1976) 1-33; idem, "Exploring New Directions," in *The Hebrew Bible and Its Modern Interpreters*, ed. D. A. Knight (Chico, CA: Scholars, 1985) 181-183.

traditional milieu.[6] The biblical texts pose more problems in this regard, since even the earliest Hebrew poetry may be viewed as a literary interaction with the poetry of oral tradition.[7] When one considers the prose narratives of the Bible, as for example in the J and E sources of the Tetrateuch, an important factor must be considered, that is, the reshaping of the traditional stories by the literary composers. If the hypothesis is granted that there existed in ancient Israel a lively and complex tradition of oral storytelling, then a central problem in the evaluation of biblical narrative becomes the nature and extent of the interaction between the literary composers and the oral tradition.

I submit that there is much to be investigated on both sides of the problem. The literary art of the biblical composers has begun to be examined in recent years,[8] as have the traces of oral tradition underlying the biblical narratives.[9] In this section I will examine the second part of the problem, the traces of oral tradition, in the context of the birth stories in biblical and Ugaritic epic and in connection with the revelation at Bethel in Genesis 28. The question of oral narrative is difficult to investigate with regard to the biblical narratives alone; it seems that by widening our focus to include other West Semitic narrative we can draw conclusions that will be more reliable and instructive.

---

[6]See F. M. Cross, "Prose and Poetry in the Mythic and Epic Texts from Ugarit" *HTR* 67 (1974) 1-15; see also the cautionary remarks of D. R. Hillers and M. H. McCall, Jr., "Homeric Dictated Texts: A Reexamination of Some Near Eastern Evidence" *Harvard Studies in Classical Philology* 80 (1976) 19-23.

[7]See the remarks of R. C. Culley, *Oral Formulaic Language in the Biblical Psalms* (Toronto: University of Toronto, 1967) 113-114.

[8]E.g., M. Sternberg, *The Poetics of Biblical Narrative* (Bloomington: Indiana University, 1985); R. Alter, *The Art of Biblical Narrative* (New York: Basic Books, 1981); M. Fishbane, *Text and Texture* (New York: Schocken, 1979); J. P. Fokkelman, *Narrative Art in Genesis* (Amsterdam: Van Gorcum, 1975).

[9]See above, n. 5.

The Birth Story

Lord has observed that one of the problems in dealing with oral narrative is the structure of our concepts concerning literary activity. We are simply unaccustomed to thinking of narrative as a protean art; we think in terms of "authors" and "texts." Lord writes:

> Our real difficulty arises from the fact that, unlike the oral poet, we are not accustomed to thinking in terms of fluidity. We find it difficult to grasp something that is multiform.[10]

In oral tradition a story has as many authors as it has singers; it has as many creations as it has performances. The stories change with each performance, yet there is stability of form, of essential plot and essential themes. The types of changes from performance to performance tend to fall into the categories of expansion or compression of ornamentation, addition or omission of material, changes of order in a sequence, substitution of one theme for another, etc.[11] But the changes do not distort the tale, since the tale only exists in multiforms. If we cannot speak of an "original" tale in oral tradition, then, as Lord notes, "we cannot correctly speak of a 'variant,' since there is no 'original' to be varied. Yet songs are related to one another in varying degrees; not, however, in the relationship of variant to original."[12]

A final general observation is in order before moving on to the birth stories in biblical and Canaanite traditions. An important characteristic of oral narrative is the primacy of story over character. That is, the "essential story" can draw into its orbit any number of different *dramatis personae*, yet the story is still recognizable in spite of a changeable cast of characters. Vladimir Propp reached the same conclusions in his study of Russian folktales, and this insight has been of some importance in recent

[10]Lord, *Singer of Tales*, 100.
[11]Ibid., 102-123.
[12]Ibid., 101.

37

literary theory.[13] Lord's remarks on this aspect of oral story are pertinent to the West Semitic narrative traditions:

> The fact that the same song occurs attached to different heroes would seem to indicate that the story is more important than the historical hero to which it is attached. There is a close relationship between hero and tale, but with some tales at least the *type* of hero is more significant than the *specific* hero. It is convenient to group songs according to their story content, or thematic configurations, because songs seem to continue in spite of the particular historical hero; they are not connected irrevocably to any single hero.[14]

The birth stories of the biblical and Canaanite traditions conform remarkably well to Lord's description of the workings of oral tradition. Since what we have are texts and not recordings of oral performances, circumspection is required before labelling our texts reflections, on one level or another, of oral traditional narrative. Nonetheless, as will become evident in our discussion, the model of oral narrative explains more cogently than any other the close relationship of the stories in terms of the stability of essential story and the divergence of particular details and emphases. The literary artistry of the composers undoubtedly played a central role in the details and final shape of the narratives, yet I believe that the intentions of the composers were, to a large extent, grounded in the oral traditions on which they drew.

ISRAELITE BIRTH STORIES

The birth story of Jacob and Esau, which will form the central point of my discussion, begins with the following verse (from the J source):

[13]V. Propp, *Morphology of the Folktale*, trans. L. Scott (Austin: University of Texas, 1968); see also A. J. Greimas, *Sémantique structurale* (Paris: Larousse, 1966; ET: *Structural Semantics*, trans. D. McDowell, R. Schleifer, and A. Velie [Lincoln: University of Nebraska, 1983]); C. Bremond, *Logique du récit* (Paris: Seuil, 1973).

[14]Lord, *Singer of Tales*, 120.

> Isaac entreated Yahweh on behalf of his wife, for she was
> barren, and Yahweh responded to his entreaty, and
> Rebekah his wife became pregnant (Gen 25:21).

The verb "to entreat" (עָתַר) has a cultic meaning: it is used in the
Qal or Hiphil, as here, of supplication to Yahweh or, in the
Niphal, of Yahweh's response to supplication.   The Arabic
cognate noun ʿaṯīrat means "an animal slaughtered for sacrifice,"
indicating the possible semantic range of this term, though there
is no explicit indication of sacrifice in the Hebrew usage. In any
case, the entreaty of Isaac has cultic associations, and Yahweh's
response is presumably given in the context of cult.   In the
following verse (v. 22), Rebekah is in pain because of the
struggling of the children in her womb, and the text tells us that
"she went to inquire (לִדְרֹשׁ) of Yahweh. Again, the word "to
inquire" is a *terminus technicus* used of cultic oracles,[15] and
Yahweh's oracular response follows in the text (v. 23). The cultic
dimension of the narrative is played down in the text, but the
words used still convey the sense of cultic entreaty and cultic
oracle.

Another aspect of the story that is implicit rather than
explicit is the reason for Isaac's entreaty for a son. Of course, that
information would have been part of the traditional heritage of
the author and audience of the tale; the desire for a son and heir
would hardly have needed to be openly voiced. Nonetheless, it is
interesting to note the depth of this desire, that it can remain
implicit and yet still be so central to the dynamics of the tale. The
story, after all, is about the eponymous ancestor of Israel; if the
possibility of his birth is placed at risk, then the very existence of
the audience is endangered. The birth of the patriarch is an issue
that concerns the very essence of the Israelites. It seems that what
is not said is a more potent presence than the little that is said;
this is the quality of biblical narrative that Erich Auerbach
described as "fraught with background."[16] It is an intriguing issue
whether this quality of narrative originates with the oral style or
the written style; all we can say is that it is characteristic of
what we have.

[15]Gunkel, *Genesis*, 269; S. Wagner, "דָּרַשׁ" *TDOT*, 3.302.

[16]E. Auerbach, *Mimesis: The Representation of Reality in Western Literature*,
trans. W. R. Trask (Princeton: Princeton University, 1953) 8-23.

Several other biblical narratives are related to the account of the birth of Jacob and Esau. As many commentators have noted,[17] the birth stories of Isaac, Joseph, Samson, and Samuel all show signs of a similar design in terms of the essential story, though details and emphases are different. Such a relationship of similarity and difference suggests that we are indeed dealing with stories which in the oral tradition were multiforms of each other, and the relationship of multiformity is preserved in the literary compositions of the various authors. A constant motif in all of these stories is the barrenness of the mother, described with only one exception by the word עֲקָרָה, "barren."[18] It is Yahweh's prerogative to open the womb, thus demonstrating his power, and also signaling the divinely ordained origin of the child, who even at birth is a special figure. Gunkel comments on this motif:

> The long infertility of the mother before the birth of the
> child is a beloved story motif: how ardently has the child
> been longed for! The child is from the beginning a gift from
> God; no wonder that, later, so much becomes of him![19]

The story of the birth of Isaac to Abraham and Sarah is more elaborate than the story of the birth of Jacob and Esau, but the essential elements are still recognizable. The notice of Sarah's barrenness (עֲקָרָה) is given briefly at the end of Abraham's genealogy in Gen 11:30 (J): "And Sarai was barren; she had no child." This notice foreshadows the need for Yahweh's intervention, since Abraham's special mark is to become the father of a "great nation" (גּוֹי גָּדוֹל; Gen 12:2). The theme of Abraham's childlessness is picked up again in Gen 15:1-6 when, after Yahweh again promises Abraham great reward, Abraham responds: "My lord, Yahweh, what can you give me, since I continue being childless?" (15:2). He adds, "You have given me no

---

[17]E.g., Gunkel, *Genesis*, 182, 268; more recently, R. Alter, "How Convention Helps Us Read: The Case of the Bible's Annunciation Type-Scene," *Prooftexts* 3 (1983) 115-130.

[18]Gen 11:30 (Sarah: J); Gen 25:21 (Rebekah: J); Gen 29:31 (Rachel: J); Judg 13:2,3 (wife of Manoah). In the only exception, the story of Hannah, we are told that "Yahweh had shut her (Hannah's) womb" (וַיהוה סָגַר רַחְמָהּ; 1 Sam 1:5). The word עֲקָרָה is not used of Hannah. Note, however, that in the psalm placed in Hannah's mouth in 1 Samuel 2, the word עֲקָרָה occurs: 1 Sam 2:5, "the barren woman bears seven."

[19]Gunkel, *Genesis*, 268.

offspring, so one of my servants will be my heir" (15:3). The problem of inheritance is specifically pointed out by Abraham as the cause for his distress, and Yahweh responds in kind: "That one will not be your heir; your own offspring will be your heir" (15:4). The problem of inheritance and of a proper heir is paramount.

The desire for a son is picked up again in Genesis 16 with a new twist: the childlessness now blends into the theme of the rivalry between Sarah and Hagar. Sarah had borne no children, so she offers her maidservant, Hagar, to bear children in her stead (16:1-2). The blending of the themes of barrenness and of the rivalry of the wives (or half-wives) occurs in two other multiforms of this story: in the birth of Joseph (Rachel vs. Leah) and in the birth of Samuel (Hannah vs. Peninnah). The legal background of the childless wife providing a substitute in order to provide an heir has been well-documented by Near Eastern legal texts;[20] the point of the story in Genesis 16, however, is not to document a legal practice, the point is to illustrate the various conflicts and repercussions that arise as a result of the lack of an heir. The problem is at once the necessity and the impossibility of the birth of Isaac, for as long as Sarah is barren the birth of Isaac remains suspended. In Genesis 16 the theme of rivalry is mixed into the story, aligning the story with the other rivalries in the patriarchal and other narratives, and introducing the figure of Ishmael, who in various ways functions as Isaac's opposite and who will produce a lineage of his own.

The birth story of Isaac proceeds at its own leisurely pace, interspersed with other stories and mixed with other themes. While entertaining some strangers, Abraham and Sarah receive the promise of a son, first from the strangers (18:10), and then from Yahweh (18:13-14), both from the J source. The story itself appears to be composite, but the promise is the same (v. 10: לְשָׂרָה וְהִנֵּה־בֵן; v. 14: וּלְשָׂרָה בֵן). The P source preserves its own promise of a son in 17:15-22. Finally, in 21:1-3 (J and P), Sarah bears Isaac. The story has taken ten chapters to tell, interwoven with other tales, but it has finally come to good issue. The contrast with the brief account of the birth of Jacob and Esau could not be greater, yet the essential lines of the stories are the same, adapted as they are to different circumstances and different configurations of themes.

[20]See, e.g., Speiser, *Genesis*, 119-121.

The story of the birth of Joseph is more briefly related, though it also brings in the theme of rivalry as in the Isaac birth story. The rivalry and the barrenness are presented in poignant terms in 29:30-31 (J): "[Jacob] loved Rachel more than Leah . . . when Yahweh saw that Leah was unloved, he opened her womb; but Rachel was barren." Rachel becomes envious of her sister, and she cries to Jacob: "Give me children, or I will die!" (30:1; E). Jacob becomes angry and replies: "Can I take the place of God, who has denied you fruit of the womb?" (30:2; E). This scene of less than domestic bliss conveys a nuanced picture of the patriarch and his young wife tangling with the problem of the lack of offspring. The immediacy of the characterizations should remind us that the birth story is not simply an inert block of narrative text or a "fixed folkloric archetype,"[21] it is rather a supple means of conveying character and conflict, as well as foreshadowing the importance of the child to be born.

After the device of the concubine is again resorted to, and after the tragicomic story of the mandrakes is told, the text relates in nearly poetic tones: "Then God remembered Rachel, and God heeded her, and he opened her womb. She conceived, and she bore a son" (30:22-23; E). Interestingly, whereas in the stories of the birth of Isaac and of the birth of Jacob and Esau it is the father who explicitly asks for offspring, in the case of the birth of Joseph it is the mother, Rachel, who pleads for a son. Rachel, however, pleads to Jacob instead of to Yahweh, occasioning Jacob's anger and his sharp retort.[22] The variation in the actions and characterizations in each of these episodes illustrates the multiformity and the expressiveness of the narratives.

The other two examples of the birth story in the Hebrew Bible are found in the Deuteronomistic work (Deuteronomy - 2 Kings). The stories of the birth of Samson (Judges 13) and the birth of Samuel (1 Samuel 1) are from other hands than the composers of the Tetrateuchal sources, an item that substantiates our

---

[21]The phrase is Alter's (*Biblical Narrative*, 62). One of the faults of Alter's book is his undervaluing of the artistic complexity of oral narrative; the same criticism applies to his otherwise valuable article, "How Convention Helps Us Read," 115-130.

[22]See the remarks of Alter, *Biblical Narrative*, 186-188.

hypothesis of a rich oral narrative tradition on which the various literary composers drew.[23]

The story of the birth of Samson begins with the expected notice of the barrenness of the mother: "[Manoah's] wife was barren (עֲקָרָה) and had borne no children" (Judg 13:2). Surprisingly, we are not told the name of Manoah's wife, and, also surprisingly, there is no mention of a plea for offspring. The theme of barrenness is found in the story, signalling the impending intervention of Yahweh to bring about the birth of the child, but since lineage is not a specific concern in the Samson story, as it was in the patriarchal stories, the desire for an heir is not explicitly voiced. Thus, the different status of Samson's heroic identity is already indicated in the introductory features of his birth story.

The next difference is the substitution of the "angel of Yahweh" (מַלְאַךְ-יהוה; 13:3) for Yahweh himself in the announcement of the impending birth of the child: "you will conceive and bear a son" (13:3). The announcement is made to the woman alone, later to be repeated in the presence of both Manoah and his wife (13:8-22). The repetition and elaboration of the event is a typical feature of oral narrative,[24] here preserved in literary form. The presence of the "angel of Yahweh" instead of Yahweh has often been seen as an indication of the later composition of this story relative to the J narratives; this may be so, but chronology is less important here than is a recognition of the essential multiformity of the birth story episodes, characterized by varying degrees of continuity and change.

In addition to the features that are distinctive in the Samson birth story, a number of elements establish a continuity with the narrative traditions preserved in the Tetrateuchal sources. The asking of the name of the angel and the angel's refusal to disclose it (13:17-18) is a multiform of the similar theme in the story of Jacob's wrestling with his divine adversary in Gen 32:30-31. Manoah's comment that "We will surely die, for we have seen God" (13:22) has analogues in Gen 32:31, Exod 19:21, 33:20, and Judg 6:22-23. Also, though perhaps less specific, the offer of a meal to the visiting angel (13:15) has a counterpart in the offering of a meal to the divine visitors in Genesis 18, whose task is to announce

[23]Compare also the story of Elisha and the Shunammite woman in 2 Kgs 4:8-37, which, while clearly a multiform of the story of Elijah and the widow of Sidon in 1 Kgs 17:7-24, also contains elements of the traditional birth story.

[24]See Lord, *Singer of Tales*, 173.

the birth of a son, Isaac, to the childless couple, Abraham and Sarah.

These lines of continuity establish a linkage between the story of the birth of Samson with the other traditional birth stories in the Tetrateuch, though the tone and the specific configuration of details give the story a cohesion of its own. Another of the new details presented in the Samson story is the identity of the hero as a Nazirite. This element establishes a continuity with the other Nazirite birth story in the Hebrew Bible, the birth of Samuel.

Although Samuel is born a Nazirite, with the promise that no razor will touch his head (1 Sam 1:11),[25] nonetheless the story of his birth shares more affinities with the patriarchal birth stories than with the birth story of Samson.[26] The story begins with the notice of Elkanah's two wives: "Peninnah had children, but Hannah had no children" (1 Sam 1:2). The rivalry set up here is parallel to the other rivalries of the women in the stories of the birth of Isaac (Sarah vs. Hagar), and in the birth of Joseph (Rachel vs. Leah). The Rachel vs. Leah rivalry is particularly close to the situation of Hannah and Peninnah, for, as the text relates in v. 5, "he loved Hannah, but Yahweh had closed her womb," setting up a perfect parallel to the situation of Rachel in Gen 29:30-31.[27] The Samuel story brings out even more of the personal nature of the rivalry, relating that "her rival used to taunt her . . . year after year, when she went up to the Temple of Yahweh; she used to taunt her, and she would cry and would not be able to eat" (vv. 6-7).[28]

At the Temple of Yahweh, Hannah pleads to Yahweh for a son and pledges to offer him to Yahweh's service as a Nazirite.[29] The

---

[25]A Qumran fragment (4QSam[a]) of 1 Sam 1:22 explicitly calls Samuel a *nzyr*; see F. M. Cross, Jr., "A New Qumran Biblical Fragment Related to the Original Hebrew Underlying the Septuagint" *BASOR* 132 (1953) 15-26.; see also the Greek text of 1 Sam 1:11. On the Nazirite elements in the birth stories of Samson and Samuel, see P. K. McCarter, Jr., *I Samuel* (AB; Garden City, NY: Doubleday, 1980) 53-54, 61, 65.

[26]McCarter and other commentators underemphasize the relationship between Samuel's birth story and the patriarchal birth stories. See McCarter's cursory remarks: *I Samuel*, 64.

[27]Note the thematic correspondences: "he loved Rachel more than Leah . . . but Rachel was barren" (Gen 29:30-31); "he loved Hannah, but Yahweh had closed her womb" (1 Sam 1:5).

[28]For a discussion of the textual difficulties of v. 6, see McCarter, *I Samuel*, 52-53.

[29]See above, n. 25.

scene in the Temple where Eli, the priest, accuses the woman of drunkenness has a nice touch of irony, for the woman has just promised that her son, as a Nazirite, will abstain from drink. Hannah replies to Eli: "I have not been drinking wine or beer, but I have been pouring out my spirit to Yahweh" (v. 15). Eli asks Yahweh to grant her request, and in v. 19 we find that "Yahweh remembered her," just as he had remembered Rachel in Gen 30:22. Hannah conceives and bears a son, and she names him Samuel (v. 20).

The Nazirite element links the birth of Samuel to the birth of Samson, but the themes of rivalry, of the overt desire for a son, and of Yahweh "remembering" the barren woman, link the story of Samuel with the patriarchal birth stories. Another set of details, interestingly enough, establishes a linkage with a lost birth story, that of Saul.[30] The word plays on the root שאל, "to ask," in vv. 17, 20, and 27-28 suggest that the child's name, as in other birth narratives, ought to be similar to the root. The naming of the child in v. 20 raises our suspicion: "She named him Samuel (שְׁמוּאֵל), 'for from Yahweh I requested him (שְׁאִלְתִּיו).'" The two words are somewhat similar, having three letters (שׁ, א, and ל) in common, yet the word plays in the biblical text are generally closer than this. The suspicion that vestiges of Saul's birth story have been borrowed into the account of Samuel's birth become a virtual certainty when the chapter closes with Hannah's statement: "as long as he lives, he is dedicated (שָׁאוּל) to Yahweh" (v. 28), clearly alluding to the name of Saul (שָׁאוּל).

Various scholars point to 1 Sam 9:1, the beginning of the story of Saul's career, as a likely place for a birth story of Saul to have been told,[31] and indeed it seems plausible that, at some point in the literary history of the narratives, a devaluation of Saul in favor of Samuel occurred,[32] motivating a literary borrowing of details from the one story to another. It seems likely that a birth story for Samuel already existed, since so many of the details are appropriate for Samuel, such as the association with the cult and the priesthood, but it does appear that a literary mixing has taken place.

---

[30]See McCarter, *I Samuel*, 62-63, 65.

[31]Ibid., 65.

[32]Ibid., 18-21.

The birth story of Samuel, therefore, has continuities on several levels with the other birth stories in the Israelite tradition. It shares Nazirite elements with the birth of Samson, themes of rivalry and of entreaty with the patriarchal birth stories, and details of word play with the lost birth story of Saul. The barrenness of the mother is a constant in all of the extant stories, so that the narrative can bring into play various types of tension and conflict until Yahweh's intervention is secured, and so that the special nature of the child is intimated by the very act of being born.

UGARITIC BIRTH STORIES

The comparison of the Ugaritic narratives with the biblical stories has continued apace since the discovery of the Ugaritic epics in the early 1930's.[33] The birth stories in the Kirta[34] and Aqhat epics have received due attention,[35] but it seems that some of the presuppositions involved in the comparison of the Ugaritic and biblical texts have not been fully examined. The remarks of Julius Obermann, whose treatment of the similarities of the Ugaritic and biblical birth stories is exemplary, are typical in their statement of the basis for comparison:

> In the main, the [Ugaritic] scene may be said to exemplify the general significance of the Ugaritic texts as a whole: They provide us with a new background for the religious and literary folklore of Palestine and the Old Testament - a much older background in point of time than that of

[33]For a discussion of the history of research on the Ugaritic texts, see especially A. Caquot, M. Sznycer, and A. Herdner, *Textes ougaritiques. Tome I: Mythes et légendes* (Paris: Cerf, 1974) 25-48, and the introductions to each of the texts.

[34]For the vocalization of *krt* as Kirta, see W. F. Albright, *Yahweh and the Gods of Canaan* (New York: Doubleday, 1968) 118.

[35]See especially J. Obermann, *How Daniel was Blessed with a Son: An Incubation Scene in Ugaritic* (New Haven: American Oriental Society, 1946) esp. 28-30; Cross, *Canaanite Myth and Hebrew Epic*, 177-183; and R. J. Clifford, "The Word of God in the Ugaritic Epics and in the Patriarchal Narratives," in *The Word in the World*, ed. R. J. Clifford and G. W. MacRae (Cambridge: Weston College, 1973 7-18; see also C. Westermann, "The Significance of the Ugaritic Texts for the Patriarchal Narratives," in *The Promises to the Fathers*, trans. D. E. Green (Philadelphia: Fortress, 1980) 165-186.

Phoenicia, and a much closer one in point of space than that
of Egypt or Babylonia.[36]

The point of the comparison is that Ugaritic texts show us a
"background" for the biblical materials.   But what kind of
"background" is this?   Richard Clifford, in another valuable
treatment of the Ugaritic and biblical birth stories, delineates the
nature of the relationship between the two bodies of narrative
more explicitly:

> If these suggestions are valid, the Ugaritic epics let us see
> something of the primitive forms and shape of the
> patriarchal tales, before they are taken up and given a new
> meaning and broader setting.[37]

In Clifford's view, the Canaanite traditions exemplified by the
Ugaritic epics are "taken up" by the Israelites and "given a new
meaning." While this approach to the comparison of Ugaritic and
Israelite materials is legitimate and, indeed, more thoughtful
than most, I question whether it is explicit enough.

It seems to me that the concept of the multiformity of an oral
tradition is the key to understanding the nature of the
relationship of the biblical and Ugaritic materials. The Ugaritic
birth stories are traditional multiforms from the northern
Canaanite cultural sphere, committed to writing sometime prior to
1365 B.C.E.[38] The biblical exemplars of the birth story are also
reflections of oral traditional narratives, with all their features
of multiformity, composed in the southern Canaanite (more
specifically, Israelite) cultural sphere in the period between the
10th-6th centuries B.C.E.[39] The earliest biblical sources for the
birth stories were set down in writing perhaps not more than two
centuries after the last of the Ugaritic tablets ceased to be in use

---

[36]Obermann, *How Daniel was Blessed*, 28.

[37]Clifford, "Word of God," 15.

[38]On the dating of the find-sites of the Ugaritic epic tablets, see R. North,
"Ugarit Grid, Strata, and Find-Localizations" *ZDPV* 89 (1973) 146; J.-C. Courtois,
"Ugarit Grid, Strata, and Find-Localizations. A Re-assessment" *ZDPV* 90 (1974)
106-107, and references.

[39]See, e.g., the discussion of Cross, "The Epic Traditions of Early Israel," in
The Poet and the Historian: Essays in Literary and Historical Biblical Criticism,
ed. R. E. Friedman (Chico, CA: Scholars, 1983) 13-39.

(circa 1175 B.C.E.).[40] In speaking of the oral performances of the two bodies of narratives, it may be appropriate for purposes of comparison to regard them as two variant traditions, one slightly earlier and to the north, and one slightly later and to the south. Cultural as well as linguistic differences separate the two traditions, but these differences, I submit, do not constitute a difference in essence or in kind. Innovations in the religious and political structures of early Israel do not indicate that there is an unbridgeable historical gulf between Canaanite and Israelite cultures; just as Hebrew is a Canaanite language, so we may regard the early Israelite narrative traditions as a variety of Canaanite narrative.[41]

The relation between the Ugaritic birth stories and the biblical birth stories is not that of "background" to "foreground," or of "primitive forms" that are "taken up" by Israel. The relation is one of continuity punctuated by various sorts of change, precisely the type of relationship that oral tradition tends to generate between any neighboring cultures sharing a common heritage. The biblical narratives and the Ugaritic narratives are, taking into account the cultural, geographic, and temporal differences, multiforms of each other.

KIRTA

The Kirta epic begins with an extended narration of King Kirta's need and desire for an heir. Kirta had previously had a wife and numerous children, but his wife died,[42] and their children all perished: some through disease, some at sea, some in battle, etc.[43] A poignant picture of Kirta's sadness follows in the text:

[40]I presume that, in addition to the epistolary and economic tablets preserved from the last days of Ugarit, mythic and epic tablets were also still in use.

[41]Note Gunkel's remark, made thirty years prior to the discovery of the Ugaritic epics: "die Vätersage [ist] im wesentlichen kanaanäisch" (Genesis, xlii).

[42]Literally, "she departed" (*tabi'at*), parallel in use to the English euphemism. Cf. the Arabic *halaka*, "to die," a semantic development from the Proto-Semitic √*hlk*, "to go."

[43]For commentary on the text, see Caquot, et al., *Textes ougaritiques*, 503ff.

yaʿin ḥatikahu kirta
   yaʿin ḥatikahu rašša
maʾda gurdašu ṭibtahu
wabitummi hin šipḫu yiʾtabid
   wabipuḫayyirihu yāriṯu
yaʿrub biḥadrihu yabkiyu
   biṯanî rigamīma wayidmaʿu
tinnatikna ʾudmaʿātihu
   kamā ṯiqalīma ʾarṣaha
   kamā ḫamišāti miṭṭatahu
bimā bakāyihu wayīšan
   bidamāʿi niḥāmimatu
šinatu taluʾannu wayiškab
niḥāmimatu wayiqmaṣ
wabiḥulumihu ʾilu yarada
   biḏhrati ʾabū ʾadami
wayiqrab bišaʾāli kirta
maʾʾatta kirta kī yabkiyu
   yidmaʿu nuʿmānu ġalmu ʾili

Kirta saw his offspring;
   he saw his offspring crushed,
   his dynasty utterly destroyed.
In its entirety the family perished,
   in its totality the succession.
He entered his chamber weeping,
   while repeating his words he cried.
His tears poured out
   like shekels to the ground,
   like five-shekel pieces onto his bed.
While weeping he fell asleep,
   while crying (he found) slumber.
Sleep overcame him and he lay down,
   slumber, and he reclined.
In his dream El came down,
   in his vision the Father of Humanity.
He approached, asking Kirta:
"What is wrong with Kirta that he weeps?
   that the Gracious One, the Lad of El, cries?"[44]

Kirta answers El that he is not weeping because of a desire for power or riches, but because he desires heirs, without which power and riches are pointless. He says to El:

[44]*CTA* 14.21-41. My vocalization of the Ugaritic is, of course, conjectural, based as it is on incomplete lexical and comparative data. It should not be confused with the *ipsissima verba*, rather an exercise in Northwest Semitic philology.

līmā 'anāku kaspa
    wayarqa ḫurāṣi
yada maqāmīha
    wa'abdê 'ālami
ṯalāṯa susawī-mi markabati
    bitarbaṣi banī 'ammati
[tin baḥīma 'aqniya
[tin ṯa'aḥīma 'ama"ida

What need have I of silver,
    or shining gold,
a household serf,
    two perpetual slaves,
three chariot horses
    from the stable of the craftsmen?
[Grant that] I may beget sons,
    [grant that] I may multiply offspring.[45]

In certain respects Kirta's initial situation resembles the "frame" story of the book of Job,[46] but it also shares affinities with the birth stories in the Israelite tradition. In Gen 15:1-6, Yahweh appears to Abraham in a vision (מַחֲזֶה) in which Yahweh promises Abraham great riches, but Abraham replies: "My lord Yahweh, what can you give me, since I continue being childless?" Yahweh thereupon promises to Abraham that he will have a child to be his heir. The narrative themes of the dream or vision, the divine offer of riches, and the request for offspring are shared by the Kirta and the Abraham stories. The weeping of the parent who requests a child is a detail found in the story of Hannah's request for a child in the Temple of Yahweh (1 Sam 1:10), and indeed several scholars have suggested that Kirta's weeping and oracle-dream take place in a sanctuary,[47] a possibility which would align the cultic context of the request with Isaac's entreaty of

---

[45]CTA 14.52-58. The stichometry and translation of these lines are based on a forthcoming treatment by F. M. Cross.

[46]See the remarks of M. H. Pope, in Wörterbuch der Mythologie, ed. H. W. Haussig (Stuttgart: Klett, 1965) I.294.

[47]E.g., Obermann, How Keret was Blessed, 10 n. 13; J. C. Greenfield, "Some Glosses on the Keret Epic" Eretz Israel 9 (1969) 62; see however the cautionary remarks of A. Caquot, "Les songes et leur interprétation selon Canaan et Israel," in Les songes et leur interprétation (Sources orientales II; Paris: Seuil, 1959) 105; also K. Jaroš, Die Stellung des Elohisten zur kanaanäischen Religion (OBO 4; Göttingen: Vandenhoeck & Ruprecht, 1982) 34-35.

Yahweh and with Rebekah's inquiry of a cultic oracle in Gen 25:21-22. Of course, divine revelation in dreams is a common theme in various story contexts in the biblical traditions, as for example in the revelation to Jacob at Bethel (Genesis 28; also a cultic context), and in the revelation to King Abimelek (Gen 20:3-7), which, interestingly enough, involves the barrenness of his wife and his slave girls.

The story of Kirta continues with El's lengthy instructions in the dream to Kirta, relating the actions he must undertake in order to acquire a wife and offspring. Kirta must first offer a sacrifice, then provision the army in preparation for an extended military campaign to the city of Udm, where dwells King Pabil and his lovely daughter Hurriya. Kirta is then to refuse various types of ransom and declare to King Pabil:

> padā ʾēna bibêtiya tatin
>   tin liya māṭta ḫurriya
>   nuʿmata šipḫi bukuraka
> dūka nuʿmu ʿanati nuʿmuha
>   kamā tôsami ʿaṭtarti tôsa[muha]
> dū-ʿuqquha ʾibbu ʾiqnîʾi
>   ʿap[ʿapā]ha sappū ṭarmila
>   taḫgurāni [ʾu]ḳma
> ʾašliwa biṣāpî ʿênêha
> dā-biḫulumiya ʾilu yatin
>   biḏrtiya ʾabū ʾadami
> kī-talidu šipḫa likirta
>   waġalma liʿabdi ʾili

> Give me what is not in my house:
>   give me Lady Hurriya,
>   the fairest of your family, your first-born;
> whose fairness is like the fairness of Anat,
>   whose beauty is like the beauty of Astart,
> whose neck is pure as lapis lazuli,
>   whose eyes shine like jewels,
>   clothed in carnelian.
> I will rest in the gaze of her eyes.
> This in my dream El granted,
>   in my vision the Father of Humanity.
> She will bear offspring for Kirta,
>   a son for the servant of El.[48]

---

[48]*CTA* 14.142-153. The transcription of the first word of line 151 as *ktld* rather than *wld* is a proposal of S. D. McBride.

Kirta then awakens and follows El's instructions, and finally acquires as his wife the Lady Hurriya. The theme of the military campaign as a means to acquire a wife is not found in the other birth story traditions, but, as has been noticed,[49] there is an affinity in the episode of the bride-quest in Genesis 24, in which Abraham instructs his servant to seek a bride for Isaac in the city of Nahor in Aram-naharaim. Abraham states that "(Yahweh) will send his angel (מַלְאָכוֹ) before you, and you will take a wife for my son from there" (Gen 24:7, cf. 24:40). The elements of the instructions guaranteed by the god, the journey and return, and the acquisition of a bride are shared by both stories. Of course, we expect a description of the beauty of the future bride, and we are not disappointed, though the description is less elaborate than the Ugaritic tale. The biblical text simply states that "the girl was very beautiful" (וְהַנַּעֲרָ טֹבַת מַרְאֶה מְאֹד; Gen 24:16).

After Kirta returns with his new wife Hurriya, there is a fragmentary scene in which El, in the midst of the divine assembly, blesses Kirta's marriage and promises him offspring, naming in particular the eldest son, Yassib:

> ʾaḫ]ra magaya ʿi[da]tu ʾilīma
> [wa]lyaʿni ʾalʾiyā[nu] baʿlu
> [ ]tbaʿ la-laṭīpānu [ʾilu dū-]paʾidi
> la-tabarrika [kirta] ṭāʿa
>   la-tamurra nuʿmāna [galma] ʾili
> kāsa yaʾḫud [ʾilu bi]yadi
>   karpāna bimi [yamīni]
> barrāku-mi yabarrik [ʿabdahu]
>   yabarrik ʾilu kirta [ṭāʿa]
>   [yamur-]mi nuʿmā[na] galma ʾili
> ʾa[ttata tiqqaḫ yā-kirta
>   ʾattata tiqqaḥ bêtaka
>   galmata tašaʿribu ḥaẓīraka
> talidu šabʿa banīma lika
>   watamānī tittaminu-mi lika
> talidu yaṣṣiba galma
>   yīnaqu ḥalba ʾaṯirati
>   maṣāṣu ṯadê batūlati [ʿanati]
>   mušêniq[tā ʾilīma]

[Then] the assembly of the gods arrived,

[49]S. B. Parker, "The Historical Composition of KRT and the Cult of El" *ZAW* 89 (1977) 165.

and Mighty Baal said:
"Come now, Kind [El, the] Compassionate,
May you bless [Kirta] the Noble,
    may you show favor to the Gracious One, [Lad] of El."
[El] took a cup in his hand,
    a flagon in his [right hand];
he blessed [his servant],
    El blessed Kirta the [Noble],
    [he showed favor to] the Gracious One, Lad of El:
"You have [taken a wife], O Kirta,
    you have taken a wife into your house,
    you have brought a maiden into your court.
She will bear you seven sons,
    eight she will produce for you.
She will bear Yassib the Lad,
    who will drink the milk of Asherah,
    who will suck the breasts of the Virgin [Anat],
    the two wet nurses [of the gods]."[50]

El goes on to list various daughters that Hurriya will bear, and
declares that "even to the youngest girl will I grant the blessing of
the first-born" (*ṣaḡaratihinna ʾabakkiruna*) indicating the breadth of
his blessing to Kirta's offspring.[51]

The themes of blessing and promise, so prominent in the biblical
birth stories, are evident in this episode of the Canaanite tale,
indicating once again that the various stories exist in a
relationship of continuity, punctuated by the types of change that
would exist in the different narrative contexts. Kirta is a king in
the Ugaritic story, and as such he commands an army in order to
acquire a wife. In the biblical stories the patriarchs are herdsmen
and farmers;[52] accordingly, the bride-quest in Genesis 24 is
conducted by an individual rather than an army. In early Israelite
traditions only adversaries, such as Abimelek in Genesis 20, are
kings.[53] Such changes are to be expected given the different

---

[50]*CTA* 15.1.11-28.

[51] There is no indication here of the motif of the "exaltation of the youngest,"
contra J. Gray, *The KRT Text in the Literature of Ras Shamra* (Leiden: Brill, 1964) 4,
10, 60; see the remarks of Gibson, *Canaanite Myths and Legends*, 92 n.1.

[52] On the social status of the patriarchs in the biblical narratives, see
especially N. K. Gottwald, *The Tribes of Yahweh* (Maryknoll, NY: Orbis, 1979)
451-453.

[53] See, however, Genesis 14 in which Abram is depicted as, at the very least, a
powerful chieftain; for discussion see J. Emerton, "The Riddle of Genesis XIV" *VT* 21

societal structures of Ugarit and early Israel. Nonetheless, the numerous continuities are clear: the themes of need and desire for heirs, the close relationship between the childless parent and the chief god (El or Yahweh), the divine blessing and bestowal of offspring, etc. In broad outline and in numerous individual details, the Kirta story shares affinities with the birth stories of the Israelite tradition.

AQHAT

The Aqhat epic also shares a number of affinities with the other birth stories in the Canaanite and Israelite traditions. The childless parent, Danel, is apparently a king,[54] like Kirta, but kingship is not a central concern as it is in the Kirta epic. Danel is pictured sitting at the entrance of the gate, judging the cases of the widows and orphans,[55] just as Job declares that he had done in his city.[56] Remarkably, Danel is listed, along with Job and Noah, as an exemplar of virtue by the prophet Ezekiel (Ezek 14:14,20), and elsewhere Ezekiel cites Danel as a paradigm of wisdom (Ezek 28:3).[57] Danel is regarded in Canaanite and Israelite tradition as a virtuous man, and as such Danel comes closer to the status of the Israelite patriarchs and heroes than does Kirta.

The Aqhat epic opens with Danel offering sacrifices to the gods and then lying down to sleep, a sequence that he repeats for six days. The scene of the sixth day transitions into a picture of the divine assembly where, on the seventh day, Baal intercedes with El on Danel's behalf:

[ḫā]mīš(t) ṯādīt(t) yômu
ʾuzr [ʾilīma] danʾilu

(1971) 403-439; see also the somewhat overstated remarks of C. H. Gordon, *The Common Background of Greek and Hebrew Civilizations* (New York: Harper and Row, 1965; originally published as *Before the Bible*, 1962) 143, 155.

[54]Danel is referred to as *mlk* in CTA 19.152.

[55]CTA 17.5.4-8.

[56]Job 29:12-13; see M. Pope, *Job* (AB; Garden City, NY: Doubleday, 1973) 212; J. C. L. Gibson, "Myth, Legend and Folk-lore in the Ugaritic Keret and Aqhat Texts" VTSup 28 (1975) 66-67.

[57]See S. Spiegel, "Noah, Daniel, and Job," in *Louis Ginzberg Jubilee Volume* (New York: American Academy for Jewish Research, 1945) 305-355; M. Noth, "Noah, Daniel und Hiob in Ezekiel XIV" VT 1 (1951) 251-260; and recently, B. Margalit, "Interpreting the Story of Aqhat" VT 30 (1980) 361-365.

ʾuzr ʾilīma yalaḥḥim
[ʾuzr] yašqiyu banī qudši
yaddi ṣītahu [dan]ʾilu
   yaddi ṣītahu yaʿli wayiškab
  [yaddī] miʾzarata pa-yalun
maka bišābī(t) yômi-mi
wayiqrab baʿlu biḥannatihu
ʾabyānūtu [daḥ]ʾilu mutu rapiʾi
   ʾanaḫa ġazru [mutu] harnamayyi
dū-ʾêna binu lihu kamā ʾaḫḫīhu
   wašuršu kamā ʾarayīhu
bal ʾiṭa binu lihu kamā ʾaḫḫīhu
   wašuršu kamā ʾarayīhu
ʾuzrm ʾilīma yalaḥḥimu
   yašqiyu banī qudši
la-tabarrikanannu la-ṯôru ʾilu ʾabūya
   tamurranannu la-bāniyu binwāti
wayakun binuhu bibêti
   šuršu biqirbi hēkalihu

A fifth, a sixth day,
Danel made an offering [to the gods],
   an offering to the gods to eat,
   [an offering]to the Sons of the Holy One to drink.
Danel took off his cloak,
   he took off his cloak, ascended, and lay down,
   [he took off] his loincloth and spent the night.
Then on the seventh day,
Baal approached with his plea:
"Danel, the Man of Rapi, is unhappy,
   the Hero, [Man] of the Harnamite, sighs;
he has no son like his brothers,
   nor heir like his kinsmen;
no son for him like his brothers,
   nor heir like his kinsmen.
He has given offerings to the gods to eat,
   offerings to the Sons of the Holy One to drink.
May you bless him, O Bull El my father,
   may you show him favor, O Creator of Creatures;
so that there might be a son in his house,
   an heir in the midst of his palace.[58]

El listens to Baal's plea and responds favorably:

[biyadi] yaḫud ʾilu ʿabdahu

[58]*CTA* 17.1.12-27.

yabarrik [danʾilla muta rapiʾi
yamur ġazra [muta harlnamayyi
napša yaḫi danʾilu [mutu rapiʾi
   brita ġazru mutu harnamayyi
[   ] huwa muḫḫu
   liʿiršihu yaʿli [   ]
bimā našāqi ʾattatihu [harāt]
   biḫabāqihu ḫamḫamatu
[lkn yālittu
   ḫamḫamatu [... limuti ralpiʾi
wayakun binuhu [bibêta]
   [šuršu] biqirbi hēkalihu

El took his servant [by the hand],
   he blessed [Danel], the Man of Rapi,
   he showed favor to the Hero, [Man of the] Harnamite:
"Let Danel, [the Man of Rapi], be revived in spirit,
   the Hero, Man of the Harnamite, in life-breath.
[   ] he himself
   let him mount his bed . . .
When he kisses his wife [she will conceive],
   when he embraces her she will (become) pregnant . . .
[   ] she will bear,
   she will (become) pregnant . . . [for the Man of] Rapi;
so that there might be a son [in his house],
   [an heir] in the midst of his palace.[59]

The situation of a man with no offspring is familiar in the various multiforms of the birth story. Danel desires a son, so he offers sacrifice to the gods and sleeps, presumably waiting for a dream oracle. On the seventh day, a propitious day in the formulaic conventions of Canaanite and biblical traditions,[60] Danel gets results. Danel's entreaty to the gods is explicit, while Kirta, it seems, receives his dream revelation by accident, much as does Jacob in his dream revelation in Genesis 28. Interestingly, Kirta is instructed by El to make a sacrifice as the first of his required tasks; in the biblical stories Manoah offers a sacrifice in the presence of the angel of Yahweh (Judg 13:19-20), and Abraham offers a sacrifice and has a dream oracle after Yahweh promises

[59]*CTA* 17.1.35-44.

[60]S. E. Loewenstamm, "The Seven-Day Unit in Ugaritic Literature" *IEJ* 15 (1965) 121-133.

him the birth of an heir (Gen 15:7-20).[61] Isaac's entreaty and Rebekah's inquiry of an oracle in Gen 25:21-22 also belong to the cultic setting of the request for an heir, as does Hannah's prayer in the Temple of Yahweh in 1 Sam 1:9-18. The Danel episode is the most extended narration of the cultic acts accompanying the request for an heir, but hints and traces from the other stories indicate the importance of the cultic context, though it is more often implied than explicitly stated.

Another feature is less explicit in the Aqhat epic than in the other birth stories. In the biblical stories the theme of the barrenness of the woman seems to be a traditional constant. Yahweh's task is to open the wombs of the women in order for the special child to be born. In the Kirta epic the birth of offspring is dependent on the acquisition of a wife, so El instructs Kirta how to acquire the proper wife. In the Aqhat epic the cause of the childlessness of Danel is not stated; he has a wife, but we do not know if the wife is barren or if Danel is sterile or impotent. The fact that we are not told is of interest; it seems that the fact of childlessness is more important than its cause, however embellished the cause might be in other birth stories.

This absence of information once again indicates the fluidity in the general structure of the birth story: there is no definite fixed sequence of events and causes that the narrative must relate; the essential story is multiform, taking on different shape in different tellings and in different contexts. The setting up of a chart to delineate the specific action sequence of a tale and its variants, as is the tendency of many critics,[62] simply misses the point of the multiformity of traditional narratives. What we may see as a missing element in the Aqhat epic is probably better described as a sign of the variability in an oral narrative tradition. That is to say, the story itself is fully told; it is only our modern notion of textual fixity that inclines us to believe that something is missing.

[61]See Obermann, *How Daniel was Blessed*, 28 n. 64. In its present setting the sacrifice and dream oracle of Gen 15:7-20 are connected with the promise of land, not with the promise of offspring. The promise of an heir which precedes in 15:1-6 may indicate a more extensive original connection. On the traditions of the "promises to the patriarchs," see the overview of C. Westermann, *The Promises to the Fathers*, 95-163.

[62]See, e.g., the chart of birth stories in D. Irvin, *Mytharion: The Comparison of Tales from the Old Testament and the Ancient Near East* (AOAT 32; Neukirchen-Vluyn: Neukirchener, 1978) 138.

For the story, it is enough to say that with El's blessing, Danel and his wife will have a son.

The story of the birth of Jacob and Esau and the other biblical birth stories share a number of traits with the Ugaritic birth stories. The proximity in time, space, language, and culture leads us to conclude that the various stories are related to each other as multiforms in the continuous tradition of oral narrative in the Canaanite-Israelite sphere. The affinities on the level of narrative also present the possibility of a number of other levels of affinity: cultic, economic, political, etc. For example, F. M. Cross has discussed at length the continuities between the Canaanite god El and the Israelite god Yahweh; this level of continuity is evident in the multiforms of the birth stories in Canaan and Israel: El/Yahweh is the god who grants heirs, blesses his favored ones, heals the barren and the sick, and guides in battle.[63] In the Jacob cycle, Yahweh is referred to as the אֲבִיר יַעֲקֹב, "the Bull of Jacob," just as El is *ṯôru ʾilu,* "Bull El."[64] Other similarities in epithets and in the terms of description abound in the texts.[65] The revelations in dreams and the aspect of El and Yahweh as "personal gods" to their chosen suppliants are further aspects of the continuities on the level of cult and pantheon.[66]

The narratives that we have from Ugarit and from Israel relate innumerable bits of information about the religious cult, political and economic practices, onomastic and lexical items, prosodic techniques, and modes of storytelling.[67] To the teller of the tales and to the audience, the cultural and historical aspects of the tale were undoubtedly secondary, part of the unspoken heritage linking the audience to the narrator. The primary point was the tale

[63]Cross, *Canaanite Myth,* 44-75, 177-194, esp. 182-183; idem, "אֵל" in *TDOT* I.242-261.

[64]Gen 49:24; see Cross, *Canaanite Myth,* 4 n. 6; and P. D. Miller, Jr., "Animal Names as Designations in Ugaritic and Hebrew" *UF* 2 (1971) 177-186.

[65]See Cross, *op cit.*

[66]On dreams, see Caquot, "Les songes," 99-124; Jaroš, *Stellung,* 31-50. On personal religion, see Cross, *Canaanite Myth,* 75 n. 120; H. Vorlander, *Mein Gott: Die Vorstellungen vom persönlichen Gott im Alten Orient und im Alten Testament* (AOAT 23; Neukirchener-Vluyn: Neukirchener, 1975) 184-215; R. Albertz, *Persönliche Frömmigkeit und offizielle Religion: Religionsinterner Pluralismus in Israel und Babylon* (Stuttgart: Calwer, 1978) 77-91.

[67]See especially L. R. Fisher, S. Rummel, et al., eds., *Ras Shamra Parallels,* vols. I-III (AnOr 49-51; Rome: Biblical Institute, 1972, 1975, 1981).

itself, the stories of the sufferings and triumphs of the legendary heroes of the past. In the stories, life is related, not simply historical data. In the terms of the tale, the important moments occur at the point of an impasse or a resolution. Danel's emotions are the significant facts of the birth episode in the Aqhat epic when he discovers that his gods had granted his plea:

> bidlanʾilil panūma tišmaḫū
> waʿalê yiṣhal piʾital
> wayapruq liṣba wayiṣḫaq
> paʿnê lihudumi yatpud
> yiššaʾu ğīhu yaṣīḫu
> ʾatibuna ʾanāku waʾanūḫuna
> watanūḫu biʾirtiya napšī
> kī-yuladu binu liya kamā ʾaḫḫīya
> wašuršu kamā ʾarayīya

> Danel's face was glad,
>   and above his forehead shone.
> He opened his mouth and laughed,
>   placed his feet on a footstool,
>   raised his voice and shouted:
> "Now I can sit and relax,
>   the spirit in my breast can relax;
> for a son will be born to me like my brothers,
>   an heir like my kinsmen."[68]

The story itself, we might say, is the thing.

---

[68]*CTA* 17.2.8-15.

Revelation at Bethel

In the course of his journey to Udm to acquire the hand of the Lady Hurriya, Kirta comes to a shrine of Asherah where he makes a vow:

> ṯamma yaddu[r ki]rta ṯāʿu
> ʾi ʾiṯata ʾaṯiratu ṣurri-mi
>   waʾilatu ṣidyāni-mi
> himma ḫurriya bêtaya ʾiqqaḥa
>   ʾašaʿriba ġalmata ḥaẓiraya
> ṯinêha klaspa-mi ʾatina
>   waṯalāṯaha ḫurāṣa-mi

> There Kirta the Noble made a vow:
> "As Asherah of Tyre lives,
> and Elat of Sidon,
> if I take Hurriya into my house,
> if I bring the maiden into my court,
> I will give double her (price) in silver,
> and triple her (price) in gold."[69]

Kirta does eventually take Hurriya into his house, but in his new state of satiety he apparently neglects to fulfill his vow, and Asherah prepares to exact vengeance.[70] Kirta falls sick, and only El's intervention by means of a healing goddess finally saves him.[71]

The Jacob story pursues different themes to different conclusions, but there is a striking convergence in the story of the revelation at Bethel in which Jacob makes a vow to the deity:

> Jacob made a vow, saying: "If God is with me and protects me on this road on which I go, and gives me bread to eat and clothes to wear, and if I return safely to the house of my father, then Yahweh will be my god, and this stone which

---

[69]*CTA* 14.199-206; see W. F. Albright, "A Vow to Asherah in the Keret Epic" *BASOR* 94 (1944) 30-31.

[70]*CTA* 15.3.25-30.

[71]*CTA* 15.4 - 15.6.

61

> I set up as a massebah will be a temple of God, and of all
> that you give to me, I will give a tenth to you." (Gen 28:20-
> 22)

Aside from the grammatical and source complexity of the text
(note the shift from third person address to second person address,
and the shift from Elohim to Yahweh to Elohim), we notice a
similarity to the Ugaritic text in the vow to a deity in the course
of a journey to another land, a journey that will culminate in the
acquisition of a wife.[72] There is no mention of the theme of the
bride-quest in the Bethel story, and the repercussions of the vow
are different,[73] but there is an essential similarity in the theme of
the hero's acquisition of divine aid at a sacred place in the course
of his journey.

We can, I believe, gain a general insight into the nature of West
Semitic epic by viewing Kirta's vow to Asherah and Jacob's vow to
Elohim/Yahweh as examples of a common repertoire of stock
narrative themes and episodes. The forms of tradition manifest
themselves in particular ways in the two stories and carry specific
implications - for instance, Kirta is shown to be fallible while
Jacob is ultimately faithful - but the essential stability of the
forms remains intact. The stability of the forms and their function
as meaningful indicators in a story are illustrated by the
continuities between the two events in the Kirta and Jacob
narratives.

In his vow Jacob reveals his concern for his safety in his travels,
and he shows his desire to return to the house of his father. Jacob
is depicted as vulnerable and afraid, as well he might since his
journey is, in the J version, a flight for his life.[74] Jacob's night

---

[72]The common features of Gen 28:20-22 and *CTA* 14.199-206 have been noted and
discussed by R. J. Clifford, *The Cosmic Mountain in Canaan and the Old Testament*
(Cambridge: Harvard University, 1972) 107; idem, "The Word of God in the
Ugaritic Epics and in the Patriarchal Narratives," in *The Word in the World*, ed.
R. J. Clifford and G. W. MacRae (Cambridge: Weston College, 1973) 13-14; and L. R.
Fisher, "Two Projects at Claremont" *UF* 3 (1971) 27-31; idem, ed., *Ras Shamra
Parallels*, vol. II (AnOr 50; Rome: Biblical Institute, 1975) 147-152; and see the
remarks of S. B. Parker, "The Vow in Ugaritic and Israelite Narrative Literature"
UF 11 (1979) 698-700.

[73]In Gen 35:1-7 (E) Jacob returns to Bethel and builds an altar, while Kirta
apparently neglects his vow.

[74]Gen 27:41-45 (J); cf. Gen 35:1 (E). The P variant (Gen 27:46 - 28:9) in which
Jacob sets out on a bride-quest is later in the history of the source documents, but the
antiquity of the bride-quest theme in Israelite and Canaanite traditions is evident

vision at Bethel is therefore fitting in its narrative context: the hero is at a low point, in fear for his life, and traveling to a strange land. At the moment of his greatest vulnerability, Jacob acquires a divine benefactor, Yahweh/Elohim, and begins a relationship with deity that will come to characterize Jacob as the hero and patriarch that he is destined to be. In the J version of the story, Bethel is where Jacob acquires the promise of land, descendents, and divine blessing (vv. 13-16). In the E version, Jacob becomes more explicitly a cult founder (v. 22) and establishes a reciprocal relationship with deity (vv. 20-21). Here is Jacob's rise to glory, the first flowering of his heroic identity.

In addition to the continuity of these themes - the vow, the acquisition of divine aid, the journey *cum* bride-quest - other aspects of the symbolism of Jacob's sojourn at Bethel warrant a close investigation, since in the compressed narration of the episode many themes are hinted at rather than developed explicitly. First of all, we notice that Jacob comes upon Bethel unknowingly; he simply stops to spend the night as the sun goes down (v. 11). A similar circumstance leads to Jacob's next direct encounter with deity, the wrestling match at Penuel in Genesis 32. The place name Bethel, "house (temple) of El," is an explicitly cultic name, as is Penuel, "face (presence) of El." Jacob's two direct encounters with Yahweh/Elohim are arranged symmetrically, the first on the way from Beersheba to Haran, the second on the homeward journey. Both encounters can be viewed as rites of passage[75] in a geographical and spiritual sense: Jacob is passing through the threshold of his native land,[76] while at the same time entering into a new phase of his heroic identity. In the encounter at Bethel, Jacob is told of his identity as patriarch and acquires a special relationship with Yahweh/Elohim, his patron deity. In the encounter at Penuel, Jacob receives his severest test:

from its multiforms in Genesis 24 (J) and in the Kirta epic; see the remarks of Parker, "Historical Composition of KRT," 165.

[75]See A. van Gennep, *The Rites of Passage*, trans. M. B. Vizedom and G. L. Caffee (Chicago: University of Chicago, 1960); V. Turner, "Betwixt and Between: The Liminal Period in *Rites de Passage*," in *The Forest of Symbols: Aspects of Ndembu Ritual* (Ithaca: Cornell University, 1967) 93-111.

[76]According to the directions of Jacob's route, Bethel and Penuel would roughly correspond to the high points from which Jacob would descend into the Jordan rift valley on his exit from and return to the promised land. Compare the more mythological geography of the passage of Gilgamesh through the gates of Mount Mashu, the cosmic mountain at the edge of the world, where fierce scorpion-men guard the passage: Gilg. IX.ii-iv; *ANET*, 88-89.

the deity wrestles with him, and only after surviving through the night does he receive his new name and new identity as "Israel." At the start of both encounters Jacob is alone and apparently vulnerable; at the end of both, Jacob emerges as a man with a promise and a destiny to fulfill.

The place names Bethel and Penuel also suggest a continuity between the Israelite cult and the Canaanite cult. The form of a place name בֵּית + *DN* is common is Syro-Palestine and indicates that El in the name Bethel (בֵּית-אֵל) refers originally to the Canaanite high god, El. Other such local place names mentioned in the Hebrew Bible include: בֵּית-עֲנָת, בֵּית חוֹרֹן, בֵּית-דָּגֹון, and שֶׁמֶשׁ בֵּית.[77] In all of these forms the divine name is a proper name, thus we are justified in reading the Bethel story as, at least in part, a reflection of an old tradition of the founding of a Canaanite cult place.[78]   Gunkel's remark that the patriarchal stories are "essentially Canaanite"[79] finds some support in the story of Jacob's founding of the cult place of the "House of El."[80]

The "messengers of God" (מַלְאֲכֵי אֱלֹהִים) in v. 12 are related to the minor members of the Canaanite pantheon who perform tasks for their superiors, as in the two "messengers" (*malʾakāmi*) of Yamm,[81] the two servants of Baal, Gapnu and Ugaru,[82] or Asherah's servant, Qadišu-wa-Amruru, also called Daggay.[83] In Israelite religion the "messengers" (מַלְאָכִים) of Yahweh perform various tasks,[84] and, like the Canaanite gods, are members of the divine assembly.[85]

[77]For other examples of place names *bēt-DN* in the ancient Near East, see H. A. Hoffner, "בַּיִת" *TDOT* 2.107-116. For the antiquity of several Syro-Palestinian sites with this name form, see Y. Aharoni, *The Archaeology of the Land of Israel*, trans. A. F. Rainey (Philadelphia: Westminster, 1982) 56.

[78]See Clifford, *Cosmic Mountain*, 105: "The story explicitly tells of the origin and ideology of a Canaanite shrine, the pre-Israelite holy place at Bethel."

[79]See above, n. 41.

[80]See above, p. 58, on Cross's remarks on the continuities of El and Yahweh.

[81]*CTA* 2.1.22-42.

[82]*CTA* 3.3.33; 4.7.54; 4.8.47; 5.1.12; 8.6-7.

[83]*CTA* 3.6.11; 4.4.8,13,16-17.

[84]For the tasks of the divine מַלְאָכִים in Israelite lore, see Gen 19:1,15; Gen 32:2; Exod 14:19; Judg 6:11-22; Judg 13:3-23; etc.; see T. H. Gaster, "Angel" *IDB* 1.129-134.

[85]See most recently, E. T. Mullen, Jr., *The Divine Council in Canaanite and Early Hebrew Literature* (HSM 24; Chico, CA: Scholars, 1980); Cross, *Canaanite Myth*, 186-190; and references cited in both.

The "ladder" (סֻלָּם) that Jacob sees in his dream (v. 12), on which the "messengers of God" are ascending and descending, is an item that is unknown elsewhere in Israelite or in Canaanite texts. Interestingly, it is found in a Mesopotamian text, the myth of Nergal and Ereshkigal.[86] In a Neo-Assyrian tablet of the myth, we find Anu sending a messenger, Kaka, to the underworld to deliver a message to Ereshkigal. Kaka then descends the *simmelat šamāmi*, "the staircase of heaven."[87] In the course of myth, we find the gods Namtar and Nergal also ascending and descending the *simmelat šamāmi*.[88] The Akkadian word *simmiltu*, "staircase," is cognate with Hebrew *sullām*, via a metathesis of the liquids *l* and *m*.[89] It seems that in the mythological traditions of the two cultures, more than just the word was cognate, but also the concept of the "staircase of heaven." The divine messengers of Gen 28:12 are simply performing the task that gods elsewhere in the Semitic world perform: they travel on the available route of transport from heaven to earth and beyond. The uniqueness of Genesis 28 is that Jacob is allowed to witness this passage between the cosmic realms. The בֵּית-אֵל is where the heavenly and earthly realms meet; it is an *axis mundi*, a place of the incursion of the sacred into the profane world.[90] Here is an appropriate place for Jacob to learn of his sacred identity and of his divine benefactor.

A final remark on the symbolism of Genesis 28 will take us beyond the sphere of ancient Semitic cultures and into the realm of prehistory and even biology. In v. 11 we find Jacob taking a stone and placing it under his head in preparation for sleep. Jacob then has his dream vision of the ladder and of the divine beings

[86]O. R. Gurney, "The Sultantepe Tablets: VII. The Myth of Nergal and Ereshkigal" *Anatolian Studies* 10 (1960) 105-131; trans. by A. K. Grayson in *ANET*, 507-512. The relevance of this text to Genesis 28 was first noted by A. R. Millard, "The Celestial Ladder and the Gate of Heaven (Gen28.12,17)" *ExpTim* 78 (1966) 86-87.

[87]Nergal and Ereshkigal (STT I no.28) col i.16'.

[88]STT I no.28, col. v.13',42' (Namtar); col. vi.18' (Nergal); etc.

[89]Cf. Arabic *sullam* and Jewish Aramaic *sūlmā*, but Syriac *sebbeltā*, Mandaic *sumbiltā*, and Neo-Syriac *simmiltā*. The variation between masculine *slm* and feminine *sml* seems to have appeared quite early in the history of the Semitic languages, judging from the clear variation in the cognates (esp. Arabic, Hebrew, and Akkadian). On the metathesis of *l* and *m*, see S. Moscati, et al., *An Introduction to the Comparative Grammar of the Semitic Languages* (Wiesbaden: Harrassowitz, 1969) 63. Note a similar metathesis within Hebrew: *śimlāh* and *śalmāh*.

[90]See M. Eliade, *The Myth of the Eternal Return*, trans. W. R. Trask (Princeton: Princeton University, 1954) 12-17.

ascending and descending. Upon awakening, Jacob sets up the stone
as a מַצֵּבָה and anoints it with oil (v. 18). Finally, Jacob promises
that, if he returns safely, he will make the מַצֵּבָה into a "temple of
God" (בֵּית אֱלֹהִים), a cultic site. In these references to the stone, all
from the E source, we have a tantalizing glance into a cultic
practice that appears to be widespread in the ancient world.[91]

The מַצֵּבָה or "standing stone" is a frequent item in the biblical
text. It is used for several purposes: to mark a cultic site,[92] to mark
a tomb,[93] or to mark a boundary.[94] The word and the concept are
cognate with the pre-Islamic *nuṣb*, which was a stone set up at
cultic sites.[95] The Phoenician term *mṣbt* is another cognate word; it
denotes a funerary stele.[96] All of these terms indicate a stone that
is "set up" for one purpose or another. The common signification
that all of these uses share is that the stone marks a liminal or
marginal place, whether a sacred area or a geographical
threshold.

The stone as a marker of liminal places is found in Mesopotamia
and Greece as well. The *kudurru* is a stone set up at boundaries in
Mesopotamia; it generally contains an inscription that proclaims
the owner's legal title to the land.[97] In Greece the "herm" is a
phallic statue that is set up in front of a house, in the market
place, at crossroads, and at the frontiers; it marks borders and
thresholds.[98]

Pouring oil on stones is also found in Greece, as it is in Hittite
culture. Oil is poured on the *omphalos* at the holy site of Delphi,
and travellers pour oil on stones at crossroads.[99] In Hittite ritual

[91]On the מַצֵּבָה, see especially C. F. Graesser, "Standing Stones in Ancient
Palestine" *BA* 35 (1972) 34-63; idem, "Studies in *Maṣṣēbôt*," (unpublished Harvard
dissertation, 1969). In the remarks that follow, I am indebted to the discussion of
W. Burkert, *Structure and History in Greek Mythology and Ritual* (Berkeley:
University of California, 1979) 35-43.

[92]Gen 35:14; Exod 24:4; cf. Josh 4:19-24, and Josh 24:26-27.

[93]Gen 35:20; 2 Sam 18:18; cf. *CTA* 17.1.27-28.

[94]Gen 31:45,51-52; Isa 19:19.

[95]See W. Robertson Smith, *Lectures on the Religion of the Semites* (London:
Black, 1889) 201-203.

[96]*KAI* 34.1; 35.1; 53.1; 60.5,6; 100.1; 163.2.

[97]See J. A. Brinkman, "Kudurru," *Reallexikon der Assyriologie*, vol. VI (Berlin:
de Gruyter, 1983) 267-274.

[98]Burkert, *Greek Mythology and Ritual*, 39-41.

[99]Ibid., 42.

the ḫuwaši-stones are often washed and anointed with oil.[100] Walter Burkert suggests that the function of these libations is essentially the same as the setting up of the stones: libations serve to "mark" a place as significant. Burkert notes that "stains of oil on a stone remain visible for quite a long time."[101] The function of libations of oil in the Greek cult of the dead follows the same principle: the libation leaves a "mark" indicating that the tomb is being cared for by the living relatives.[102]

The function of marking territory by means of stones and libations appears to be an archaic trait in human societies. Borders, sacred sites, tombs, crossroads - these are all liminal places that call for special marking. Crossing thresholds, whether sacral or geographical, is an act that involves danger and risk, whether physical or spiritual. Cultures, therefore, develop ways to mark these thresholds and to navigate their passage.[103]

In Genesis 28, Jacob marks the holy place with the appropriate materials and vows to return and construct a בֵּית אֱלֹהִים at the site of the holy stone. Yet the roots of Jacob's impulse to set up a מַצֵּבָה are not limited to the sphere of human culture. Other animals mark their territories: mammals, reptiles, birds, etc.[104] The concern to mark boundaries and thresholds is not limited to *homo sapiens*; here is an impulse that is rooted in the biology of many species. In humans this impulse takes on many forms, both sacred and secular, but the impulse itself appears to be innate; it is one of the features that define us as human animals.

[100]See A. Goetze, *Kleinasien* (Munich: Beck, 1957) 168.

[101]Burkert, *Greek Mythology and Ritual*, 42.

[102]Ibid., 42.

[103]See van Gennep, *Rites of Passage*; Turner, "Betwixt and Between."

[104]Burkert, *Greek Mythology and Ritual*, 43; on territoriality in insects, birds, fish, reptiles, and mammals, see the overview in R. A. Wallace, *Animal Behavior: Its Development, Ecology, and Evolution* (Santa Monica, CA: Goodyear, 1979) 326-343, and references.

2. Epic and Cult

The relationship between sacred narrative (myth or epic) and sacred actions (ritual) has been an ongoing concern of biblicists, classicists, and anthropologists since the pioneering researches of Robertson Smith and Frazer in the late nineteenth and early twentieth centuries.[1] Robertson Smith's view that myth originally derived from ritual has had an important influence on scholars of biblical and other ancient texts, as in the "Cambridge school" of classicists,[2] and the "Myth and Ritual school" of Near Eastern scholars.[3] The primary tenet of this approach stressed that the "thing said" (*legomenon*) is a secondary construct fully determined by the "thing done" (*drōmenon*).[4] The "thing done" in the Near Eastern context tended to be either the annual ritual of enthronement or the seasonal fertility rituals, according to followers of the "myth and ritual" approach. Although the excesses of the "myth and ritual" approach have long since been admitted,[5] one still finds scholars arranging various mythical texts according to minute and conjectural indices of vegetation

[1]W. Robertson Smith, *Lectures on the Religion of the Semites* (London: Black, 1889; J. G. Frazer, *The Golden Bough: A Study in Comparative Religion* (London: Macmillan, 1890).

[2]E.g., J. Harrison, *Prolegomena to the Study of Greek Religion* (Cambridge: Cambridge University, 1903); G. Murray, *Four Stages of Greek Religion* (New York: Columbia University, 1912; the later edition [1925] was extended to *Five Stages of Greek Religion*); F. M. Cornford, *From Religion to Philosophy* (London: Arnold, 1912).

[3]See S. H. Hooke, ed., *Myth and Ritual* (Oxford: Clarendon, 1933); idem, ed., *Myth, Ritual and Kingship* (Oxford: Clarendon, 1958); I. Engnell, *Studies in Divine Kingship in the Ancient Near East* (Uppsala: Almqvist & Wiksells, 1943); T. H. Gaster, *Thespis: Ritual, Myth and Drama in the Ancient Near East* (New York: Schuman, 1950).

[4]For this formulation, see J. Harrison, *Themis: A Study of the Social Origins of Greek Religion* (Cambridge: Cambridge University, 1912) 327-331.

[5]See H. Frankfort, *The Problem of Similarity in Ancient Near Eastern Religions* (Oxford: Clarendon, 1951); J. Fontenrose, *The Ritual Theory of Myth* (Berkeley: University of California, 1966); G. S. Kirk, *Myth: Its Meaning and Function in Ancient and Other Cultures* (Berkeley: University of California, 1970) 8-31; J. W. Rogerson, *Myth in Old Testament Interpretation* (Berlin: de Gruyter, 1974) 66-84; also Burkert, *Structure and History in Greek Mythology and Ritual*, 35-58.

imagery or kingship imagery,[6] and one occasionally finds other scholars describing a myth as a "libretto" to cultic rituals,[7] even when little or nothing is known of the performative context of the myth in question.

The conjectural density of approaches that link epic or myth in general to specific cultic acts render such approaches suspect. There are, nonetheless, numerous grounds on which sacred narrative and sacred acts can be seen to converge. For example, in the Bethel narrative discussed above, Jacob performs certain unmistakably cultic acts within the context of the narration. Even if Jacob is unaware of the cultic import of his actions, the audience is well aware that he is acting according to the requirements of cult. The linkage between the cult place of Bethel and the patriarch Jacob is part of the explicit message of the narrative. The question posed here is not when or whether the Bethel narrative was acted out, but how Jacob is acting out cultic concerns within the context of the narrative. The question shifts from the field of history to the field of narrative dynamics.

In other texts the interaction of cult and narrative takes on more subtle forms. In the two instances discussed below, the densely textured narrative dynamics are seen to include various allusions to cultic practice and belief in which the cultic dimension adds an important level of significance to the narrated acts. The conflict between Aqhat and Anat, I will argue, is only poorly understood unless the metaphors and symbols evoked by the two antagonists are recognized as redolent with cultic allusion. A double meaning is communicated by these allusions in which a promise of life becomes a veiled metaphor for the threat of death. In the episode of Jacob's deception of Isaac, the donning of animal skins by Jacob becomes not only an assumption of a false, opposite identity, but also a ritual play on the role of the sacrificer and the sacrificed and on the nature of the ritual blessing.

The common features of the Jacob narrative and Canaanite epic stressed in this section are not the overt similarities of the birth stories, but are more of the order of a background essence, a ritually

---

[6] E.g., J. C. de Moor, *The Seasonal Pattern in the Ugaritic Myth of Ba'ru* (AOAT 16; Kevelaer: Butzon & Bercker, 1971).

[7] E.g., Cross, *Canaanite Myth*, ix.

charged dimension of significance, in which the actions and sayings of the characters take on a doubled aspect. Anat says something, Jacob does something, Aqhat and Isaac respond, all contributing to a narrative design in which traces of ritual, death, and taboo remain.

Aqhat and Anat

The conflict between Aqhat and Anat centers on Anat's desire for Aqhat's divine bow. The sexual component of this desire has been debated in recent years,[8] but, in spite of the specter of Freudian reductionism, I think that the sexual tenor of the narrative is incontestable. In CTA 18.1.24, Anat exclaims to Aqhat: ʾatta ʾaḫī waʾana ʾalḫātukal, "You are my brother and I am [your sister],"[9] a phrase that echoes the diction of love poetry in the ancient Near East.[10] In an episode in the amours of the god El,[11] the imagery of shooting a bird using the language of archery (note the characteristic verb yari in line 38: "he shot [with a bow]") is mixed in with a scene of conception and pregnancy. Just as El shoots a bird and sets it on the hot coals (lines 38-39), so he seduces the two goddesses (line 39). The imagery of hunting and cooking naturally blends in with the imagery of sex.

In addition to the sexual resonance of Anat's desire for Aqhat's bow, there is also the dimension of the hunt, of rivalry, and of death. As P. Xella has convincingly demonstrated for the Aqhat epic, the relationship between the young hunter and the goddess of the hunt is fraught with danger and leads often to a significant reversal: the young hunter becomes the hunted, the prey of the goddess of the hunt.[12] The Greek story of the hunter Aktaion provides an analogy for the cooperation of the levels of sex and hunting in the confrontation between the young hunter and the

[8]D. R. Hillers, "The Bow of Aqhat: The Meaning of a Mythological Theme," in *Orient and Occident. Essays Presented to C. H. Gordon*, ed. H. A. Hoffner, Jr. (AOAT 22; Neudirchen-Vluyn, Neukirchener, 1973) 71-80; see also H. H. P. Dressler, "Is the Bow of Aqhat a Symbol of Virility?" *UF* 7 (1973) 217-220; and below, pp. 90-92.

[9]Following the restoration of C. H. Gordon (*apud CTA*, 85 n. 8).

[10]See, e.g., Cant 4:9,10,12; 5:1; and M. H. Pope, *Song of Songs* (AB; Garden City, NY: Doubleday, 1977) 69-85.

[11]*CTA* 23.37-53.

[12]P. Xella, "Una 'rilettura' del poema di Aqhat," *Problemi del mito nel vicino oriente antico* (Naples: Istituto Orientale di Napoli, 1976) 61-91.

goddess of the hunt.[13]   In the version of the story preserved by
Euripides, Aktaion boasts that he is a better hunter than Artemis;
she then transforms him into an animal and his own hunting dogs
kill him.[14]   In another version Aktaion's affront is his proposal to
marry his aunt Semele;[15] in another he proposes to marry Artemis
herself.[16] And in the late version made famous by Ovid, the young
hunter's fault is to see the goddess naked.[17]   In all of these
multiforms of the story, the young hunter's affront is punished by
his death at the behest of the goddess. The language of sex and
the language of the hunt are variations on each other in these
stories; both are facets of the complex and dangerous relationship
between the young hunter and the goddess of the hunt. The
antiquity of these twin themes, sex and the hunt, has been traced
to prehistoric times by W. Burkert;[18] its continuous expressive force
is substantiated by its presence in Greek tradition, in Near Eastern
tradition, and in the fascination these traditions still exert today.

The themes of sex and hunting, both signaled by the conflict
over Aqhat's bow, converge in the eventual fate of the young
hunter: his death. The end of the hunt is the death of the prey; in
this case the prey is the young hunter Aqhat: the hunter becomes
the hunted. The scene of Aqhat's refusal of the bow to Anat and
her attempt to bribe him with eternal life is one of the more
moving scenes in Ugaritic epic and, I will argue, one of the most
subtle.[19] After Aqhat refuses a bribe of silver or gold for his bow,

[13]See M. C. Astour, *Hellenosemitica* (Leiden: Brill, 1965) 163- 173; W. Burkert,
Homo Necans: The Anthropology of Ancient Greek Sacrificial Ritual and Myth,
trans. P. Bing (Berkeley: University of California, 1983) 111-116; see also J.
Fontenrose, *Orion: The Myth of the Hunter and the Huntress* (Berkeley: University
of California, 1981) 33-47.

[14]Euripides, *Bacchae* 337-340.

[15]According to Hesiod (new fragment), Stesichorus, and Akusilaos, *apud*
Burkert, *Homo Necans*, 112 n. 12.

[16]Diodorus Siculus IV.81.3-5.

[17]Ovid, *Metamorphoses* III.138-252; Nonnos, *Dionysiaca* V.287- 551.

[18]Burkert, *Homo Necans*, 116.

[19]For the inspiration of the interpretation that follows, I am indebted to T.
Abusch's treatment of a related episode in the Mesopotamian Gilgamesh epic:
"Ishtar's Proposal and Gilgamesh's Refusal: An Interpretation of *The Gilgamesh
Epic*, Tab. 6, Lines 1-79" *HR* 26 (1986) 143-187 (originally presented at the annual
meeting of the American Oriental Society, March, 1983); see below, n. 38.

and after Anat refuses his offer to contribute the materials for a new bow, Anat raises the stakes:

wataʿni batūlatu ʿanatu
ʾiriš ḫayyīma la-ʾaqhatu ġazru
ʾiriš ḫayyīma waʾatinuka
balmôta waʾašalliḫuka
ʾašaspiruka ʿimma baʿli šanāta
ʿimma banū ʾili tasappiru yaraḫīma
kī-baʿlu kī-yaḫawwiyu yaʿašširu
ḫawwūya yaʿašširu wayašqiyunhu
yabuddu wayašīru ʿalihu
naʿīmu [wayaḳniyunannu
ʾap ʾanāku ʾaḫawwiyu ʾaqhata ġazra

wayaʿni ʾaqhatu ġazru
ʾal tašrugunī yā-batūlatu-mi
dam liġazri šaragūki ḫaḫḫūma
mutu ʾuhrayatu mahu yiqqaḫu
mahu yiqqaḫu mutu ʾaṯriyatu
sapsaga yussaku lira ʾši
ḫurṣa liẓāri qudqudiya
[walmôta kulli ʾamūtu
waʾana môta-mi ʾamūtu
[ʾap malṭni rigma-mi ʾargumu
qištūma [qištu] māhirīma
hitta taṣūdūna taʾnaṭatu [bihu]

[galm tišḫaq ʿanatu
wabilibbi taqniyu [taḫbūlatu]
ṯubu liya la-ʾaqhatu ġazru
ṯubu liya walika [ʾargumu]
himma la-ʾaqriyuka binatībi pišʿi
[   ] binatībi gaʾāni
ʾašaqīluka taḫtu [paʿnêya] ʾanāku
nuʿmānu ʿimqu našīma

And the Virgin Anat replied:
"Ask for life, O Aqhat the Hero,
    ask for life and I will give it to you,
    deathlessness, and I will bestow it on you.
I will make you count the years with Baal,
    you will count the months with the Sons of El.
When Baal gives life, he makes a feast,
    makes a feast for the life-given and gives him drinks;
he sings and chants over him,
    the singer serenades him.
So will I give life to Aqhat the Hero."

And Aqhat the Hero replied:
"Do not lie to me, O Virgin,
    for to a Hero your lies are filth.
A mortal - what does he get in the end?
    What is the destiny of a mortal?
Glaze will be poured on my head,
    ashes on the top of my skull.
As all men die, so I will die,
    yes, I too will surely die.
And this too I will say:
Bows are weapons for warriors.
    Do women now hunt?"

Anat laughed aloud,
    and plotted in her heart:
"Heed me, O Aqhat the Hero,
    heed me while I speak to you.
Surely I will meet you on the path of rebellion,
    [   ] on the path of pride.
I will make you fall beneath my feet,
    O lovely one, strongest of men."[20]

The general scholarly understanding of this passage renders the text literally: Anat attempts to bribe Aqhat with immortality, he vehemently rejects her promise as a lie, and Anat plots revenge.[21] Surely this interpretation is intended by the text; the actions of the characters are consistent, occasioning no sense of being misled. Yet, I submit, there is a subtext here, a reservoir of imagery that the Ugaritian would not have missed, that contributes to the vehemence and the substance of Aqhat's reply and to the inevitability of Anat's subsequent murder of the young hunter.

The imagery that I refer to is given in Anat's description of the existence of the "life-given:"

When Baal gives life, he makes a feast,
    makes a feast for the life-given and gives him drinks;

[20]*CTA* 17.6.25-45.

[21]H. L. Ginsberg's reading of the scene and its context is representative ("The North- Canaanite Myth of Anat and Aqhat" *BASOR* 97 [1945] 5): "[Aqhat's] bow excites the cupidity of that ferocious warrior-goddess, the virgin Anat; and failing to induce Aqhat to surrender it to her in exchange for either riches or immortality, she goes and denounces, perhaps even traduces, him to El."

> he sings and chants over him,
>> the singer serenades him.[22]

The immediate image is of the young hunter, now immortal, participating in the divine feast, similar to the scene described in RS 24.252 where the gods are seated at a feast, eating and drinking:[23]

> ... bihaddi rāʿiyi
> dū yašīru wayaḏammiru
>> bikinnāri waṯulbi
>> bitupi wamaṣiltêmi

> ... with Haddu the shepherd,
> who sings and plays
>> on the lyre and the flute,
>> on the tambourine and the cymbals.[24]

The feasting of the gods is a common theme in Ugaritic literature and occurs on any number of occasions. Of interest is the feast of the gods to celebrate Kirta's wedding, at which El blesses Kirta with a peculiar expression:

> maʾdu rama kirta
>> bitôk rapiʾī ʾarṣi
>> bipuḫri qibbūṣi ditāni

> May Kirta be highly exalted
>> in the midst of the Rephaim of the earth,
>> in the council of the assembly of Ditanu.[25]

---

[22]lines 30-32.

[23]On RS 24.252, see A. Caquot, "La tablette RS 24.252 et la question des rephaim ougaritiques" *Syria* 53 (1976) 295-304; M. H. Pope, "Notes on the Rephaim Texts from Ugarit," *Essays on the Ancient Near East in Memory of Jacob Joel Finkelstein*, ed. M. de J. Ellis (Memoirs of the Connecticut Academy of Arts & Sciences 14; Hamden, CT: Archon, 1977) 169-170; C. E. L'Heureux, *Rank Among the Canaanite Gods: El, Ba'al, and the Repha'im* (HSM 21; Missoula: Scholars, 1979) 169-181, and references.

[24]lines 3-4. On the presence of "Haddu the shepherd" in this passage, see the arguments of A. J. Ferrara and S. B. Parker, "Seating Arrangements at Divine Banquets," *UF* 4 (1972) 37-39.

[25]*CTA* 15.3.13-15 and 15.3.2-4. On the West Semitic tribal name Ditānu/Didānu, see J. J. Finkelstein, "The Genealogy of the Hammurapi Dynasty" *JCS* 20 (1966) 101; E. Lipinski, "Ditanu," in *Studies in Bible and the Ancient Near*

The feasting of the gods and the reference to the "Rephaim of the earth" establishes a connection on the levels of theme and diction with a number of other texts, the so-called "Rephaim texts" (CTA 20 - 22),[26] in which the Rephaim (*rpʾum*), who are also called "gods" (*ʾilnym*),[27] are depicted as feasting in the "banquet house" (*bt ʾikl*) in the "heart of Mount Lebanon" (*bʾirt lbnn*).[28] The identity of these Rephaim is debated, but it is becoming increasingly clear that the Rephaim are the deified shades of the dead kings and warriors, similar to the later usage of the term in Hebrew and Phoenician.[29]

A recently discovered Ugaritic funerary text makes the identification of the Rephaim more explicit. In the course of the text of RS 34.126,[30] the "Rephaim of the earth / assembly of Didanu" (*rpʾi ʾars / qbs ddn*) are called up, and various dead kings are identified as Rephaim (*rpʾum*). The text appears to relate the burial ritual for the Ugaritic king Niqmaddu, and the other kings who are summoned are apparently his ancestors. It seems clear that the Rephaim of the earth (*rapiʾu ʾarsi*) are the shades of dead kings, bearing in mind the common use of the word *ʾarsu*, "earth," to signify "the underworld."[31] In lines 15-16 there is a reference to the ritual feeding of the shade of the dead king:

East Presented to S. E. Loewenstamm, eds. Y. Avishur and J. Blau (Jerusalem: Rubinstein, 1978) 91-110.

[26]On the Rephaim texts and the problem of the Ugaritic Rephaim, see the works cited above, n. 23, and below, n. 30; see also A. Caquot, "Rephaïm," *Supplément au dictionnaire de la Bible*, Vol. X, ed. H. Cazelles and A. Feuillet (Paris: Letouzey & Ané, 1985) 334-357; M. H. Pope, "The Cult of the Dead at Ugarit," in *Ugarit in Retrospect*, ed. G. D. Young (Winona Lake, IN: Eisenbrauns, 1981) 159-179, and references.

[27]*CTA* 20.1.2; 21.1.4; 22.1.4; etc.

[28]*CTA* 22.2.25.

[29]*KAI* 13.8 and 14.8; Isa 14:9; 26:14,19; Ps 88:11; Prov 2:19; 9:18; 21:16; Job 26:5, etc.

[30]On RS 34.126, see especially W. T. Pitard, "The Ugaritic Funerary Text RS 34.126" *BASOR* 232 (1978) 65-75; idem, "RS 34.126: Notes on the Text" (forthcoming); P. Xella, *I testi rituali di Ugarit*, vol I (Rome: Consiglio Nazionale delle Ricerche, 1981) 279-287; P. Bordreuil and D. Pardee, "Le rituel funéraire ougaritique RS 34.126" *Syria* 59 (1982) 121-128; B. A. Levine and J.-M. de Tarragon, "Dead Kings and Rephaim: The Patrons of the Ugaritic Dynasty," *JAOS* 104 (1984) 649-659, and references.

[31]On *ʾarsu* as "underworld" in Ugaritic, see *CTA* 4.8.8-9; 5.6.25; 19.141; etc.

ṭūlḫanu maliʾaⅼ
wayiblaʿu

The table is full,
and he devours.[32]

A series of sacrifices and a benediction follow.

The theme of the feasting of the royal dead and the rite of
sacrifice that actualizes this theme are part of the conceptual
background for another West Semitic burial inscription, that of
the eighth century Aramaic king Panammu I.[33] In this text the
king instructs his heir to sacrifice to Hadad and to remember the
name of Panammu, saying:

taʾkul nabš panammū ʿim hadad
watašti nabš panammū ʿim hadad

May the spirit of Panammu eat with Hadad,
and may the spirit of Panammu drink with Hadad.[34]

There are a number of other traces of the cult of the dead
ancestors in Ugaritic and other West Semitic texts,[35] but the
continuities in theme and diction are clear enough to allow us to
return to Anat's description of the life of the "immortal" in her
exchange with Aqhat.

The subtext of Anat's promise to Aqhat and the reason for the
vehemence of his response is, I suggest, inherent in the imagery

---

[32]For a discussion of lines 15-16, see Pitard, "Funerary Text," 70; Bordreuil and
Pardee, "Le rituel funéraire," 126. According to Pitard's recent collation ("Notes on
the Text") the final letter of *ml[ ]* could be either *ʾ* or *k*. For the purpose of the
present discussion the difference is negligible: "the table is full" or "the table of the
king." For memorial stelae depicting the deceased sitting at a banquet table, see
ANEP, 630-637.

[33]*KAI* 214; see J. C. Greenfield, "Un rite religieux araméen et ses parallèles"
RB 80 (1973) 46-52; and Caquot, "La tablette RS 24.252," 303.

[34]lines 21-22.

[35]*CTA* 17.1.32-33; Ps 106:28; see, in general, C. F. A. Schaeffer, *The Cuneiform
Texts of Ras Shamra-Ugarit* (London: Oxford University, 1939) 46-56; Pitard,
"Funerary Text"; and Greenfield, "Un rite religieux." The West Semitic institution
of the *marzēaḥ* is relevant here: the *marzēaḥ* is a guild or club with responsibilities
for the burial and ritual well-being of its members; see recently Pope, "Cult of the
Dead," and references.

that Anat uses to describe the existence of the "life-given."
According to the themes of the Ugaritic narrative, Anat is
describing not merely the life of the immortal gods, but also the
precise state of the existence of the royal dead, the *rapi²ū ²arṣi*, who
feast with Baal - the divine dead.[36] Aqhat as the son of a king
would be intimately aware of the terms of such a description, as
would the immediate audience of the text. Faced with a promise
of immortal life that resonates with images of the life of the
royal dead, how could Aqhat do other than explode with anger at
the ruse of the goddess: "Do not lie to me, O Virgin, / for to a Hero
your lies are filth." Aqhat goes on to describe explicitly the fate
of mortals: death and a ritual burial, complete with glaze and
ashes poured on the head of the deceased.[37] Aqhat's emphasis on
the funerary rites makes explicit his awareness of the subtext of
Anat's promise: she promises life, but at the core of her promise is
a very real threat of death. Aqhat recognizes the subtext of
Anat's promise and exposes it, thus setting into motion the process
that will end with a fulfillment of the promise, that is, with his
death.[38]

[36]See the king list in RS 24.257, verso, in which the names of the former kings
of Ugarit are prefaced by *²ilu*, "god." Note the references, in the recto text, to
"flutes" (*ṯlbm*) and "his tambourines" (*tph*), apparently played "for the Gracious
One" (*ln²m*). K. A. Kitchen ("The King List of Ugarit" *UF* 9 [1977] 139-141) has
pointed out the similarites with RS 24.252 and RS 34.126 and has concluded that
the list of dead, deified kings and the reference to flutes and tambourines have to do
with a ritual for the dead kings; see also Xella, *Testi rituali*, 288-291.

[37]The practice of pouring plaster on the skulls of the dead is a phenomenon of
Neolithic religion in Syro-Palestine (see J. Cauvin, *Religions néolithiques de Syro-
Palestine* [Paris: Maisonneuve, 1972] 43-47). Although it is odd that such an archaic
trait would be remembered in the Late Bronze Age, no other plausible explanation
of the text is available. For the unambiguous reading of *sapsaga* as "glaze," see H.
A. Hoffner, Jr., "Ugaritic *pwt*: A Term from the Early Canaanite Dyeing Industry"
JAOS 87 (1967) 300 n. 5, and references; *contra* M. Dietrich, O. Loretz, and J.
Sanmartin, "Die angebliche Ug.- He. Parallelle SPSG // SPS(J)G(JM)" *UF* 8 (1976)
37-40. The possible relevance of the Neolithic custom was first pointed out by E. M.
Good, "Two Notes on Aqhat" *JBL* 77 (1958) 73-74. On unusually archaic survivals in
Greek epic, see Burkert, *Greek Mythology and Ritual*, 29-34, and *passim*.

[38]In a paper influential on the present study (see above, n. 19), T. Abusch noted
a similar dynamic in the oft-compared episode in the Gilgamesh epic in which
Ishtar proposes marriage to Gilgamesh. Abusch convincingly demonstrated that
the images Ishtar uses to entice Gilgamesh have connections with traditional
descriptions of the king of the underworld (which in fact is Gilgamesh's role in the

context of cult). In the epic, Gilgamesh then recites a list of Ishtar's past lovers, all of whom she had killed, thus exposing her intent. Ishtar turns away to plot Gilgamesh's downfall, obtaining Anu's permission for her acts. The continuities between the Mesopotamian and Ugaritic stories, if my argument is correct, thus extend to the implicit intent of the goddess's verbal imagery (a description of the afterlife, conveying a threat of death to the hero) and to the motive for the hero's vehement refusal.

A more distant parallel exists in the relationship between Odysseus and the goddess Kalypso in the *Odyssey*. The goddess promises Odysseus immortality if he will stay with her as her bedmate, but her allusions to the stories of Orion and Iasion, both of whom were killed as a result of being the lovers of goddesses (*Odyssey* V.116-136), point to an omminous fate for Odysseus if he were to remain. On this point, see G. Nagy, *The Best of the Achaeans: Concepts of the Hero in Archaic Greek Poetry* (Baltimore: Johns Hopkins University, 1979) 202-203.

The Deception of Isaac

Archaic and cultic elements are important in the Jacob cycle as well as in the Canaanite epics. The cultic elements in the Bethel story have been discussed above. A more subtle degree of influence can be detected in the highly compressed story of Jacob's deception of Isaac in Genesis 27. Gunkel and Robertson Smith already noticed cultic elements in this story; I wish to expand on their remarks.

The first question concerns the nature of the "tasty meal" (מַטְעַמִּים) that Isaac requests from Esau in v. 4. Isaac states that Esau must hunt some wild game with his quiver and bow and then prepare a "tasty meal" from it, in order that (בַּעֲבוּר) Isaac may give the blessing to Esau. Robertson Smith noted that this episode "has all the air of a sacrificial scene."[39] Gunkel also remarked that "originally it may have been concerned with a sacrificial meal" and cited a similar episode in the Balaam story where Balaam commands Balak to offer a sacrifice before Balaam blesses the people of Israel (Num 23:1).[40] If the dynamics of these stories are the same, then we can perhaps infer that it is the sacrificial meal itself which allows the נֶפֶשׁ of Isaac (v. 4) to pronounce the divine blessing, as in the case of Balaam's oracles.

Jacob's subversion of Isaac's wishes, in this case, takes on a double level of transgression. Not only is he breaking his father's command to Esau, but he is also actively tampering with the nature of the "tasty meal." Instead of hunting a wild animal for the meal, he offers domesticated goats (גְּדָיֵי עִזִּים; v. 9). In this, Jacob's deed reflects the traditional Israelite system of sacrifice in which *only* domestic animals were suitable.[41] The polarity between domestic and wild animals, between the preferred and the forbidden, highlights the polarity between Jacob, the domestic man "who dwelled in the tents," and Esau, the brother he

---

[39]W. Robertson Smith, *Lectures on the Religion of the Semites* (London: Black, 1889) 467.

[40]Gunkel, *Genesis*, 283.

[41]Lev 1:2.

supplants, who is "a skilled hunter, a man of the fields" (Gen 25:27).

The polarity of Jacob and Esau in this scene is mirrored by the polarity of the parents, Isaac and Rebekah. As mentioned in Gen 25:28, Isaac loves Esau because he has a taste for game (בְּפִיו כִּי-צַיִד), but Rebekah loves Jacob. The father-mother dichotomy serves to heighten the contrast between the two brothers; indeed, the two parents are at cross-purposes over the beneficiary of Isaac's blessing.

The point of the polarity, however, goes deeper than the family alliances. As with many instances of thesis and antithesis, the result is a synthesis, fraught with tension as it may be. Rebekah clothes Jacob in Esau's finest garments (Gen 27:15), and then she covers his hands and the "smooth part of his neck" (חֶלְקַת צַוָּארָיו) with the skin of the goats. The polarity of smooth skin versus hairy skin is touched upon here: these are important characteristics of Jacob versus Esau. In v. 11 Jacob states that Esau is a "hairy man" (אִישׁ שָׂעִר) but that he is a "smooth man" (חָלָק אִישׁ). He fears that Isaac will touch him and know him for a "trickster" (מְתַעְתֵּעַ). The diction here is significant. The "smooth" aspect of Jacob functions on two levels: first he is smooth-skinned, second he is a trickster. The Hebrew adjective חָלָק can convey both nuances of the English word "smooth."[42] For Jacob to wear the hairy skins to cover his "smoothness," therefore, is an act that reverberates on several levels.

An additional aspect of Jacob's wearing of the skins was pointed out by Robertson Smith. He noted a possible ritual dimension in the sacrificer wearing the skins of the sacrificial animal.[43] He collected a number of instances of this practice in the ancient world, two of which are particularly notable. The first is a reference in Lucian's *De Dea Syria* to one of the preliminary rites of the pilgrims to Hierapolis, the holy city of the Syrian Goddess. Lucian writes of the pilgrim's activities:

ἀνὴρ εὖτ᾽ ἂν ἐς τὴν ἱρὴν πόλιν πρῶτον ἀπικνέεται, κεφαλὴν

---

[42]The double meaning of Jacob's "smoothness" was pointed out to me by Philip Kimball. For the lexical data, see *BDB*, 325 s.v. חָלָק.

[43]Robertson Smith, *Lectures*, 467.

μὲν ὅδε καὶ ὀφρύας ἐξύρατο, μετὰ δὲ ἱρεύας ὄιν τὰ μὲν
ἄλλα κρεουργέει τε καὶ εὐωχέεται, τὸ δὲ νάκος χαμαὶ
θέμενος ἐπὶ τούτου ἐς γόνυ ἕζεται, πόδας δὲ καὶ κεφαλὴν
τοῦ κτήνεος ἐπὶ τὴν ἑωυτοῦ κεφαλὴν ἀναλαμβάνει.

Whenever someone is about to come to the Holy City, he
shaves his head and his eyebrows. Then after sacrificing a
sheep, he carves it and dines on the other parts. The fleece,
however, he lays on the ground and kneels upon it, and the
feet and the head of the animal he puts on his own head.[44]

The "smoothness" of the sacrificer and the wearing of the skins are
notable. Robertson Smith also remarked on a late custom attested
for the Cyprian Aphrodite, a goddess with a number of Semitic
traits.[45] According to Joannes Lydus: πρόβατον κωδίῳ ἐσκεπασμένοι
συνέθυον, "They sacrifice sheep together, while they are
themselves covered with sheepskins."[46]

Also of interest in this context are two Assyrian reliefs, one from
the ninth century B.C.E. and one from the eighth, in which men
are depicted in some sort of ritual ceremony wearing lion masks
and draped in lion skins.[47] The purpose of the religious ceremony
involved is obscure, as is the symbolic connotation of the lion skin,
though we can infer a ritual significance to the wearing of the
skins, probably connected with the symbolism of hunting and
death.

With these examples of ritual acts involving the wearing of
animal skins in the Semitic and Mediterranean sphere, it becomes
plausible to suggest that Jacob's donning of the skins of the
sacrificial animal is a residue of a ritual dimension, a dimension
that neatly complements the other polarities in the text. Just as

[44]*De Dea Syria*, eds. H. W. Attridge and R. A. Oden (Missoula: Scholars, 1976)
para. 55, pp. 56-57.

[45]On the Cyprian Aphrodite, see Robertson Smith, *Lectures*, 469-479; and more
recently W. Burkert, *Griechische Religion der archaischen und klassischen Epoche*
(Stuttgart: Kohlhammer, 1977) 239-240 and references.

[46]Joannes Lydus, *De Mensibus*, 4.65; for the emendation see Robertson Smith,
Lectures 469-479; and W. Burkert, *Homo Necans: The Anthropology of Ancient Greek
Sacrificial Ritual and Myth*, trans. P. Bing (Berkeley: University of California,
1983) 115.

[47]See R. D. Barnett, "Lions and Bulls in Assyrian Palaces," in *Le palais et la
royauté*, ed. P. Garelli (Paris: Geuthner, 1974) 443-444 and pl. VII; and H. Frankfort,
The Art and Architecture of the Ancient Orient (London: Penguin, 1958) pl. 94A

Jacob "becomes" Esau by wearing his clothes and receiving his blessing, so the sacrificer "becomes" the sacrificed animal by wearing the skins of the animal.[48] The sense of transformation is not explicit, it is rather a metaphorical transformation - Jacob "becomes" his brother, the sacrificer merges with the sacrificed, but only for the sake of the blessing bestowed by his blind father. Jacob is the "smooth" man who, for a moment, takes on the traits of his opposite twin and, wrapped in the symbols of the ritual, collects the blessing due him. Of course, the transformation is only momentary; when Esau finds out, Jacob is forced to flee, for fear of his life.

[48]For the archaic roots of this sacrificial symbolism, and for other Greek examples, see Burkert, *Homo Necans*, 113-116.

3. A Literary Interlude

In the above sections I have discussed the types of multiformity that characterize Israelite and Canaanite traditional narrative, and I have discussed the interaction of epic and cult in the narratives. No discussion of ancient narrative would be complete, however, without some attention to the issue of literary art. The stories, after all, are artfully stylized communicative acts; yet attention to the literary dimension remains a generally neglected task.

Recent treatments of biblical narrative have emphasized the literary nature of the texts. For example, Robert Alter's book begins with the simple question: "What role does literary art play in the shaping of biblical narrative? A crucial one. . . ."[1] Alter goes on to substantiate his claim through numerous close readings of texts. Canaanite narratives have yet to be treated as literary texts, though there are a few notable exceptions.[2] The following statement is typical of treatments of Canaanite narratives: "Canaanite myths . . . are characterized by their extreme prolixity; no doubt the literary tradition is chiefly at fault, but even so the myths that have survived are relatively uninteresting."[3] Such a view may be justified, or may simply be a result of a poor reading of the texts.

In the following discussion I will sketch the roles of two of the female protagonists in Canaanite and Israelite epics. The literary configurations in which Pughat and Rachel play their parts reveal the artistic and stylistic integrity of both Canaanite and Israelite narrative and display as well the continuity of thematic concerns that link the two traditions. While Canaanite and

---

[1]Alter, *Biblical Narrative*, 3.

[2]See especially P. Xella, "Una 'rilettura' del poema di Aqhat," *Problemi del mito nel vicino oriente antico* (Naples: Istituto Orientale di Napoli, 1976) 61-91, esp. 85-89; S. B. Parker, "The Historical Composition of KRT and the Cult of El" *ZAW* 89 (1977) 161-175; and G. Del Olmo Lete, *Mitos y leyendas de Canaan* (Madrid: Cristiandad, 1981) 31-62 and *passim*.

[3]G. S. Kirk, *Myth: Its Meaning and Functions in Ancient and Other Cultures* (Berkeley: University of California, 1970) 221.

Israelite narrative may, in places, reach different levels of literary achievement, the conclusion is nonetheless inescapable that art, as well as insight, was a central concern of the composer, and that this concern was a constant in Canaan and in Israel.

Pughat and Rachel

Pughat, the sister of Aqhat in the Aqhat epic, is described as "she who carries water,/ who brushes the dew from the barley,/ who knows the course of the stars" (*ṭākimatu maya / ḥāsipatu liša⁽āri ṭalla / yādi⁽atu halīka kabkabīma*).[4] In these words Pughat is characterized as an ideal type, like the wife whose "worth is far beyond that of rubies" in Prov 31:10-31.[5] Pughat is diligent, responsible, and intelligent, and as such is a proper daughter for Danel, the wise patriarch, and a proper sister for the hero Aqhat.

Toward the end of the Aqhat epic, Pughat resolves to avenge her brother's death by killing Yatpan the warrior, who, with the goddess Anat, had killed Aqhat. Pughat says to her father Danel:

> la-tabarrikanī ʾalīku burraktu
> tamurranī ʾalīku namrartu
> ʾamḫaṣu māḫiṣa ʾaḫīya
> ʾakallī-mi kāliya ⁽ūla ʾummatiya

> Bless me, that I may go blessed,
>   favor me, that I may go favored.
> I will kill the killer of my brother,
>   destroy the destroyer of the son of my family.[6]

After she takes leave of Danel, she washes in the sea, and she applies a special type of rouge.[7] She then puts on her clothing:

> ... tilbaš nipāṣa ǵazri
> tašit ḫallāpa bilnšgiha
> ḫarba tašit bita⁽ratiha
> wa⁽alê tilbaš nipāṣa ʾattati

---

[4]*CTA* 19.55-56; cf. *CTA* 19.50-52, 19.199-200.
[5]See J. Gray, *The Legacy of Canaan* (VTSup 5; Leiden: Brill, 1965) 253-254.
[6]*CTA* 19.194-197.
[7]*CTA* 19.203-205.

> She put on a hero's clothes,
>   she placed a knife in her sheath,
>   she placed a sword in her scabbard,
>   and over all this she put on a woman's clothes.[8]

Pughat then proceeds to the dwelling of Yatpan and, when the text breaks off, is apparently serving wine to Yatpan. It would seem that Pughat, like similar heroines in Israelite tradition (Jael, Judith), will kill the adversary after she has lulled him into submission with wine and her beauty.[9] When the text breaks off, Yatpan is still boasting of his might: "the hand that killed Aqhat the Hero / can kill a thousand of the enemies of (my) Lady" (*yadu maḫaṣat ʾaqhalta ġazraʾ timḫaṣu ʾalpa-mī ʾêbī šitti*).[10] The text would suggest that Yatpan's boast is in vain.

The symmetries in Pughat's role are notable. She will kill her brother's killer; in order to do so she will dress in a warrior's garb, while dressed outwardly as a woman. Commentators have noted a parallelism of role here with the goddess Anat, who in the Baal myth avenges her brother Baal's death by killing Mot, her brother's killer.[11] This parallelism of role is important to Pughat's persona, but the parallelism with Anat is even more pervasive, as Delbert Hillers has suggested in a provocative article.[12]

Hillers has proposed a sexual meaning for the encounter between Aqhat and Anat in the Aqhat epic. Aqhat's bow, he argues, is a masculine sexual symbol, since bows function as such in various ancient Near Eastern texts, particularly in proverbial expressions and incantation texts. Anat's desire for Aqhat's bow is sexual, Hillers contends, at least on a symbolic level, and his loss

[8]*CTA* 19.205-208.

[9]On the similarities of the stories of Jael, Judith, and Pughat, see M. H. Pope, in *Wörterbuch der Mythologie*, 243-244; T. H. Gaster, *Thespis: Ritual, Myth and Drama in the Ancient Near East* (New York: Schuman, 1950) 260; and S. B. Parker, "Toward an Interpretation of AQHT" (delivered at the annual meeting of the Society of Biblical Literature, 1980) 14-15.

[10]*CTA* 19.220-221.

[11]See Caquot, et al., *Textes ougaritiques*, 409-415 and references.

[12]D. R. Hillers, "The Bow of Aqhat: The Meaning of a Mythological Theme," in *Orient and Occident. Essays Presented to C. H. Gordon*, ed. H. A. Hoffner, Jr. (AOAT 22; Neukirchen- Vluyn: Neukirchener, 1973) 71-80.

of the bow and his death are equally symbolic and fraught with psychological tension. Hillers writes: "The mythological theme springs from man's experience of woman as attractive, yet threatening to his sexuality and his life."[13]

Hillers's Freudian etiology of the myth seems to be somewhat reductive. Myths are not simply allegories for sexual conflicts or tensions, just as they are not simply allegories for meteorological phenomena. Myths are complex narratives that express and define a whole range of human emotions, cultural beliefs, and practical conflicts, while at the same time performing the important functions of entertainment and education. Sexual themes can often be found in myths, but to reduce the myth to a symbolic commentary on sex is to lose much of the richness of the narrative.

Hillers does point out, however, an important aspect of the goddess Anat. "Anath," Hillers observes, "is beautiful and sexy, that she is also a ferocious warrior is the most obvious part of her character. An Egyptian text adds explicit evidence for the transvestite nature of Anath; she is called '. . . Anat the divine, thou the victorious, woman acting as a warrior, clad as men and girt as women.'"[14] While I doubt that Anat is explicitly depicted as a transvestite, the Egyptian text accentuates the polarities in Anat's character: she is a beautiful woman and she is a savage warrior.

On the figure of Pughat, Hillers notes that there is an interesting balance in the Aqhat epic between Pughat and Anat. Anat, on the one hand is "deceiving, violent, emasculating, the one who turns a man into a woman; opposing her and perhaps victorious in the end is Pughat, the sister, wise, compassionate, and loyal, who turns herself into a man in the cause of justice."[15] Hillers pushes the symmetry a bit too far in his comparison, but much of the symmetry stands. Pughat does not turn herself into a man, but she dresses as a male warrior - as does Anat in the Egyptian text - and she kills a man; Anat does not emasculate a

[13]Hillers, "Bow of Aqhat," 78; see the critical remarks of H. H. P. Dressler, "Is the Bow of Aqhat a Symbol of Virility?" *UF* 7 (1975) 217-220.

[14]Hillers, "Bow of Aqhat," 74.

[15]Ibid., 80.

man, but she threatens and kills him. Both figures exact vengeance on their adversary; sexual undercurrents may be at play in both encounters; and in both the woman acts as a warrior.

The parallels between Pughat and Anat are significant in the character dynamics of the Aqhat epic. Equally important, I submit, are the symmetries in the scenes in which the two acts of vengeance take place. This type of symmetry is less on the level of character than on the level of literary structure. The symmetry of scenes is an example of the literary art of Canaanite narrative.

In the scene where Aqhat is killed by Anat and Yatpan, he is eating a meal in the pavilions of Qarit Abilim, the city of the moon god.[16] According to a broken passage, it may be related that Yatpan lives in Qarit Abilim, but other readings of the passage are possible.[17] In any case, Aqhat is seated, eating a meal:

> nuʿmānu ġazru šata ṯrm
> w[   ] ʾištʾir bidadīma
> wanʿrs [   ]

> The Gracious One, the Hero, took a meal
> and . . . honey,[18] in the pavilions,
> and cake[19]. . .[20]

Anat then tells Yatpan her plan. While Aqhat is eating, Anat will fly among the vultures, apparently in the form of a bird, and will release Yatpan, who is also in the form of a bird, above Aqhat's head. Yatpan will then strike Aqhat on the head until he dies. Anat commands:

> hullimannu ṯinê-mi qudquda
> talāta ʾid ʿalê ʾudni
> šupuk kamā šaʾiyi dama
> kamā šāḫiti libirkêhu

[16]*CTA* 18.4.7-8,14-15; cf. 19.163-164.

[17]*CTA* 18.4.7-8: *yṯb yṯp . . . qrt ʾblm*; see H. L. Ginsberg, in *ANET*, 152b.

[18]The translation "honey" is conjectural. The word *ʾištʾir* occurs elsewhere in a letter (*PRU* II, 83.3) where it designates a liquid commodity, measured by the *kadu*, listed along with *šamnu*, "oil." See Caquot, et al., *Textes ougaritiques*, 438.

[19]I follow Caquot, et al., (*Textes ougaritiques*, 438) in the conjectural translation "cake," relating the word to Hebrew עֲרִיסָה, "course meal, dough."

[20]*CTA* 18.4.14-15.

taṣ'ī kamā rūḫi napšuhu
    kamā 'iṭṭali brluhu
    kamā quṭri bi'appêhu

Strike him twice on the skull,
    three times over the ear;
make his blood run, like a slaughterer,
    (run) to his knees, like a butcher.
His breath will leave him like wind,
    his life-breath like spittle,
    like smoke from his nostrils.[21]

Anat and Yatpan then proceed to put the plan into action, and Aqhat is killed.

The aspects of this scene that I would note are: the situation of the victim who is eating in the pavilions, the disguise of the killers, and the description of the murder in terms of the slaughter of an animal. The hunter Aqhat is here hunted by birds of prey and is killed while eating, as an animal is killed.

In the fragmentary scene in which Pughat is about to kill Yatpan, similar reversals and symmetries are found. Yatpan is the man who "killed Aqhat the Hero" and who "can kill a thousand of the enemies of (my) Lady,"[22] yet here he will be killed by a single enemy, a woman, the sister of Aqhat. In this scene he is pictured in his pavilions (*bidadīka*),[23] and he is grateful that Pughat has come so that she can serve him wine. While he is in his cups, Pughat presumably will deal him the killing blow. Pughat, as mentioned above, is washed and rouged and dressed in women's clothes, but beneath her clothes are a sword and warrior's clothing. At the time when she deals the blow she will undoubtedly uncover her warrior garb. Pughat is in disguise, a woman concealing a warrior's weapons and gear, and she attacks her adversary in his pavilion while he is occupied with drink. The parallels with the scene of the murder of Aqhat are evident.

Yet the parallels go a step further. The rouge that Pughat had applied is part of her disguise: it is a cosmetic, and thus

[21]*CTA* 18.4.22-25; cf. 18.4.33-37.
[22]*CTA* 19.220-221.
[23]*CTA* 19.213.

highlights her feminine appearance, yet rouge is also applied
when one is about to perform an animal sacrifice, as when Kirta
offers a sacrificial sheep to El and Baal.[24] The rouge is part of the
symbolism of the scene: Pughat is dressed as a woman, but she is
prepared to kill Yatpan as an animal is killed.

The symmetry of the two scenes gives us a sense of the drama
and complexity of the narrative. In certain ways Pughat's murder
of Yatpan mirrors Anat's and Yatpan's murder of Aqhat. The
dynamics of male and female, hunter and hunted, appearance and
disguise, sex and death are all represented in the twin death
scenes with various twists and hints of subsidiary themes. Pughat
is, on the one hand, linked to Anat in her guise as avenging
warrior, uniting "male" and "female" traits, yet on the other hand
she is linked to Aqhat, whose murder she avenges. Pughat is
shown to be successful where Aqhat failed: she overcomes the
adversary and sets matters right. Although the epic is named for
Aqhat,[25] it is Pughat who finally takes on the role of hero (*ǵzr*):
she is his successor and his counterpart. But the narrative does not
tell us this overtly: it guides us to this conception through the
symmetries and ironies implicit in its narrative art.

A similar complex of symmetries and ironies occurs in the Jacob
cycle in the roles of Jacob and Rachel. As has often been noticed,
the relationship between Jacob and Esau is mirrored by the
relationship between Rachel and Leah.[26] Jacob and Rachel are
each the youngest child, while Esau and Leah are the eldest. In
each pair the siblings are in conflict, with the youngest eventually
ascendent. The themes of the rights of the first-born, the conflict
between two siblings, and deeds of trickery recur in the two sets of
relationships.

[24]*CTA* 14.62-64,156-158.

[25]Note the superscription, *li-ʾaqhati*, "concerning Aqhat," in *CTA* 19.1.

[26]See, e.g., M. Buber, "Leitwortstil in der Erzählung des Pentateuchs," in
Werke. Band II: Schriften zur Bibel (Munich: Kösel, 1964) 1140; Fokkelman,
Narrative Art in Genesis, 139-141; J. G. Gammie, "Theological Interpretation By
Way of Literary and Tradition Analysis," in *Encounter with the Text: Form and
History in the Hebrew Bible*, ed. M. J. Buss (Philadelphia: Fortress, 1979) 118; and
R. E. Friedman, "Deception for Deception" *Bible Review* 2 (Spring, 1986) 22-31, 68.

The rivalry between Rachel and Leah centers on Jacob's love and the bearing of offspring. Leah marries Jacob first and bears his first son (Gen 29:32), yet Rachel, the younger of the two, is the one whom Jacob loves (Gen 29:30). The rivalry between Rachel and Leah is drawn in a tragicomic vein in the episode of the mandrakes (Gen 30:14-17), in which Rachel loses the battle of fertility once again. Finally Rachel bears Joseph who will be Jacob's favorite (Gen 37:3). The rivalry between Jacob and Esau centers on the blessings and privileges of the first-born. Esau is born first, though not without a struggle (Gen 25:22-26), but it is Jacob who finally acquires the blessing with the help of his mother, who loves him more than she loves his brother. In both rivalries the father supports the rights of the first-born: Isaac loves Esau (Gen 25:28), though he mistakenly gives the blessing to the disguised Jacob (Gen 27:27-29); Laban protects the first-born rights of Leah and brings her to Jacob's nuptial tent under the cover of darkness in place of Rachel (Gen 29:23).

These repetitions and polarities are central to the literary dynamics of the text, and they reveal the complex artistry in the characterizations of Jacob, Rachel, and the others. The subtlety of these dynamics is well illustrated by a comparison of two scenes, one involving Jacob and Isaac, the other involving Rachel and Laban. The symmetries and ironies in these two scenes have been noted briefly by other scholars; I wish to place them in a wider perspective by setting them against other West Semitic narrative traditions. As will become clear, the literary dynamics involved are very similar to the Ugaritic narrative discussed above. The similar style of literary art will suggest a continuity of artistic concerns in the two bodies of narrative.

In Genesis 27, Jacob acquires the blessing of his father Isaac. Isaac is incapacitated because he is old and blind, and Jacob deceives Isaac into believing that he is Esau by wearing Esau's clothes and by covering his neck and hands with goat-skins. Rebekah is the one who plans the deception, and Jacob is initially hesitant. In v. 12, Jacob protests: "But if my father feels me (יְמֻשֵּׁנִי), I will appear to him as a trickster, and he will curse me and not bless me." Rebekah reassures him, and Jacob goes through with the scheme. Sure enough, Isaac does feel him; in vv. 21-22 the text relates: "Isaac said to Jacob, 'Come closer, my son, so I might feel you (וַאֲמֻשְׁךָ), to see if you are my son Esau or not.' And Jacob drew near to Isaac his father, and he felt him (וַיְמֻשֵׁהוּ), and he said, 'The voice is the voice of Jacob, but the hands are the hands of Esau.'" Jacob survives the scene and deceives his father, coming away with the patriarchal blessings of fertility, sovereignty, and Yahweh's favor.

In Genesis 31 a similar scene occurs, but the actors this time are Laban and Rachel. Unbeknownst to her father or to her husband, Rachel has stolen Laban's teraphim, the household gods, just as she and the rest of Jacob's family are preparing to flee Haran (v. 19). The teraphim are cult statues that ensure general blessings for the household, and, as is now clear from recently discovered Akkadian legal texts, they also ensure the proper passage of the family blessing and inheritance from one generation to another.[27] In stealing the teraphim, it seems that Rachel has placed herself on the level of Jacob, whose trickery enabled him to inherit *his* family blessing.

The parallels between Jacob's acquisition of the blessing and Rachel's theft of the teraphim continue, in an ironic style, in the text. Laban pursues the fleeing family, and, in a poignant cry, asks Jacob: "Why did you steal my gods?" (v. 30). Jacob, unaware that Rachel had stolen the teraphim, replies: "Whoever you find that has the gods, that person will not live!" (v. 31). Jacob appears indignant that Laban would accuse him or his kin of such a crime.

Laban then searches the tents. After checking the tents of Jacob, Leah, and the two maidservants, the action slows down:

> He left Leah's tent and he went into Rachel's tent. Now Rachel had taken the teraphim and had placed them in a camel cushion and sat on them; and Laban felt (וַיְמַשֵּׁשׁ) around the whole tent, but he did not find them. And she

[27] See most recently J. Huehnergard, "Biblical Notes on Some New Akkadian Texts from Emar (Syria)" *CBQ* 47 (1985) 428-431; and M. A. Morrison, "The Jacob and Laban Narrative in Light of Near Eastern Sources" *BA* 46 (1983) 155-164, esp. 161-162; see also M. J. Selman, "Comparative Customs and the Patriarchal Age," in *Essays on the Patriarchal Narratives*, eds. A. R. Millard and D. J. Wiseman (Leicester: Inter-Varsity, 1980) 101, 110; M. Greenberg, "Another Look at Rachel's Theft of the Teraphim" *JBL* 81 (1962) 239-248; and A. E. Draffkorn, "*Ilāni/Elohim*" *JBL* 76 (1957) 216-224.

said to her father, "Let not my lord be angry that I cannot rise before you, for the way of women is upon me." So he searched, but he did not find the teraphim (Gen 31:33-35).

In this scene Rachel steals the teraphim, the symbols of the family inheritance and blessing, and through a clever ruse she deceives Laban so that he will not find them. The use of the verb "to feel" (משש) in v. 34 (also in v. 37) seems to be an overt literary reminiscence of Isaac "feeling" Jacob (משש) in Gen 27:12,22. Several commentators have noted the verbal correspondence and the ironic reversal in this scene,[28] yet I believe that the ironies and symmetries in this scene have not been fully appreciated.

Rachel is seated in her tent, immobile, because, she says to Laban, "the way of women" is upon her. Commentators have noted the disrespect that that this conveys toward the teraphim, for in biblical times menstrual blood was regarded as a pollution (Lev 15:19-24).[29] The humor and irony of this act are apparent: only by polluting the idols can Rachel keep possession of them and retain the family blessing. On another level, Rachel's immobility places her in a similar posture as blind Isaac in Genesis 27; there it is he who sits while Jacob comes forward so that Isaac can feel him (Gen 27:21). In Gen 31:34 it is Rachel who sits while Laban moves about, feeling through the tent. The inversion of immobile/mobile and deceiver/deceived is notable in the two scenes and suggests another level of ironic reversal.

Interestingly, the relation of the heroine to the hero in the Jacob cycle is similar to the relation in the Aqhat epic. Rachel deceives her father, acquires the family blessing, and is not found out. Jacob, on the other hand, deceives his father, acquires the family blessing, and *is* found out. Jacob then flees for his life (Gen 27:43). Rachel, though she too is fleeing, has triumphed over her victim without being discovered. In a similar manner, Pughat triumphs over her adversary, while Aqhat lies fallen. The theme

[28]E.g., M. Fishbane, *Text and Texture* (New York: Schocken, 1979) 51; J. P. Fokkelman, *Narrative Art in Genesis* (Amsterdam: Van Gorcum, 1975) 170; see also K. P. Bland, "The Rabbinic Method and Literary Criticism," in Literary Interpretations of Biblical Narratives, eds. K. R. R. Gros Louis, et al. (New York: Abingdon, 1974) 22.

[29]E.g., Gunkel, *Genesis*, 348.

of revenge in the Pughat episode corresponds to the revenge in Rachel's deception: in both the heroine's actions avenge past wrongs perpetrated on the hero. Significantly, in both the heroine comes out unblemished,[30] placing her on a level that the hero had not attained.

The symmetries of character, motivation, and action in the relation between Rachel and Jacob communicate to the audience that she is indeed a proper counterpart for Jacob. Her actions display the same independence and guile that mark him as a "trickster" hero; she is the appropriate "trickster" heroine. The symmetries between Rachel and Jacob are wide-ranging, and in their complex relationship the themes and artistry of the narrative come to full life.

In terms of the Jacob cycle, the role of Rachel highlights the complexity of the biblical narrative art; in terms of West Semitic narrative, the continuities of structure and the love of symmetries and ironies in the persons of Pughat and Rachel highlight the continuity of Canaanite and Israelite narrative art. Artistry is not, of course, an end in itself in these narratives; the importance of Pughat and Rachel in these stories speaks also of the significance of the heroine, a figure who is not only the counterpart of the hero, whether as sister or wife, but who also, at crucial moments, goes beyond him.

[30]In the case of the Aqhat epic we presume that Pughat is successful in her act of vengeance, but, as noted above, the tablet is broken. The related story traditions of Jael and Judith (see above, n. 9) support this surmise.

Part III

The Jacob Cycle and Israelite Epic

In order to come to a clear understanding of the Jacob cycle, it is necessary to do more than merely compare it with Ugaritic epic. We must measure the Jacob cycle against the standards of its own culture, that of ancient Israel. To set a story against the background of its own identity - this is perhaps an idealistic goal, yet it seems reasonable and even necessary.[1] To make this goal more manageable, I will compare the Jacob cycle with some Israelite traditions that seem to be closely related and will trace the features that distinguish Jacob as a traditional hero of Israel.

I will be using the word "hero" of Jacob in a conscious manner; not in the casual way in which the word is used in modern rhetoric or in literary criticism (though I do not exclude these usages), but more specifically in the ancient use of the word. "Hero" (*hērōs*) in ancient Greek refers to a figure who is significant not only because of the powerful or extreme qualities exhibited in epic, but also because of the identity of the hero as a founder of cities and cult places, as an ancestor of numerous kinship lines, and as a figure involved in religious worship.[2] The Israelite heroes were not directly worshipped in cult, so there is an important difference; but the general sense of the hero, as one who shaped both the political and religious realities that sustain the present world, is a significant common ground. The Ugaritic and Mesopotamian heroes belong also to this common ground, though variation exists

[1]See E. D. Hirsch, Jr., *The Aims of Interpretation* (Chicago: University of Chicago, 1976).

[2]On Greek heroes, see G. Nagy, *The Best of the Achaeans: Concepts of the Hero in Archaic Greek Poetry* (Baltimore: Johns Hopkins University, 1979); W. Burkert, *Greek Religion*, trans. J. Raffan (Cambridge, MA: Harvard University, 1985) 203-208.

in the specific relationship between the hero and the cult in each of these cultures.[3]

In this chapter I will investigate Jacob as an Israelite hero from two basic perspectives. In the first, I will investigate Jacob from the vantage point of his conflicts and interactions with his various adversaries. The strange encounter at Penuel with the deity will be the focus of one discussion; the other will focus on the dynamics of Jacob's relationship with his brother Esau. Both of these discussions will bring in comparative material from other Israelite and Near Eastern traditions in order to highlight implicit traditional resonances that might otherwise be missed. In the second part of the chapter, I will discuss at length the common patterns and themes that emerge when the Jacob cycle is compared to the stories of Moses. The similar shape of the two traditions will give rise to a more detailed understanding of the origin and development of both traditions, and will trace a perspective through which questions about the larger sphere of Israelite narrative traditions may be broached.

---

[3]On the relationship between Ugaritic heroes and cult, see the discussion and references above, pp. 73-81; on the relationship between Mesopotamian heroes and cult, in particular for the figure of Gilgamesh, see W. G. Lambert, "Gilgameš in Religious, Historical and Omen Texts and the Historicity of Gilgameš," in *Gilgameš et sa légende*, ed. P. Garelli (Paris: Klincksieck, 1960) 39-52.

1. The Hero and the Other

An essential tension exists between the hero and his/her adversary. The French philosopher Alain has phrased this relationship succinctly:

> The object that belongs to the hero and shapes the hero is the enemy; that is to say, the equal, the much-praised equal, the rival, a rival whom he judges worthy of himself. Therefore there can be no complete hero without a solemn war, without some provocation, without the long anticipation of another hero, subject of fame and legend.[4]

The nature of the adversary and the nature of the encounter with the adversary are determining factors in the emergence of a hero's identity. Achilles is unthinkable without Hektor, as is Beowulf without Grendel. The array of adversaries that a hero encounters defines the essence of the hero's nature: Gilgamesh encounters first Enkidu, then the monster Huwawa, the goddess Ishtar, the sacred Bull of Heaven, and finally death itself, each of these encounters contributing to the understanding of Gilgamesh's character and destiny.

So too with Jacob. Jacob's adversaries on the human level are primarily Esau and Laban. Jacob's nature as a trickster is manifested in his encounters with these two, as he tricks Esau (and his father Isaac) out of the blessing of the first born, as Jacob is tricked by Laban into marrying *his* first born, and as Jacob finally tricks Laban in return in his sly acquisition of Laban's flocks.[5]

Jacob also has a divine adversary. In Genesis 32, Jacob wrestles with a "man" (אִישׁ) in the darkness, who he later realizes is none other than Elohim himself (v. 31). Why does Jacob wrestle with God? Perhaps the traditional nature of the hero's identity might

---

[4]Alain, *The Gods*, trans. R. Pevear (New York: New Directions, 1974 [1934]) 113.

[5]On the theme here of the trickster tricked, see Gunkel, "Jakob" *Preussische Jahrbücher* 176 (1919) 354; Fokkelman, *Narrative Art in Genesis*, 126-130; Friedman, "Deception for Deception," 24-27.

give us a clue. If the hero is defined by the adversary, then the greater the adversary, the greater the hero. It is fitting, in this context, for the great patriarch to encounter the great god in single combat. How else would we know how great the hero is? The self is defined by the other; the other, in religious terms, is God; therefore mythological encounters are inevitable. In this sense I would agree with Heraclitus' defense of tradition, as reported by Aristotle:

> Ἡράκλειτος ἐπιτιμᾷ τῷ ποιήσαντι 'ὡς ἔρις ἔκ τε θεῶν καὶ ἀνθρώπων ἀπόλοιτο,' οὐ γὰρ ἂν εἶναι ἁρμονίαν μὴ ὄντος ὀξέος καὶ βαρέος οὐδὲ τὰ ζῷα ἄνευ θήλεος καὶ ἄρρενος ἐναντίων ὄντων.

> Heraclitus rebukes the poet who wrote "Would that strife might perish from among gods and men": for there would be no harmony without high and low notes, nor living creatures without male and female, which are opposites.[6]

The hero and the other are also opposites; from their encounter comes the harmony we call epic.

---

[6]Aristotle, *Eudemian Ethics*, 1235a, 25-29; see G. S. Kirk and J. E. Raven, *The Presocratic Philosophers* (Cambridge: Cambridge University, 1957) 193-196; W. K. C. Guthrie, *A History of Greek Philosophy. Vol. I: The Earlier Presocratics and the Pythagoreans* (Cambridge: Cambridge University, 1962) 446-449.

Encounter at Penuel

Jacob's encounters with his various adversaries form the heart of his heroic identity. In what may be regarded as the climax of his career - the granting of his new name, "Israel," which signals his initiation into his new identity as ancestor of a nation - the divine adversary gives as a reason for the change of status: וַתּוּכָל כִּי-שָׂרִיתָ עִם-אֱלֹהִים וְעִם-אֲנָשִׁים, "for you have contended with God (or 'gods') and with men and have prevailed" (32:29). The Greek versions of this passage preserve what may have been the original reading of the Hebrew as a poetic bicolon: "for you have contended with God / and with men you have prevailed."[7] A passage from the oracles of Hosea indicates that the description of Jacob's contendings may have been poetic and formulaic in its conservatism of phrase and parallelism:

בַּבֶּטֶן עָקַב אֶת-אָחִיו
וּבְאוֹנוֹ שָׂרָה אֶת-אֱלֹהִים
וַיָּשַׂר אֶל-מַלְאָךְ וַיֻּכָל

> In the womb he supplanted his brother,
> and as a man he contended with God,
> he contended with an angel and prevailed (Hos 12:4-5).

The continuity of expression between the Genesis passage and the Hosea passage (note especially the placement of the verbs שׂרה and יכל) indicates the central importance of Jacob's conflicts with his various adversaries and suggests as well the possible oral formulaic nature of this description of Jacob's exploits.[8] Esau

---

[7]The Greek reads: ὅτι ἐνίσχυσας μετὰ θεοῦ καὶ μετὰ ἀνθρώπων δυνατός. On the parallelism in Gen 32:29b, see R. Coote, "The Meaning of the Name Israel" *HTR* 65 (1972) 137-142; and F. I. Andersen and D. N. Freedman, *Hosea* (AB; Garden City, NY: Doubleday, 1980) 610.

[8]On the relationship between the Hosea passage and the Genesis traditions, see Andersen and Freedman, *Hosea*, 597-600; P. Ackroyd, "Hosea and Jacob" *VT* 13 (1963) 245-259; E. M. Good, "Hosea and the Jacob Tradition" *VT* 16 (1966) 137-151; F. Diedrich, *Die Anspielungen auf die Jakob-Tradition in Hosea 12,1 - 13,3* (Wurzburg: Echter, 1977); and recently S. L. McKenzie, "The Jacob Tradition in Hosea XII 4-5" *VT* 36 (1986) 311-322.

figures as the first of Jacob's adversaries; Laban is the second major adversary. Interestingly and paradoxically, Jacob's third major adversary, the mysterious שִׁיא, "man," of Gen 32:23-33, is identified by Jacob in v. 31 as none other than אֱלֹהִים, "God." At this point, it seems, Yahweh is not only Jacob's benefactor and protector, he is also Jacob's adversary.

Hermann Gunkel, James Frazer, and others have suggested that the story of Jacob's encounter with a divine adversary stems from older traditions of battles between divine beings and heroes.[9] Gunkel adduced various nocturnal encounters between heroes and demons, monsters, and gods from a number of cultures;[10] Frazer adduced a number of instances from other cultures where heroes do battle with river-gods.[11] Both types of divine adversaries are found in ancient West Semitic mythology, as we know from texts discovered since the time of Gunkel and Frazer. One of the most important adversaries of Baal in Canaanite myth is the god known as Prince Sea/Judge River (*zubūlu Yammu/ṭāpiṭu Naharu*) in the parallelism of Canaanite poetry.[12] Various reflexes of Sea/River as a divine adversary of Yahweh are found in Israelite traditions.[13] The category of nocturnal demons is also found in West Semitic lore. A seventh century B.C.E. Phoenician incantation from Arslan Tash names various night demons: "Fliers" (*ʿpt*), "Crushers" (*pḥṣt*), and the god Sasam.[14] Part of the incantation reads:

[9]For a résumé of the views of various scholars, see F. van Trigt, "La signification de la lutte de Jacob près du Yabboq," in B. Gemser, J. Hoftijzer, et al., *Studies on the Book of Genesis* (OTS 12; Leiden: Brill, 1958) 280-309; and Westermann, *Genesis 12-36,* 624-635.

[10]Gunkel, *Genesis* (3rd ed., 1910) 364-365.

[11]J. G. Frazer, *Folk-Lore in the Old Testament* (London: Macmillan, 1919) II. 410-425; reprinted in T. H. Gaster, *Myth, Legend, and Custom in the Old Testament* (New York: Harper & Row, 1969) I. 205-210.

[12]E.g., *CTA* 2.3.9-23; 2.4.15-30, etc.

[13]See U. Cassuto, "The Israelite Epic," in *Biblical and Oriental Studies II,* trans. I. Abrahams (Jerusalem: Magnes, 1975) 69-109; Cross, *Canaanite Myth and Hebrew Epic* 112- 144; J. Day, *God's Conflict with the Dragon and the Sea: Echoes of a Canaanite Myth in the Old Testament* (Cambridge: Cambridge University, 1985).

[14]*KAI* 27; see especially the treatment of F. M. Cross and R. J. Saley,"Phoenician Incantations on a Plaque of the Seventh Century B.C. from Arslan Tash in Upper Syria" *BASOR* 197 (1970) 42-49; see also A. Caquot, "Observations sur la première tablette magique d'Arslan Tash" *JANES* 5 (1973) 45-

šs[m] ˀl yptḥ ly
wˀll ẏrd lmzzt
yṣˀ šmš l ssm
ḥlp wldr ʿp

As for Sasam, let (the house) not be opened to him,
And let him not come down to (my) door posts.
The sun rises, O Sasam:
Disappear, and fly away home.[15]

The latter phrase is reminiscent of the request of Jacob's divine
adversary in v. 27: "let me go, for dawn is breaking" (כִּי עָלָה הַשַּׁחַר
שַׁלְּחֵנִי). I would stress that Jacob's adversary is neither a night
demon nor a river-god; Jacob names him in v. 31 as Elohim.
Nonethless there are thematic continuities in the Penuel encounter
with traditional images of other conflicts and other gods.

Another strain of narrative tradition, perhaps more central
than the traditions of nocturnal demons or river-gods, may be seen
in the conflict between Jacob and his divine adversary. Because of
the essential monotheism of Yahwistic religion,[16] it would seem
that any significant divine role in the epic would have to be
played by Yahweh, thus the paradoxical dimension of Yahweh's
appearance as divine enemy.[17] Nonetheless, Yahweh appears
elsewhere as a divine adversary, as, for example, in the strange
encounter in Exod 4:24-26 where Yahweh seeks to kill Moses.
Although this passage is particularly obscure,[18] it seems to
manifest the theme of Yahweh's occasionally adversarial
relationship with his chosen hero. Another example of this

---

51. On the god Sasam, see *KAI* vol. II, 44; and W. Fauth, "SSM BN PDRŠŠA" *ZDMG*
120 (1970) 227-256. The doubts recently expressed by J. Teixidor and P. Amiet (*Aula
Orientalis* 1 [1983] 105-109) concerning the authenticity of the inscription are not
compelling, palaeographically or stylistically.

[15]Cross and Saley, "Phoenician Inscription" 46-47 (lines D.1-8).

[16]Perhaps "monotheism" is an inaccurate term to describe the concept of
Yahweh in Israelite religion, but other terms, such as "henotheism" are equally
problematic; for an insightful statement on the plurality of the concepts of Yahweh
in ancient Israel, see Max Weber, *Ancient Judaism*, trans. H. H. Gerth and D.
Martindale (New York: Macmillan, 1952) 133-135.

[17]See the remarks of R. Barthes, "The Struggle with the Angel," *Image-Music-
Text*, trans. S. Heath (New York: Hill and Wang, 1977) 140.

[18]See below, pp. 158-161.

relationship may be seen in Genesis 22 where Yahweh "tests" (נִסָּה;
v. 1) Abraham by commanding him to sacrifice his only son Isaac.[19]
Abraham passes his test, Isaac is spared, and the result is that
Abraham and his descendents are blessed. In the story of Jacob's
encounter with his divine adversary, Jacob survives the danger, as
do the other heroes, and he receives the blessing of his new name
and heroic identity. The polarity of Yahweh as benefactor and
Yahweh as adversary is central to these traditions, and may be an
indication of a level of narrative meaning that we have yet fully
to grasp.

   An additional clue to the paradoxical relationship between
Yahweh and these heroes (Jacob, Abraham, Moses) may be found in
a neighboring epic tradition, that of the Mesopotamian hero
Gilgamesh. Gilgamesh draws on the aid of numerous gods in the
course of his adventures, but none so constantly as the sun-god
Shamash.[20] In the Old Babylonian version of the epic, Gilgamesh
implores Shamash:

> allak Šamaš . . .
> ullânu lušlima napi[šti]
> terranni ana kārim š[a Uruk]
> ṣillam šuku[n elīya]
>
> I am going, Shamash, . . .
> from there let me return safely;
> bring me back to the shores [of Uruk];
> place your protection [over me].[21]

Gilgamesh appeals to Shamash in his role as the patron-god of
travelers, but their relationship seems to be more complex than
this. In a Hittite fragment, Shamash intercedes on Gilgamesh's
behalf in the council of the gods;[22] in the Standard Babylonian
version he eventually becomes the one who initiates Gilgamesh's

---

[19]Speiser (*Genesis*, 256) remarked on the similarity of the testing of Abraham
and Jacob in these passages.

[20]On the relationship between Gilgamesh and Shamash, see Tigay, *Evolution
of the Gilgamesh Epic*, 76-81.

[21]Gilg. Y. 217-220; for the Yale tablet, see R. C. Thompson, *The Epic of
Gilgamesh: Text, Translation, and Notes* (Oxford: Clarendon, 1930) 25-29; *ANET*,
78-81.

[22]*ANET*, 85-86.

heroic quest to slay Humbaba.[23] In the Old Babylonian version, the elders of Uruk pray, "May Shamash cause you to reach your goal" (*lišakšīdka irnittaka Šamaš*),[24] and they add, "This night may there be a word at which you rejoice" (*mušītka awat taḫaddû*),[25] a foreshadowing of dream omens in which Shamash is involved.

In another Old Babylonian text, a dream omen is described, apparently sent from Shamash and from Gilgamesh's father and personal god Lugalbanda.[26] Part of the text recounts Gilgamesh's narration of the dream to his friend Enkidu:

> ibrī šuttam aṭṭul kī la‹p›tat kī nemat kī dalḫat
> anāku rīmī ṣērim aṣṣabtanim
> iššassīšu qaqqaram ilette tarbuʾtašu iqattur šamê . . .
> ina pānīšu anāku altūd
>
> My friend, I saw a dream: how troubled, how [?], how disturbing,
> I fought a wild bull of the steppe.
> At his cry he split the earth, his dust storm darkened, the sky . . .
> Then I bent down (in defeat) before him.[27]

After a few fragmentary lines, Enkidu interprets the dream:

> ilum ibrī ša nellaku . . . šum
> ul rīmum-ma nukkur mimma
> rīmu ša tāmuru Šamaš nāṣirum
> ina dannatim iṣabbat qātni
>
> The god, my friend, to whom we go
> is not a bull, though it is strange.
> The bull which you saw is Shamash the guardian;
> from danger he will take our hand.[28]

---

[23]See Tigay, *Evolution of the Gilgamesh Epic*, 81; for the SB Gilgamesh, see Thompson, *Epic of Gilgamesh*, 11-70; *ANET*, 79-99, 503-507.

[24]Gilg. Y. 257.

[25]Gilg. Y. 262.

[26]Gilg. Har. B; for commentary on this difficult text, see W. von Soden, "Beiträge zum Verständnis des babylonischen Gilgameš-Epos" *ZA* 53 (1959) 215-219; see also *ANET*, 504.

[27]Gilg. Har. B. 3-6.

[28]Gilg. Har. B. 11-14.

The message of the dream appears to be the continued guidance of Shamash (and Lugalbanda).[29] The specifics of the dream are puzzling, however. Gilgamesh wrestles[30] with a bull - who at that point is an unknown adversary - he is defeated, and only after the fact does he learn that the bull was in reality Shamash, his divine guardian. The similarities with Jacob's encounter with Yahweh are arresting. Jacob wrestles with an unknown adversary, who he later discovers is Elohim, his divine patron. For Gilgamesh the encounter takes place in a dream; for Jacob the encounter occurs at night. Gilgamesh kneels down in defeat; Jacob stalemates his opponent. For all the differences and for all the similarities, there is a common mood to the encounters, at least for the interpreter: *kī laptat . . . kī dalḫat*, "how troubled . . . how disturbing."

Why does Gilgamesh wrestle with his benefactor, Shamash, who is in the form of a bull? Why does Jacob wrestle with Elohim who appears as an unknown אִישׁ? The fragmentary and/or laconic state of the texts perhaps precludes an answer, but I would suggest that the paradoxical quality of Gilgamesh's nocturnal dream encounter with his divine benefactor/adversary places this tradition in the same category as Jacob's dangerous wrestling match with Elohim in Genesis 32 and with the other instances of Yahweh's adversarial relationships with his heroes. Somehow the god-hero relationship, in Mesopotamia as in Israel, is charged with a dimension of danger. The dark side of the god-hero relationship may say something about the ambiguous nature of the hero,[31] or may say something about the nature of the hero's contendings. It may be that the shaping of the hero through his encounters is not complete until, like Job, he has contended with his god.[32]

---

[29]Gilg. Har. B. 10,15-17 concern Lugalbanda.

[30]The verbs *ṣabātu*, "to grab, seize; fight, wrestle (in Gt)," and *lâdu*, "to bend down," are both characteristic of wrestling scenes; see the wrestling encounter of Gilgamesh and Enkidu in Gilg. P. vi.11-12,16-17 (for the Pennsylvania tablet, see Thompson, *Epic of Gilgamesh*, 20-24; *ANET*, 76-78); and other wrestling references cited in *AHw* 527 (s.v. *lâdu*), and 1069 (s.v. *ṣabātu*, Gt).

[31]See below, pp. 145-148, on the morally ambiguous side of Jacob and Moses.

[32]The testing of Job belongs to the same category as the other heroic tests; the main difference is, at this later time, the testing is carried out by the שָׂטָן, not

directly by Yahweh. See also the later form of this traditional theme in Mark 1:12-13; Matt 4:1-11; and Luke 4:1-13.

Jacob and Esau

Already in their mother's womb Jacob and Esau were in conflict with each other. They "crushed each other" (וַיִּתְרֹצֲצוּ) in Rebekah's womb, causing her to cry out, in a possibly corrupt phrase, "Why me?" (לָמָּה זֶּה אָנֹכִי; Gen 25:22).[33] After consulting with Yahweh for an answer, she receives the following reply:

> Two nations are in your womb,
>> two peoples within you are divided;
> One people will be mightier than the other,
>> and the elder will serve the younger (Gen 25:23).

Finally the twins are born, Esau emerging first, all red and hairy, then Jacob, holding on to the heel of his brother. The names of the brothers are related to their origins by means of word plays. Jacob (יַעֲקֹב) is so named because his hand was holding the heel (עֲקֵב) of Esau. Esau's name is more tenuously related to the image of a hairy mantle (אַדֶּרֶת שֵׂעָר) that is used to describe his hairy appearance. Neither of these folk etymologies is linguistically correct,[34] but, of course, such is not their intention. Both names point to characteristics that will distinguish the lives of the two brothers. Esau is a hairy man, a man of the hunt and of nature.

---

[33]Note the idiom in Gen 27:46 (P), also uttered by Rebekah: לָמָּה לִּי חַיִּים, "why should I live?" A haplography is possible in the consonantal text of Gen 25:22: אנכי [יחיה] למה זה, "why should I live?," triggered by homoioteleuton. Alternately, the phrase might simply be a terse idiomatic expression.

[34]The name יַעֲקֹב is a hypocoristic form, "May DN protect." The root ʿqb, "to protect," is found in Amorite, Ethiopic, and Old South Arabic. The name form yaʿqub-ʾil is found several times in Akkadian texts of the second millennium; in Ugarit the name yaʿqub-baʿl is attested. The form yaʿqub-DN is also found several times in Egyptian sources of the second millennium. For a recent review of the data, see Thompson, *The Historicity of the Patriarchal Narratives*, 43-50, and references. On the yaʿqub-har scarabs, see R. Giveon, "Yaʿqob-har" *Göttingen Miszellen* 44 (1981) 17-20; see also A. Kempinski, *Syrien and Palästina (Kanaan) in der letzten Phase der Mittelbronze IIB-Zeit (1650-1570 v. Chr.)* (Wiesbaden: Harrassowitz, 1983) 74-75, and references.

The name עֵשָׂו appears to be from the root ʿsy/w, but the form is unusual; cf. the Old South Arabic name ʿysw (apud KB, 741 s.v. עֵשָׂו).

Jacob is a heel-grabber, a usurper, who soon will supersede his brother by means of deception and intrigue.

The following verses in Gen 25:27-28 give a succinct portrait of the two brothers as they grow up, emphasizing the traits that distinguish the two brothers: "The youths grew up, and Esau was a man skilled in the hunt, a man of the fields, while Jacob was a mild man (אִישׁ תָּם)[35] who stayed in the tents." The text goes on to provide crucial familial information: "Isaac loved Esau, because he had a taste for game, while Rebekah loved Jacob." The traits and alliances of the two brothers will be highlighted in the episode of the deception of Isaac in Genesis 27; it is characteristic of biblical narrative art that elements which will be crucial in a later episode are briefly mentioned, almost alluded to, well before the key episode.[36]

The story of Esau's sale of his birthright for a bowl of pottage expands on the differences of the two brothers. Jacob is the one who stays indoors, cooking a pot of stew, while Esau is engaged in an unsuccessful hunt. The encounter between the two brothers takes place on Jacob's domestic terrain, and it is therefore not surprising that Jacob acquires the desired birthright from his hungry brother. Esau is depicted as a thoughtless, crude man,[37] while Jacob is shrewd and manipulative. In the conflict between the man of the hearth and the man of the hunt, it is the man of the hearth who wins.

Before examining more closely the polarity of traits that define the two brothers, let us briefly consider other pairs of brothers with whom Jacob and Esau have been compared. One obvious comparison is with the birth story of the twin brothers Perez and Zerah in Gen 38:27-30. During labor, one child, Zerah, stretches his hand out of the womb and the midwife proclaims it the first-born, but then the hand is withdrawn and the other child, Perez,

---

[35]Note that Noah and Job are also "mild" or "complete" (תמם√) men in Israelite tradition, though the word implies more of a moral status in their cases; cf. Gen 6:9 (נֹחַ אִישׁ צַדִּיק תָּמִים; P) and Job 1:1 (וְהָיָה הָאִישׁ הַהוּא תָּם).

[36]See N. M. Sarna, "The Anticipatory Use of Information as a Literary Feature of the Genesis Narratives," in *The Creation of Sacred Literature*, ed. R. E. Friedman (Berkeley: University of California, 1981) 76-82.

[37]See the discussion of Alter, *Biblical Narrative*, 42-45.

emerges first. The prenatal conflict of the twin brothers over the place of the first-born distinctly recalls the conflict of Jacob and Esau, and in fact it seems clear that the two episodes are multiforms, rooted in the traditions of birth stories in ancient Israel. Unfortunately, we hear nothing more of the conflicts of Perez and Zerah.

The story of the blessing of Ephraim and Manasseh in Gen 48:8-20 also contains the theme of the acquisition of the first-born rights by the youngest son.[38] Significantly, it is Jacob/Israel who performs the blessing. In an obvious play on the story of the deception of blind Isaac, the text relates that "Israel's eyes were dim with age, he could not see" (Gen 48:10). But in this story, instead of the blind father being deceived by his youngest son, here the blind grandfather (Israel) deceives the father (Joseph) by bestowing the blessing of the first-born onto the youngest son (Ephraim). The twists and turns in the story show Jacob/Israel once again playing his role as the trickster, and the youngest son again is ascendent.

In the stories of Perez and Zerah and of Ephraim and Manasseh, the ascendence of the younger son functions both as a narrative theme and as a political etiology. A hierarchy is set up between the pairs of brothers and this hierarchy corresponds to a political reality in Israel. Perez was apparently a more powerful Judahite clan than Zerah,[39] just as Ephraim was dominant over Manasseh.[40] The general correspondence between epic characters and social clans or tribes is difficult to define, but it seems clear in a number of cases that political relations were articulated through the narrative relations of eponymous ancestors. The question arises, then, of the possible political level of the dealings of Jacob and Esau. After all, Jacob is named "Israel" during his struggle with his divine adversary in Genesis 32, and Esau is named "Edom" (אֱדוֹם) in Gen 25:30 after he asks for some of the "red stuff" (הָאָדֹם), the lentil stew. Can we legitimately infer that the

---

[38]See also the stories of Joseph and David for this theme. The conflict between the elder son, Cain, and the younger son, Abel, is also relevant here. Yahweh's choice of the sacrifice of the younger son is likely a variation on this theme.

[39]See, e.g., Num 26:20-21; 1 Chr 9:4-6; etc.

[40]See, e.g., Num 1:10,32-35; Josh 21:5; etc.

political relations of Israel and Edom are being articulated in the narrative?

The problems involved are complicated,[41] but we can at least sketch an approach to the major issues. In Deut 23:8, Moses commands: "Do not abhor the Edomite, for he is your brother." This command distinguishes the Edomites from the Ammonites or the Moabites, who are condemned in the verses preceding.[42] It seems, then, that Edom is distinguished from the other Transjordanian nations as a kin of Israel. In Judges 5, one of the oldest pieces of Hebrew poetry,[43] we find that Yahweh's triumphant march to save his people originates in Seir and in the plains of Edom (v. 4). Other appearances in early Hebrew poetry of the theme of the march of the Divine Warrior from the southland tend to corroborate this early linkage of Israel with Edom.[44] The listing of a place-name *Yahwi* in the region of Seir in Egyptian inscriptions from the Late Bronze Age adds a tantalizing bit of evidence to the supposition that Yahweh was an important god in the south before he became the god of Israel.[45] In any case, these data indicate the types of connections that might have linked Israel and Edom in the early period.

On the narrative side of the equation, we find that the relations between Jacob and Esau do not exactly mirror the relations of Israel and Edom. While it is true that Israel conquered Edom in the era of David, as appears to be the intent of

[41]See, e.g., J. T. S. Bartlett, "The Land of Seir and the Brotherhood of Edom" *JTS* 20 (1969) 1-20.

[42]Interestingly, the Egyptians as well as the Edomites are not to be abhorred (Deut 23:8).

[43]For the antiquity of Judges 5, see F. M. Cross, Jr., and D. N. Freedman, *Studies in Ancient Yahwistic Poetry* (Missoula, MT: Scholars, 1975) 13-21; D. A. Robertson, *Linguistic Evidence in Dating Early Hebrew Poetry* (Missoula, MT: Scholars, 1972) esp. 135-156.

[44]Cf. Judg 5:5; Deut 33:2; see Cross, *Canaanite Myth*, 85-86, esp. 86 n. 17.

[45]See R. Giveon, *Les Bédouins shosou des documents égyptiens* (Leiden: Brill, 1971) 26-28 (toponym list, Amenophis III), 74-77 (toponym list, Ramses II); see also the doubts expressed by M. Astour, *IDBSup*, 971. On the "Midianite hypothesis" in general, see R. de Vaux, *The Early History of Israel*, trans. D. Smith (Philadelphisa Westminster, 1978) 330-338; W. J. Dumbrell, "The Midianites and their Transjordanian Sucessors" (Ph.D. diss., Harvard University, 1970), and references; see also the recent remarks of B. Mazar, "Yahweh Came Out from Sinai," in *Temples and High Places in Biblical Times*, ed. A. Biran (Jerusalem: Hebrew Union College, 1981) 5-7, and discussion following.

the oracle in Gen 25:23, the characters of the two brothers do not correspond to historical reality. As Gunkel acutely pointed out, the identification of the brothers with the two nations appears to be a late phenomenon in the growth of the traditions, since aspects of the relations of the two brothers contradict the historical record: "in the story Jacob is afraid of his brother, in history Israel conquered Edom in war; in the story Esau is dumb, in history he is famous for his wisdom."[46] It seems that the different attributes of the two brothers, as well as the rather strained word plays between Esau and Edom, indicate that the traditions of Jacob and Esau were already well-formed before the brothers were identified with Israel and Edom.

The problem of the convergence of Jacob-Esau with Israel-Edom brings in its train innumerable uncertainties concerning early Israelite history and traditions, so that no definitive view can be forwarded. All we can say with any certainty is that at some point the characters were identified as eponymous ancestors of political groups, and that neither the narrative of the two brothers nor the history of the two nations can be discerned with any clarity through the other.

The pair of Ishmael and Isaac, sons of Abraham by different mothers, present a comparable narrative and political bond. The conflict over who will inherit the blessing of Abraham is not depicted as a direct conflict between the two half-brothers, but rather as a conflict between the two wives, Sarah and Hagar, in which Sarah gains the upper hand in both the J and E versions. Once again, it is the younger son, Isaac, who gains the right of the blessing and covenant of Abraham. The political dimension is once again present, as Ishmael is the ancestor of the Ishmaelites and Isaac is a patriarch of Israel. The actions of the epic characters, however, are not mere political allegories for tribal movements and affiliations. The events run more complexly than that.

For example, consider the character of Ishmael. In the J version (Genesis 16), Hagar flees into the wilderness in fear of Sarai and receives an annunciation from the angel of Yahweh. Her child, the angel says, "will be a wild ass of a man, / his hand against

---

[46]Gunkel, *Genesis* (3rd ed.) xx. On the wisdom of the Edomites, see Jer 49:7; Bar 3:22-23; and Job.

everyone, / and everyone's hand against him" (Gen 16:12). In the E version (Gen 21:9-21), Hagar again is wandering about the wilderness, sent out at Sarah's behest, and an angel of God delivers an oracle of promise concerning the child. The text relates: "And God was with the youth, and he grew up; and he dwelled in the wilderness and he became an expert bowman" (Gen 21:20).[47] As has often been noticed,[48] Ishmael is described here in similar terms as Esau, who is "skilled in the hunt, a man of the fields" (Gen 25:27). Both Ishmael and Esau are the eldest of two brothers, both are stripped of the privileges of the first-born, and both are hunters, men of the wilds. The image of Cain is also relevant here: he is the firstborn of two brothers, his offering is passed over in favor of Abel's offering, and he is cast out into the wilderness to be "a restless wanderer on the earth" (Gen 4:12).

Why are these figures of Israelite epic all men of the wilderness? What symbolic associations are being represented here? To pursue this theme, we must widen our range of investigation to include other Near Eastern traditions of brothers and counterparts: Gilgamesh and Enkidu, Horus and Seth, and Hypsouranios and Ousōos.

GILGAMESH AND ENKIDU

The relationship of Gilgamesh and Enkidu in the Mesopotamian tradition undergoes an important transformation between the Sumerian and Old Babylonian periods.[49] In the Sumerian Gilgamesh cycle, Enkidu is called the servant (*arad*; *šubur*) of Gilgamesh, while in the Old Babylonian epic he is elevated to the status of Gilgamesh's friend (*ibrum*).[50] It has been

---

[47] The term translated "expert bowman," רֹבֶה קַשָּׁת, literally "a shooter(?) (that is) an archer," is problematic; perhaps the consonants have been misdivided and we should read רַב הַקֶּשֶׁת," great of the bow" or "archer of the bow," still with the connotation "expert bowman."

[48] E.g., Gunkel, *Genesis* (3rd ed.) 192.

[49] On the history and versions of the Gilgamesh epic, see most recently Tigay, *Gilgamesh*; see also T. Jacobsen, *The Treasures of Darkness: A History of Mesopotamian Religion* (New Haven: Yale University, 1976) 195-219; and the essays in P. Garelli, ed., *Gilgameš et sa légende* (Paris: Klincksieck, 1960).

[50] See Tigay, *Gilgamesh*, 29-30.

suggested that the numerous thematic features that distinguish the Akkadian epic from its Sumerian sources were set into motion by this singular change in the status of Enkidu.[51] Enkidu's death in the Sumerian version was a sad occasion for Gilgamesh, but in the Akkadian version the death of Enkidu becomes the tragic event that utterly transforms Gilgamesh. When Enkidu dies, Gilgamesh's world is shattered; he despairs of his life in Uruk and sets out to attain immortality. In recounting this quest the epic achieves immortality, even if Gilgamesh himself does not.

The characters of Gilgamesh and Enkidu form a polarity in the Akkadian epic. Gilgamesh is a royal figure, the king of Uruk, whose fame is renowned among the lands. The incipit of the Old Babylonian version says of Gilgamesh: "he was preeminent among kings" (*šūtur eli šarrī*).[52] As king of Uruk, Gilgamesh is a man of culture, of civilized life. Enkidu's character is completely opposite. Created to be the rival of Gilgamesh to quiet his reckless energy, Enkidu is a man of nature. In the Old Babylonian version, Gilgamesh's mother interprets a dream of Gilgamesh as a sign of the coming of Enkidu:

> minde Gilgameš ša kīma kâti
> ina ṣēri iwwalid-ma
> urabbišu šadû

> No doubt, Gilgamesh, one like you
> was born on the steppe,
> the open country raised him.[53]

Enkidu is described as having a "hairy body" (*šu''uram pagaršu*);[54] he runs around the steppe with the animals;[55] he is

---

[51]See the remarks of G. Dossin, "Enkidou dans l'épopée de Gilgameš" *Académie royale de Belgique. Bulletin de la classe des lettres . . .* 42 (1956) 580-593; and Tigay, *Gilgamesh*, 29-30.

[52]Gilg. P. colophon; Gilg. I.i.27; see Tigay, *Gilgamesh*, 48, 150.

[53]Gilg. P. i.17-20.

[54]Gilg. P. iii.23. Note the similar depiction of Enkidu and Esau: Esau is an שָׂעִר אִישׁ, a "hairy man" (Gen 27:11). Hebrew *šā'īr* is cognate with Akkadian *šu''urum*; for discussion, see Speiser, *Genesis*, 196.

[55]Gilg. P. ii.12-13.

said to have been suckled on the milk of animals;[56] and he does not know how to eat bread or to drink beer.[57] Enkidu is a savage man, a model of primeval humanity,[58] untutored in the ways of culture.

G. S. Kirk has observed that the polarity of the characters of Gilgamesh and Enkidu corresponds neatly to the thematic opposition of "nature" and "culture" that Claude Lévi-Strauss has discerned in many American Indian myths.[59] In Lévi-Strauss's view, the opposition of nature/culture forms one of the basic conceptual polarities of *la pensée sauvage* that myths attempt to resolve.[60] Other polarities, such as death/life, raw/cooked, wet/dry, etc., are aligned with the nature/culture polarity, and out of the network of these relationships a limitless variety of myths are generated. While aspects of Lévi-Strauss's approach to myth are problematic,[61] the value of many of his insights is undeniable, even if often more suggestive than definitive.

Gilgamesh is, according to these terms, a man of culture while Enkidu is a man of nature. Enkidu is initiated into human culture by the harlot who teaches him the ways of sex, clothing, bread, and beer.[62] Having entered human society, Enkidu discovers that the animals of the wild no longer recognize him, and he can run with them no longer.[63] The Old Babylonian text relates Enkidu's transformation into a man of culture after he finishes his initiatory meal:

[56]Gilg. P. iii.1-2.

[57]Gilg. P. iii.6-8.

[58]On Enkidu as a *lullû* man ("primordial man"), see Gilg. I.iv.6,13,19; and Tigay, *Gilgamesh*, 202-203.

[59]G. S. Kirk, *Myth: Its Meaning and Functions in Ancient and Other Cultures* (Berkeley: University of California, 1970) 145- 151; see also Tigay, *Gilgamesh*, 209-213.

[60]For Lévi-Strauss's use of the terms "nature" and "culture," see, e.g., Lévi-Strauss, *Totemism*, trans. R. Needham (Boston: Beacon, 1963) 77-102; idem, "The Structural Study of Myth," *Structural Anthropology* (New York: Basic, 1963) 206-231.

[61]For criticism from the point of view of biblical scholarship, see Rogerson, *Myth in Old Testament Interpretation*, 101-127; see also the comments of M. Douglas, "The Meaning of Myth," *Implicit Meanings* (London: Routledge and Kegan Paul, 1975) 153- 172.

[62]Gilg. P. ii-iii.

[63]Gilg. I.iv.23-28.

šu^{ʾʾ}uram pagaršu
šamnam iptašaš-ma
awīliš īwi
ilbaš libšam
kīma muti ibašši

His hairy body
he anointed with oil;
he became like a man.
He put on clothes;
there he was, like a man.[64]

In his passage from nature to culture we see Enkidu acting out in miniature a history of the emergence of humanity. At his creation he is a representative of a former age when people "knew not the eating of bread, / knew not the wearing of garments; / the people went around with skins on their bodies. / They ate grass with their mouths like sheep, / drank water from ditches."[65] By the time Enkidu enters the city of Uruk, he has become "like a man" in the ways of culture, and to the harlot he appears even "like a god" (kīma ili tabašši)[66] - a phrase reminiscent of the passage of Adam and Eve from nature to culture in the Israelite tradition.[67]

Gilgamesh and Enkidu meet each other in a hostile encounter on Enkidu's entry into the city, and Gilgamesh proves the victor.[68]

---

[64]Gilg. P. iii.23-27.

[65]From the Sumerian myth of *Lahar and Ashnan*; text and translation in Tigay, *Gilgamesh*, 203. Compare the description of Enkidu and of primeval humanity with the description of the West Semitic god Amurru in the Sumerian composition, *The Marriage of MAR.TU*: "a tent dweller [buffeted?] by wind and rain . . . dwelling in the mountain . . . the one who digs up mushrooms at the foot of the mountain, who does not know how to bend the knee; who eats uncooked meat; who in his lifetime does not have a house; who on the day of his death will not be buried" (text and translation in Tigay, *Gilgamesh*, 201; see also G. Buccellati, *The Amorites of the Ur III Period* [Naples: Istituto Orientale di Napoli, 1966] 330-331). Enkidu, primeval humanity, and Amurru are all described in terms of nature, the opposite of culture. The savage, the foreigner, and the primeval man form a continuous image of the "other." Note the raw/cooked symbolism in the description of Amurru corresponding to the nature/culture distinction; see Lévi-Strauss, *The Raw and the Cooked*, trans. J. and D. Weightman (New York: Harper and Row, 1975).

[66]Gilg. P. ii.11.

[67]For comparisons of Genesis 2-3 with Gilgamesh, see J. A. Bailey, "Initiation and the Primal Woman in Gilgamesh and Genesis 2-3" *JBL* 89 (1970) 137-150; Speiser, *Genesis*, 26-28.

[68]Gilg. P. vi.

After the encounter they become fast friends; from opposites the two have become counterparts.

Gilgamesh and Enkidu remain inseparable throughout their adventures until Enkidu dies. At that point, torn by grief, Gilgamesh leaves Uruk and journeys into the unknown lands wearing only the skins of animals.[69] As Kirk has pointed out, here Gilgamesh reverses his character and takes on the early traits of Enkidu: Gilgamesh here becomes the man of nature, the savage man.[70] After being admonished by the sun god Shamash and by the divine alewife that "(eternal) life, which you seek, you will not find" (*balāṭam ša tasaḫḫuru lā tutta*),[71] Gilgamesh finally reaches the home of Utnapishtim where he finds that immortality is not something a mere mortal can attain. For his return trip to Uruk, Utnapishtim commands that Gilgamesh be once again clothed in the garments of human culture:

> malīšu ina mê kīma elli limsi
> liddi maškīšū-ma libil tamtum
> ṭābu lū ṣapû zumuršu
> lū udduš parsīgu ša qaqqadīšu
> tēdīqi lū labiš ṣubat bāltīšu
> adi illaku ana ālīšu
> adi ikaššadu ana urḫīšu
> tēdīqu šīpa ayy-iddī-ma
> edīšu lidiš

> Let him wash off his grime in pure water,
> let him cast off his skins, let the sea carry them away,
> that the beauty of his body may be seen.
> Let him renew the band on his head,
> let a majestic garment clothe his body,
> that he may travel to his city,
> that he may achieve his journey.
> Let not his majestic garment be discolored,
> let it be wholly new.[72]

[69]Gilg. Me. i.2; for the Meissner fragment, see Thompson, *Epic of Gilgamesh*, 53-54; *ANET*, 89-90.

[70]Kirk, *Myth*, 149.

[71]Gilg. Me. i.8; iii.2.

[72]Gilg. XI.240-246.

The Standard Babylonian version of the Gilgamesh epic ends with Gilgamesh showing the boatman Urshanabi the great walls of Uruk and taking pride in their grandeur. The Old Babylonian version might not have ended with this scene,[73] but the import of the image of the walls of Uruk fit neatly into the implication of the narrative. Gilgamesh has re-entered the realm of human culture: he is reconciled to the limitations of human life, and he takes pride in the achievements of human society. The image of the walls of Uruk is an appropriate symbol: it signifies both the boundaries of human culture and the fame that cultural achievement can bestow.[74]

In this sense the end for Gilgamesh is complementary to the end for Enkidu. On his deathbed, Enkidu cursed the harlot for first introducing him to the ravages of human culture. Then Shamash intervenes and asks Enkidu why he should curse the harlot:

> ša ušākiluka akla simat ilūti
> kurunna išqûka simat šarrūti
> ulabbišuka lubšī rabâ
> u damqu Gilgameš tappâ ušaršûka kâša

> who made you eat food fit for divinity,
> who made you drink beer fit for royalty,
> who clothed you with noble garments,
> and made you have fair Gilgamesh for a friend.[75]

Enkidu relents, acknowledging that the harlot gave him more than he had realized, and proceeds to bless her: "May [kings,] princes, and nobles love you" (*šarrāni malkī u rubê lirāmūki*).[76] At his death, Enkidu accepts his human state; like Gilgamesh, he is reconciled to the gifts and burdens of human mortality and human culture.

---

[73] See Tigay, *Gilgamesh*, 146-149.

[74] On the fame that building projects bestow, see Tigay, *Gilgamesh*, 146-149; see also A. L. Oppenheim, *Ancient Mesopotamia: Portrait of a Dead Civilization* (Chicago: University of Chicago, 1964) 257-258.

[75] Gilg. VII.iii.36-39.

[76] Gilg. VII.iv.2.

HORUS AND SETH

The conflict of the gods Horus and Seth is one of the constants of Egyptian mythology.[77] According to the theogony of Heliopolis, Seth is the uncle of Horus, although in some early Pyramid Texts Horus and Seth appear as brothers.[78] This type of mixing is not unusual in mythological traditions and gives us notice that genealogies are subject to the same kind of multiformity as other types of tradition.[79] In the conflict between Horus and Seth, the issue is the right to the kingship of the god Osiris, whom Seth had murdered. Horus defeats Seth after numerous encounters and intrigues, and becomes the "lord of heaven" and "king of the gods."[80]

As is the case with Jacob and Esau and with Gilgamesh and Enkidu, there is a notable polarity in the characters of Horus and Seth. I do not wish to infer that any of these figures can be reduced to a simple "type" of one or another quality, as in a medieval morality play, rather I wish to highlight one strand in the complex web of traditions that encompasses, to a greater or lesser degree, each of these figures. Egyptian tradition is allusive and difficult, but certain traits can be pointed out that characterize a duality for Horus and Seth.

Henri Frankfort and others have stressed the "deeply rooted Egyptian tendency to understand the world in dualistic terms as a series of pairs of contrasts balanced in unchanging equilibrium."[81]

[77]On Horus and Seth, see H. te Velde, *Seth, God of Confusion* (Leiden: Brill, 1967); E. Hornung, "Seth. Geschichte und Bedeutung eines ägyptischen Gottes" *Symbolon* 2 (1975) 49-63; and J. G. Griffiths, *The Conflict of Horus and Seth from Egyptian and Classical Sources* (Liverpool: Liverpool University, 1960).

[78]See Griffiths, *Horus and Seth*, 12-13.

[79]On the fluidity of traditional genealogies in the ancient Near East, see R. R. Wilson, *Genealogy and History in the Biblical World* (New Haven: Yale University, 1977).

[80]Translations of the New Kingdom text of "The Contendings of Horus and Seth" are found in M. Lichtheim, *Ancient Egyptian Literature. Volume II: The New Kingdom* (Berkeley: University of California, 1976) 214-223; W. K. Simpson, ed., *The Literature of Ancient Egypt* (New Haven: Yale University, 1973) 108-126; an older, abridged translation is found in *ANET*, 14-17.

[81]H. Frankfort, *Kingship and the Gods* (Chicago: University of Chicago, 1948) 19, cf. 22; see also W. Helck, "Die Mythologie der alten Ägypter," in *Wörterbuch der Mythologie*, 350; and te Velde, *Seth*, 48, 75.

Horus and Seth as a contrasting pair could be assimilated to any
number of other oppositions. For example, the separation of Horus
and Seth that ended their quarrel was linked with the separation
of heaven and earth, earth and underworld, right and left, black
and red, to be born and to be conceived, rulership and strength, life
and dominion, and other pairs.[82]

The relationship between the characters of Horus and Seth is
one of contrasts and balances. As H. te Velde observes: "Seth is the
other one opposite Horus, the royal god of Egypt."[83] Seth is a god
of confusion, an enemy of boundaries, and te Velde rightly notes
that these traits link Seth with the "trickster" figures of various
cultures.[84] Seth is born unnaturally; he kills Osiris through a
clever ruse; he engages in homosexual acts with Horus; and he
becomes pregnant by ingesting Horus' semen.[85] Seth says of
himself: "I am Seth the originator of confusion."[86] In all of these
roles, Seth is a genuine trickster figure, transgressing the cultural
codes of ethics and order.[87]

Another dimension of Seth's character has been less well
defined by Egyptologists. Seth is clearly a god of disorder and a
trickster, but it is important to recognize the conceptual duality
that underlies his various roles. Most of the traits that
characterize Seth can be subsumed under his aspect as the god of
nature, as opposed to Horus, the god of culture. Seth was

[82]te Velde, *Seth*, 60-63.

[83]Ibid., 110.

[84]te Velde, "The Egyptian God Seth as a Trickster" *Journal of the American Research Center in Egypt* 7 (1968) 37-40.

[85]In the text "The Contendings of Horus and Seth," Isis tricks Seth by spreading the semen of Horus onto some lettuce which Seth then eats, becoming pregnant. Compare with the Sumerian myth of "Enki and Ninhursaga" (trans. in *ANET*, 37-41; see the discussion of Jacobsen, *Treasures of Darkness*, 112-113) in which Enki, the Sumerian trickster god, becomes pregnant by eating plants which contain his own semen. The motif of the trickster god becoming pregnant, thus blurring the distinction between male and female, is found in other cultures as well (see below, n. 87).

[86]te Velde, "Seth as a Trickster," 38.

[87]On the trickster figure in various cultures, see P. Radin, *The Trickster: A Study in American Indian Mythology* (New York: Schocken, 1972 [1956]); G. Dumézil, *Loki* (Paris: Maisonneuve, 1948); E. E. Evans-Pritchard, *The Zande Trickster* (Oxford: Clarendon, 1967); and especially R. D. Pelton, *The Trickster in West Africa* (Berkeley: University of California, 1980).

worshiped primarily in the border regions of Egypt, and the animal representing Seth was depicted as living in the desert or in foreign lands.[88]   Seth kills Osiris in the desert, and he is driven away to the desert after the final judgement of his quarrel with Horus.[89]   From at least the time of the Middle Kingdom, Seth is viewed as the lord of foreign lands.[90]   Seth is a hunter; he kills the Apopis serpent; and the Seth animal is depicted in hunting scenes.[91]   All of these traits represent Seth as a god of the wilds, one pole of the nature/culture dichotomy.

Te Velde summarizes Seth's character in the following terms: "On the mythological level Seth is a disturber of the peace, on the cosmic level a thunder-god, and on the geographical level a foreigner."[92]   In all of these roles Seth is opposed to Horus: disturbance is opposed to order, thunder to the sun, and the foreigner to the king.   Seth is the god of the disorderly, threatening, foreign, uncivilized aspect of the cosmos, while Horus is the god of order, of civilization, of the hegemony of Egypt.

The conflict between Horus and Seth thus extends to the widest ranges of their characters.   Horus and Seth hold between them the totality of the conflicting forces of culture and nature.   It is remarkable, therefore, as H. Kees first noted, that in ancient Egypt the two gods who are separate in the mythology are often worshiped as one god in the local cult.[93]   In the Pyramid texts, the Pharoah is given the title of "Horus-Seth."   The image of the god Horus-Seth is represented as one figure with two heads: a falcon head for Horus and a Seth head.   This figure is depicted in the realm of the dead, in the land where contrasts are subsumed and the mystery of totality is revealed.[94]   As te Velde observes: "Horus and Seth are the gods who contend and are reconciled or who are separated and reunited."[95]

[88]See te Velde, *Seth*, 111, 116.
[89]Ibid., 111.
[90]Ibid., 110, 113.
[91]Ibid., 99-108, 111.
[92]Ibid., 118.
[93]Ibid., 69-70.
[94]Ibid., 69-70.
[95]Ibid., 70-71.

The contrast between Horus and Seth is in the broadest sense a contrast between the forces of culture and the forces of nature as conceived by the ancient Egyptians, ordered by an abiding belief in the duality of the cosmos and of the equilibrium of this duality. The conceptual shadings of this duality take on a form distinctive of Egyptian religion, but also, I would stress, distinctive of the common human perception of this duality, as we can see in the features that link the divine pair of Horus and Seth with the mortal pairs of Gilgamesh and Enkidu and Jacob and Esau.

HYPSOURANIOS AND OUSŌOS

Hypsouranios and Ousōos are brothers in the Phoenician traditions recorded by Philo of Byblos, a writer of the early Roman era.[96] Philo claimed that his account was a translation of an original Phoenician work by a certain Sanchuniathon, whom Philo held to be a figure of extreme antiquity. The date of Sanchuniation (Phoenician Sakkunyaton) is a matter of debate, but the authenticity of the Phoenician traditions preserved in Philo's work is generally clear.[97] Philo does, however, often overlay the Phoenician material with a Greek interpretation. For example, Philo is a Euhemerist, that is, he regards the Phoenician "gods" as originally having been famous men. He states: "Since they considered these men as benefactors and sources of many blessings, they worshiped them as gods even after they had passed on."[98]

Philo presents the two brothers Hypsouranios and Ousōos as human brothers, but it is clear from the context that the brothers are gods, descended from Beelsamēn, transparently the Phoenician

---

[96]See H. A. Attridge and R. A. Oden, Jr., *Philo of Byblos: The Phoenician History. Introduction, Critical Text, Translation, Notes* (CBQMS 9; Washington DC: Catholic Biblical Association, 1981); J. Ebach, *Weltenstehung und Kulturentwicklung bei Philo von Byblos* (Stuttgart: Kohlhammer, 1979) esp. 149-174; and A. I. Baumgarten *The Phoenician History of Philo of Byblos* (Leiden: Brill, 1981) esp. 159-165.

[97]For discussion, see Attridge and Oden, *Philo of Byblos*, 1-9; Baumgarten, *Phoenician History*, 261-268; and references.

[98]PE 1.9.29; Attridge and Oden, *Philo of Byblos*, 29-71.

high god Ba'l Šamēm.[99] The two brothers would then be lesser gods, perhaps members of local pantheons. The text relates of the two brothers:

> Εἶτά φησι τὸν Ὑψουράνιον οἰκῆσαι Τύρον καλύβας τε ἐπινοῆσαι ἀπὸ καλάμων καὶ θρύων καὶ παπύρου, στασιάσαι δὲ πρὸς τὸν ἀδελφὸν Οὔσωον, ὃς σκέπην τῷ σώματι πρῶτος ἐκ δερμάτων ὧν ἴσχυσεν συλλαβεῖν θηρίων εὗρεν.

> Then he says that Hypsouranios settled Tyre and that he invented huts made of reeds, rushes, and papyrus. He quarrelled with his brother, Ousōos, who first discovered how to gather a covering for the body from the hides of animals which he captured.[100]

The similarities between the brothers Hypsouranios and Ousōos and the brothers Jacob and Esau have long been noted: the fraternal quarrel, the association of one brother with huts or tents, and the association of the other brother with hunting. Some scholars have suggested that the Phoenician brothers are in fact distorted versions of the biblical brothers, and have seen in the name Ousōos the linguistic equivalent of Esau.[101] More recently, however, scholars have seen in the Phoenician brothers a pair of mythological figures, perhaps local to Tyre and Sidon.

The name Ousōos has been most plausibly connected with Usû, the name for old mainland Tyre.[102] Ousōos would then be the eponymous god of Tyre. In the text, however, it is Hypsouranios who first settled Tyre. Philo tells us that Hypsouranios was also called Samemroumos, transparently šamēm rūmīm, "High Heaven," in Phoenician. The name Hypsouranios is a direct Greek

[99]PE 1.10.7-10; see comments of Attridge and Oden, Philo of Byblos, 81.

[100]PE 1.10.10; Attridge and Oden, Philo of Byblos, 42-43.

[101]For a discussion of the views of the early commentators on Philo, see Attridge and Oden, Philo of Byblos, 82; Ebach, Philo von Byblos, 159-161; Baumgarten, Phoenician History, 160-161. Note that KB (741 s.v. עֵשָׂו) persists in listing Ousōos as a cognate of Esau!

[102]First argued by T. K. Cheyne, "The Connection of Esau and Usöos" ZAW 17 (1897) 189. The evidence for the correct rendering of the West Semitic sibilant as a samekh was first presented by W. F. Albright, The Vocalization of the Egyptian Syllabic Orthography (New Haven: American Oriental Society, 1934) 35 (III.E.5), 65 (XX.B.1); see also A. F. Rainey, "Toponymic Problems" Tel Aviv 9 (1982) 133. For the location of Usû, see H. J. Katzenstein, The History of Tyre (Jerusalem: Schocken Institute, 1973) 14-15, and references.

translation of the Phoenician. Interestingly, we know of a district in Sidon called *šmm rmm*, "High Heaven;"[103] accordingly some have seen in Hypsouranios an eponymous god of Sidon.[104] The apparent mix of Tyre and Sidon in the association of these two gods may be a matter of a confusion in our text or in Philo's sources, or we may not yet have enough data to properly sort out the associations.[105]

Once the Phoenician divine brothers are separated from the mortal brothers Jacob and Esau, there still remain the traits that initially suggested a connection. To say that the pairs of brothers are different is only the first step; we must then account for the similarity. As is now perhaps evident, the continuity in the traits of the two pairs of brothers derives from the traditional polarity of culture versus nature. Hypsouranios, like Jacob, is an exponent of culture: he invents huts made of reeds, rushes, and papyrus. Ousôos, like Esau, is an exponent of nature: he is a hunter of animals and invents clothing made of skins. Both Phoenician brothers share the role of culture hero by inventing items of culture, but the opposition in the types of implements that they invent still distinguishes their polarity. The two brothers quarrel, as do Jacob and Esau, as do Horus and Seth, and as do Gilgamesh and Enkidu initially. The quarrel of opposites in the Phoenician narrative tradition is resolved into a unity in the cult: Hypsouranios and Ousôos are worshiped in the cult, and annual festivals are held in their honor after their "death."[106]

Although little information is preserved of the Phoenician deities Hypsouranios and Ousôos, enough remains to trace the continuity of the nature/culture polarity in the Phoenician

---

[103]*KAI* 15; see J. Friedrich and W. Röllig, *Phönizisch-punische Grammatik* (2nd ed.; AnOr 46; Rome: Biblical Institute, 1970) para. 78d for the vocalic shift **ram > *rōm/*rūm.*

[104]See O. Eissfeldt, "Schamemrumim 'Hoher Himmel,' ein Stadtteil von Gross-Sidon," *Kleine Schriften*, vol. II (Tübingen: Mohr, 1963 [1938]) 123-126.

[105]Baumgarten (*Phoenician History*, 161-163) argues that the two brothers are both gods of Tyre, supposing that there was also a section of Tyre called *šmm rmm.* The rivalry would then be between two sections of Tyre rather than between Tyre and Sidon.

[106]*PE* 1.10.10.

tradition, similar in its own way to the nature/culture polarities in Mesopotamian, Egyptian, and Israelite traditions.

AGAIN, JACOB AND ESAU

Esau is a hunter, "a man skilled in the hunt, a man of the fields," while Jacob is "a mild man who dwelled in the tents" (Gen 25:27). Esau is "a hairy man" while Jacob is "a smooth man" (Gen 27:11). The polarity of the two brothers is many-dimensional, but the nature/culture distinction serves well to convey many of the shadings of their differences. Esau is a hairy hunter,[107] reminiscent of the hairy Enkidu and of the divine hunters Ousǒos and Seth. Jacob is a man of the tents, reminiscent of Hypsouranios, Gilgamesh, and Horus, all heroes of culture. Oddly enough, Jacob is like Seth in being a trickster figure; this aspect of Jacob's personality has caused no little difficulty in addressing Jacob's ambiguous ethics, but it is firmly a part of his character. As noted above, Jacob is a "smooth" man both physically and psychologically: he is a man of culture *and* a trickster.

The nature/culture distinction operates at a number of points in the narratives of Jacob and Esau; attention to its presence can aid us in sensing the various levels of meaning in the stories. For example, Jacob as a man of culture is twice seen preparing meals. First we see Jacob cooking his lentil stew while Esau is in the wilderness hunting. Esau arrives, famished, and asks Jacob for some of the "red stuff" (הָאָדֹם; Gen 25:30), referring to the stew not by its proper name but by its sensible quality: red. Jacob replies: "First sell me your birthright" (מִכְרָה כַיּוֹם אֶת-בְּכֹרָתְךָ לִי; Gen 25:31). Jacob embarks on a cultural activity, trade, for his cooked product, while Esau bemoans his natural state: "I am on the verge of death; what use to me is the birthright?" (וְלָמָּה-זֶּה לִי בְּכֹרָה הִנֵּה אָנֹכִי הוֹלֵךְ לָמוּת; Gen 25:32). Jacob is operating on the level of culture while Esau is operating on the level of nature. Esau is depicted here as thoughtless and driven by appetite, but the

---

[107]On the cross-cultural association of hairiness with being outside of society, see C. R. Hallpike, "Social Hair" *Man* 4 (1969) 256-264, reprinted in *Reader in Comparative Religion: An Anthropological Approach*, eds., W. A. Lessa and E. Z. Vogt (4th ed.; New York: Harper and Row, 1979) 99-105.

nuance goes deeper than that. The difference between the two brothers is contained in their very words. Esau is the one who calls the stew the color "red;" Jacob sees it as a means for his ascendence over his brother.

The second time we see Jacob involved in the preparation of a meal is in Genesis 27, the episode of the deception of Isaac. As discussed earlier,[108] the preparation of the meal involves several symbolic elements. Jacob, the domestic man, the man of culture, serves Isaac a meal of domestic goats while Esau is off hunting in the wilds for the required wild game. Once again Esau is away hunting while Jacob is at home. The substitution of the domestic son for the "wild" son neatly mirrors the substitution of the domestic goats for the wild game. The "smooth" versus "hairy" distinction is important here, for not only does Jacob mask his smooth skin with the hairy animal pelts, but the manner of it is distinctly "smooth" in its other nuance: it is a trick. The pelts of the domestic goats are the disguise for the domestic man; with them he resembles his hairy brother. In so doing Jacob recognizes himself as a "trickster" (מְתַעְתֵּעַ; v. 12).

In blind Isaac's statement, "the voice is the voice of Jacob, but the hands are the hands of Esau" (הַקֹּל קוֹל יַעֲקֹב וְהַיָּדַיִם יְדֵי עֵשָׂו; v. 22), we see the convergence of the identities of the two brothers. Isaac's sense of hearing tells him that Jacob is before him, but his senses of touch and of smell tell him that it is Esau. Jacob has, for the moment, "become" his brother Esau. The man of culture has, through his symbolic transformation, become the man of nature, and he thereby acquires the blessing. Once again, the wiles of the man of culture prove superior over the man of nature.

In a metaphorical sense we see the convergence of Jacob and Esau in the symbols of Jacob's disguise. Jacob becomes a hairy man and takes on the smell of the outdoors. The union of the traits of the two brothers is complete, but it is only momentary, and the conflict between the two escalates into Esau's threat of murder (Gen 27:41). Jacob is warned and, accordingly, he flees.

The next and last scene in which the two brothers come into contact with each other is a scene of reconciliation, in which the

[108]Pp. 83-86.

two brothers disarm their conflict. Jacob is wary of encountering Esau, and in fear he sends gifts ahead (Gen 32:14-22). Ironically, in the midst of his fear of the impending encounter with his brother, he unexpectedly encounters his mysterious adversary at the Jabbok ford, whom he afterwards identifies as Elohim himself (Gen 32:31). Even after his encounter with God, Jacob is still afraid of Esau, showing once again his hesitancy in direct encounter, preferring more subtle tactics. Esau, however, has changed, and is now a gracious, forgiving friend. The text relates: "Esau ran to him, and he embraced him, and he fell on his neck, and he kissed him, and he wept" (Gen 33:4). A sequence of quick verbal forms introduces Esau, similar to his presentation in the lentil stew scene: "and he ate, and he drank, and he rose, and he left" (Gen 25:34). This time, however, the verbs convey a sense of trust and warmth in Esau rather than his former brusque and thoughtless ways. Jacob is taken aback by Esau's affection and speaks guardedly. A sense of reconciliation is nonetheless conveyed by Jacob's choice of words in v. 11, where Jacob urges Esau to accept his gift: "Accept my gift (lit. 'blessing') which I have brought to you,[109] for God has favored me, and I have plenty." The word for "my gift" is בִּרְכָתִי, literally "my blessing," the same word as the blessing that Jacob had received from Isaac in the scene of the deception.[110] Jacob is offering to Esau "my blessing" as a gesture of reconciliation; it is not the genuine blessing of the patriarch, to be sure, but a sense of reconciliation is conveyed by the careful choice of words.

In this final scene for the two brothers,[111] Jacob and Esau are reunited, if briefly. Jacob offers his gift/blessing, and Esau accepts graciously. Jacob makes an excuse to depart from Esau's company and promises to rejoin him in Seir (Gen 33:14), but we hear no further of their meeting. The two brothers, the man of culture and the man of nature, end their feud and separate. It is appropriate that their meeting takes place on Jacob's return trip to his homeland: the journey is a rite of passage both geographically and

[109]Reading הֻבֵאת with the Samaritan text and the Greek and other versions.

[110]See Buber, "Leitwortstil," 1141; Fishbane, *Text and Texture*, 52.

[111]In the P stratum, Jacob and Esau bury Isaac in Gen 35:29.

socially. The transition is doubly marked: the journey from foreign land to home is accomplished as the brother is reconciled with brother. Unity with land and with kin are symbolically linked, forming a thematic closure within the Jacob cycle.

The polarity of Jacob and Esau, their conflicts and their reconciliation, are highlighted by the symbolic polarity of nature and culture. In the traditions of the ancient Near East, culture was a valued state and the lack of culture was disparaged. Existence before or outside of culture was depicted as a state of confusion and strife. The good qualities of nature were acknowledged, as we can see in the depiction of Enkidu, or in the description of the Garden of Eden, but in general life outside of culture was seen as an unstable existence in which humans were little more than "mere" animals. At some points in Israelite tradition we find a nostalgia for the natural state, as in the beliefs of the Rechabites,[112] but even here the longing is for a purification of cultural life and not a return to primal existence. There is a sense of the "noble savage" in Enkidu, but even he finally acknowledges the superiority of culture. The advantages of culture and the moral inferiority of the natural state are patent in the traditions of the ancient Near East. At the heart of the traditional resonances of the nature/culture polarity lies at least a part of the answer to the question of the meaning of Jacob as the eponymous ancestor, the revered patriarch, of Israel.

---

[112]On the Rechabites and the "desert motif" in biblical literature, see P. A. Riemann, "Desert and Return to Desert in the Pre-exilic Prophets" (Ph.D. diss., Harvard University, 1964); R. de Vaux, *Ancient Israel. Volume I: Social Institutions* (New York: McGraw-Hill, 1965) 13-15; and S. Talmon, "The 'Desert Motif' in the Bible and in Qumran Literature," in *Biblical Motifs: Origins and Transformations,* ed. A. Altmann (Cambridge: Harvard University, 1966) 31-63.

2. *The Life of the Hero*

In a posthumous work published in 1876, J. G. von Hahn presented an outline of what he termed the "Aryan Expulsion and Return Formula" (*Arische Aussetzungs- und Rückkehr-Formel*), a pattern that described the biographies of fourteen heroes of Greek, Roman, Indic, and Germanic cultures.[1] Von Hahn was the first scholar to note systematically the common elements shared by a number of heroic cycles; he concluded that the reason for the common features was the primacy of tradition over historical memory, defining tradition as "*gläubige Urdichtung*," "primitive poetic faith."[2] The strain of German Romanticism in von Hahn's theory has since passed out of fashion, but the investigation of common elements in various heroic cycles has continued apace.

The major works in this century in which common features of the life of the hero have been investigated include Otto Rank's *The Myth of the Birth of the Hero*,[3] Lord Raglan's *The Hero: A Study in Tradition, Myth, and Drama*,[4] Joseph Campbell's *The Hero with a Thousand Faces*,[5] and Vladimir Propp's *Morphology of the Folktale*.[6] The cultural fields treated in these studies vary from Propp's consideration of Russian folktales to Campbell's treatment of myths, epics, and folktales from virtually every major cultural area. The results of these studies agree in certain respects and conflict in others. They concur in tabulating a degree of fixity in certain traditions of the hero, but they vary widely in their

[1] *Sagwissenschaftliche Studien* (Jena, 1876); for discussions of the history of research, see A. Taylor, "The Biographical Pattern in Traditional Narrative" *Journal of the Folklore Institute* 1 (1964) 114-129; and A. Dundes, in *The Study of Folklore*, ed. Dundes (Englewood Cliffs, NJ: Prentice-Hall, 1965) 142-144.

[2] von Hahn, *apud* Taylor, "Biographical Pattern," 115.

[3] Published in 1909; English translation by F. Robbins and S. E. Jelliffe (New York: Knopf, 1959).

[4] London: Watts, 1936; see also his earlier article, "The Hero of Tradition," in Dundes, ed., *The Study of Folklore*, 144- 157.

[5] Princeton: Princeton University, 1949.

[6] Published in 1928; English translation by L. Scott (2nd ed.; Austin: University of Texas, 1968).

assessment of these common features.

Rank, a Freudian psychoanalyst, regarded the common features as a projection of the Oedipal conflict and related psychic complexes. Raglan, a "myth and ritual" scholar, viewed the common features as a remnant of an archaic ritual pattern. Campbell, an ardent Jungian, regards the various traditions of the hero as a mythic blueprint for the struggle of the psyche towards "individuation," the state of self-integration and fulfillment. Propp, a Russian Formalist, was more concerned with a purely descriptive result, and as such his work tends to be more careful than the others. He still indulged, however, in a speculation that all folktales are descended from an original story type of the kidnapping of a princess by a dragon.[7] Propp is generally more reticent than the others concerning the source of the impulse for such stories; he tentatively suggested a mix of psychological impulses, religious beliefs, and elements from the pattern of everyday life.[8]

One of the problems of these studies is the universality of the patterns discerned. Each pattern is claimed to be valid cross-culturally, yet each of the authors presents a different pattern. Clearly, there is a lack of consistency in the authors' methods. Often the patterns are discerned by a "cookie-cutter" method; once the list of elements is formulated, each story is abridged and truncated until the shape of the story fits the prearranged mold. Local variations and distinctive features are ignored. While there may be value in such a procedure, it seems that quite a bit is lost or passed over. To take an analogy from the field of linguistics, the search for language universals is legitimate and valuable, but the distinctive features of any single language are completely passed over. The method precludes consideration of a single language. In a similar fashion, the search for universals in the pattern of the life of the hero will yield interesting results, but will be unable to fathom the significance of a single heroic cycle: it is not geared to such a pursuit.

[7]Propp, *Morphology*, 114
[8]Ibid., 106-107.

In the following section I will investigate the pattern of events that forms the Jacob cycle in its present guise, composed primarily from the J and E sources.[9] As a foil for my discussion, I will consider similar and divergent features from the story of the life of Moses, also primarily from J and E. The results will be a delineation of a culture-specific pattern of narrative episodes that forms a basis for both the Jacob and Moses traditions, giving us an opportunity to perceive more clearly the nature of early Israelite narrative tradition and the nature of the figures of Jacob and Moses.

---

[9] I should point out that the episodes that I will compare are predominantly J, with occasional supplementations from E and P. Recent controversies concerning source analysis are not germane to my discussion, since neither the division of sources nor the dating of sources affects the substance of my arguments.

Jacob and Moses

Hermann Gunkel noted at the beginning of this century: "Now it is evident that Genesis contains the final setting down in writing of a body of oral tradition."[10] Since his day scholarly discussion has continued to debate questions concerning the evidence for oral traditional influence on the Genesis narratives along with the possible innovations of the literary composers/redactors.[11] Many have agreed that aspects of Gunkel's theoretical stance are no longer tenable; several key assumptions of the *Formgeschichte* school have been vitiated by recent research on oral tradition.[12]

The most important assumption that has been challenged is the primacy of the short unit of narrative over the longer narrative cycle or complex. A. B. Lord has demonstrated, on the basis of his fieldwork and analysis of South Slavic oral epic traditions, that the difference between a short narrative and a long narrative corresponds to a difference in inclination of storyteller and audience, not to a historical movement from short to complex.[13] He concludes:

> It does not in any way necessarily follow that the shortest is the oldest and the longest the latest or that the crudest is the oldest and the most polished the latest. It may be, but it is not necessarily so.[14]

A story is not a fixed entity in an oral tradition; it is composed of traditional elements and themes that can be elaborated or compressed at will, guided by "the logic of the narrative and by the consequent force of habitual association."[15] The relationship

---

[10]Gunkel, *Genesis*, ii.

[11]See the discussion above, pp. 24-32.

[12]See above, pp. 6-13, and references.

[13]Lord, *Singer of Tales*, 6, 94-98.

[14]Lord, "The Gospels as Oral Traditional Literature," in *The Relationships Among the Gospels: An Interdisciplinary Dialogue*, ed. W. O. Walker, Jr. (San Antonio: Trinity University, 1978) 43.

[15]Lord, *Singer of Tales*, 96.

between stories is characterized by the same degree of multiformity that guides a performance of an individual story:

> There is a kind of interpenetration of elements between songs, a kind of exchange from one to another, as it were. A song is a conglomerate of elements more or less loosely joined together for a time, always capable of losing some of its elements to another conglomerate with a somewhat similar, though not exactly the same, configuration. . . . An interweaving of elements in this way is the normal method of formation and of continued re-formation of "songs" in oral traditional narrative.[16]

On traditional stories of the life of a hero, Lord observes:

> In their normal tellings, oral traditional narratives about individuals, whether in verse or prose, only rarely include a single account that begins with birth and ends with death. Most commonly, the separate elements or incidents in the life of a hero form individual poems or sagas. . . . One of the reasons for this is that the several narratives cluster around the "transitional" points in the man's life: his birth, his childhood or growing up, his initiation into manhood, his marriage, his mature deeds, and his death.[17]

Traditions of the life of the hero tend to focus on the extraordinary episodes in that life; since the life of a hero is an extension of an ordinary life, it follows that the most unusual occasions of ordinary life will be enlarged and elaborated in the hero's life. The concept of "rites of passage" is important here:[18] since the hero is a liminal figure, situated on the margin of the human world and the divine world, the liminal moments in the hero's life will be the subject of great interest. Rites of passage such as birth, death, and marriage are emphasized, as are encounters with "other-worldly" benefactors and antagonists, as well as the dangerous passages from one geographic or cosmic

---

[16]Lord, "Tradition and the Oral Poet: Homer, Huso and Avdo Medjedović," in *La Poesia epica é la sua formazione* (Rome: Accademia Nazionale dei Lincei, 1970) 22.

[17]Lord, "Gospels," 39-40.

[18]See van Gennep, *The Rites of Passage*; and Turner, "Betwixt and Between."

realm to another. The stories of a hero can be told as separate episodes as occasion warrants, but the whole complex of the hero's life is always part of the tradition, as the reservoir from which individual performances are drawn.

The stories of the life of Jacob and the life of Moses in the Pentateuchal sources are ready illustrations of the complexity and multiformity that underlie the formation of a narrative cycle about the life of a traditional hero. A general pattern of episodes can be discerned that characterizes both story cycles, though the similarity of the episodic pattern is counterbalanced by the distinctive features of each individual story. I would argue that the proportion of similarity of pattern to difference of detail is strong evidence for the oral traditional origins of both story cycles, in which this type of balance of similarity and difference is expected. Jacob and Moses are distinct heroes, each with his own special attributes, but at the root of both traditions we can detect a mixing of episodes, a multiformity of deeds, through which the individual figures are marked by the tradition as special, heroic, and worthy of story.

The general sequence of episodes shared by the two story cycles is summarized in the table below. It will be noted that the pattern extends essentially throughout the Jacob cycle but is found in the Moses cycle only in Exodus 2-4. The reasons for the relative elaboration and compression of the pattern in the two cycles will be considered below; at present I would only point out that the special deeds of Moses in the deliverance of the Israelites from Egypt begin only *after* the common pattern ends, perhaps suggesting that the pattern is more closely knit to the Jacob cycle than to Moses. In any case, the pattern is now an integral part of both cycles, indicating that a common tradition underlies the present form of both story cycles.

Patterns of the Hero in Early Israel: Jacob and Moses

Jacob Story		*Moses Story*
	Special Birth	
Gen 25:21-26		Exod 2:1-10
	Youthful (Illicit/Subversive) Deed	
25:29-34 and 27:1-40		2:11-14
	Flight, as Result of Youthful Deed	
27:41-45		2:15
(P variant: 27:46-28:9)		
	Promise by Deity at Sacred Place*	
28:10-22		
	Incident at Well with Future Wife	
29:1-14		2:16-21
	Marriage and Offspring	
29:15-30:24		2:21-22
	Commissioning by Deity at Sacred Place*	
		3:1-4:17
	Return to Land of Birth (at Command of Deity)	
31:1-32:22		4:18-23
	Dangerous Encounter with Deity	
32:23-33		4:24-26
	Meeting with Brother, Arrival Home	
33:1-20		4:27-31

*Note the correspondence between the "Promise by Deity at Sacred Place" and the "Commissioning by Deity at Sacred Place."

Interpreters have often noticed the similarities of individual episodes, for example the incident at the well or the dangerous encounter with the deity,[19] but since the attention of most commentators has been focused on the individual episode rather than on the whole story cycle, the common pattern of episodes has been overlooked. The essential nature of the stories lies in the convergence of pattern and episode; both are levels of tradition that are ultimately inseparable, converging in the performance of an individual narrative.

Having stressed the importance of the whole story cycle,[20] I will proceed by comparing the individual episodes within each pattern, pointing out the various levels of continuity and discontinuity that characterize the relationship of the two story cycles.

SPECIAL BIRTH

The birth stories of Jacob and Moses show clearly the type of diversity that distinguishes the two story cycles. As I have shown earlier,[21] the birth story of Jacob and Esau is related to a number of other biblical and Ugaritic birth stories, most of which are concerned with the problem of a lack of an heir and the steps taken by the deity to resolve the crisis. Jacob is, after all, a patriarch and an ancestor, so this type of story fits his destiny well. Jacob's birth story also relates his cleverness in holding on to his brother's heel, and portrays in miniature the conflict between the two brothers over the claim of the first-born. The story is a supple means of conveying character and intention, as well as marking the hero by the special intervention of the deity.

[19]E.g., Gunkel, *Genesis*, 294-295, 326.

[20]I should note that I find unconvincing the recent attempts of M. Fishbane (*Text and Texture*, 40-62) and J. G. Gammie ("Theological Interpretation," 120-124) to describe the structure of the Jacob cycle as an elaborate chiasm. While there are certainly symmetries in the story, as in the encounters with the deity at sacred sites (Bethel, Penuel) on the flight from and the return to the promised land, the story as a whole does not conform to a rigorous chiastic scheme. On the search for elaborate chiasms in biblical narrative and poetry, see the cautionary remarks of J. Kugel, "On the Bible and Literary Criticism" *Prooftexts* 1 (1981) 224-226.

[21]Pp. 37-59.

The birth story of Moses is also related to other traditional birth stories, but the related stories in this case are not Israelite or Canaanite, but Mesopotamian and Egyptian. The birth story of Sargon, King of Akkad, contains a number of elements similar to the Moses story, as has been noted since its discovery in the last century.[22] Epic traditions of the deeds of Sargon are known from the second and first millennia B.C.E.; texts have been found in Mesopotamia, Anatolia, and Egypt.[23] As one commentator has noted: "With the possible exception of Gilgamesh, Sargon of Akkad dominated the literary tradition of Mesopotamia as no other historical figure before or after."[24] In a tablet of the Sargon legend found in Ashurbanipal's library in Nineveh, Sargon relates the circumstances of his birth:

> My mother, a high-priestess, conceived me, in secret she bore me.
> She placed me in a reed basket, with bitumen she caulked my hatch.
> She abandoned me to the river from which I could not escape.
> The river carried me along; to Aqqi, the water drawer, it brought me.
> Aqqi, the water drawer, when immersing his bucket lifted me up.
> Aqqi, the water drawer, raised me as his adopted son.
> Aqqi, the water drawer, set me to his garden work.
> During my garden work, Ishtar loved me, so that
> For 55 years I ruled as king.[25]

The similar features of the Sargon birth story and the Moses birth story are numerous. Sargon's mother is a high-priestess (*ēnetu*), while Moses' mother is a Levite. The associations of the two priestly designations are different, for an *ēnetu* priestess was

[22]On the Sargon legend in the oral and literary traditions of Mesopotamia, see B. Lewis, *The Sargon Legend* (Cambridge, MA: ASOR, 1980); supplemented by the review of J. G. Westenholz in *JNES* 43 (1984) 73-79; and especially R. Drews, "Sargon, Cyrus and Mesopotamian Folk History" *JNES* 33 (1974) 387-393. On the relation between the birth stories of Sargon and Moses, see also B. S. Childs, "The Birth of Moses" *JBL* 84 (1965) 109-122; D. B. Redford, "The Literary Motif of the Exposed Child" *Numen* 14 (1967) 209-228; and C. Cohen, "The Legend of Sargon and the Birth of Moses" *JANES* 4 (1972) 46-51; the treatment of D. Irvin ("The Joseph and Moses Stories as Narrative in the Light of Ancient Near Eastern Narrative," in *Israelite and Judaean History*, eds. J. H. Hayes and J. M. Miller [Philadelphia: Westminster, 1977] 191-193) is less useful.

[23]See Lewis, *Sargon Legend*, 109-147.

[24]Ibid., 109.

[25]Text and translation in ibid., 24-25.

prohibited from bearing children,[26] but the sacral origin of each child is emphasized by this parentage. Since Sargon's birth is illicit, his mother places him in a reed basket and abandons him in a river. Similarly, Moses' birth is illicit, by the command of Pharaoh, so Moses' mother places him in a reed basket and abandons him in a river. Both children are rescued by strangers, one by a water drawer, the other by Pharaoh's daughter. Sargon is adopted by the water drawer and is watched over by Ishtar,[27] while Moses is adopted by Pharaoh's daughter and is later chosen by Yahweh.

Another ancient Near Eastern tradition similar to the birth story of Moses is the Egyptian tradition of the birth of Horus.[28] Horus is born in the Nile marshes to Isis, and she protects him there from the anger of Seth. According to a late Ptolemaic version of this story:

> She hid [him] as 'Child-who-is-in-the-papyrus-(thicket)'
> . . . he was sailing about in a boat of papyrus, and Isis said to
> Thoth, "Let me see my son who is hidden in the marshes."
> Thoth said, "See him!"[29]

The purpose of several of these notices is to connect the birth of Horus by means of word plays with the origin of the name of the god Anubis and to identify Horus with this god.[30] Yet there are similar features with the birth of Moses. W. Helck has noted several of these common features: the papyrus craft, the hiding of the child in a marsh, the pursuing villain, and even the protecting sister (Nephthys).[31] D. Redford proposes to discount these similarities by reason of the lateness of the Egyptian text, the lateness of some of the distinctive words, and the cross-

[26]See the discussions of Cohen, "Legend of Sargon," 47-49; and Lewis, *Sargon Legend*, 38-42, and references.

[27]On the "love" of Ishtar in the Sargon legend, see Westenholz, review of *Sargon Legend*, 78-79.

[28]See W. Helck, "Ṯkw und die Ramses-Stadt" *VT* 15 (1965) 48; and Redford, "Exposed Child," 220-224.

[29]From the Jumilhac Papyrus; translation in Redford, "Exposed Child," 223.

[30]See Redford, "Exposed Child," 222.

[31]Helck, "Ramses-Stadt," 48.

fertilization of literary motifs in the Greco-Roman period;[32] but
Helck's evalution of possible narrative convergences is preferable:

> Whether in this case Egyptian mythic motifs were actually
> the effective origins of the [Moses] birth story, I would not
> venture to decide; but one should not exclude from the outset
> the possibility of Egyptian descent and limit oneself to
> Mesopotamia, especially since such Egyptian mythic
> influence is noticeable in the Hebrew sphere.[33]

The placement of the Moses story in Egypt lends credence to the
possiblity of Egyptian influence as well as Mesopotamian
influence. We need not choose one over the other; Mesopotamian
stories, Egyptian stories, and Israelite stories can all show traces
of multiform elements. Stories and themes are not the property of
one culture only; they can blend and be passed on in the oral folk
tradition until it is impossible to untie them and trace the lineage
of the parts. The birth story of Moses, I suggest, shows traces of
relatedness to both Mesopotamian and Egyptian traditions, while
itself being perfectly at home in Israelite tradition.

The birth story of Moses is also a means of characterization and
foreshadowing for the infant Moses. He is persecuted by Pharaoh
at birth just as he will be later in his career. He is cast into the
waters of the Nile to save him from Pharaoh's grasp just as he
later leads the Israelites through the waters of the Red Sea to
escape Pharaoh. As in the Jacob story, the lines of conflict are
clearly drawn as early as the hero's birth: Jacob's adversary is
Esau, Moses' is Pharaoh. The two birth stories are more than
simply multiforms of other birth stories: they are symbols of the
heroic essence of the two characters. Already at birth the two are
cast into the roles that will distinguish their careers as heroes of
the Israelites.

[32]Redford, "Exposed Child," 223-224.
[33]Helck, "Ramses-Stadt," 48.

YOUTHFUL (ILLICIT/SUBVERSIVE) DEED

Commentators have long pondered the ethical problem of Jacob's trickery of Esau and Isaac in the twin stories of his acqusition of the "birthright" (בְּכֹרָה) and the "blessing" (בְּרָכָה). Gunkel noted that "originally the two stories are variants: 'blessing' and 'birthright' are essentially identical,"[34] and suggested that the moral problem we as modern readers perceive in the stories was not necessarily felt as a problem by the original audience. He suspected that the happy ending of the story for Jacob, coupled with the earthy, humorous aspect of Jacob's trickery, made the story an enjoyable one, unencumbered by a sense of Jacob's moral culpability. Gunkel also suggested that in early Israel, morality and religion had not yet been bound together; the stories are "pre-ethical."[35]

Gerhard von Rad properly rejected Gunkel's proposals as naive. While describing Gunkel's interpretation as "a necessary counterstroke to the moral solemnity and stiff spirituality of almost all older interpretations," he emphasized the "exalted and serious" mood of the stories.[36] He noted acutely that "the narrator himself, i.e., on his own, gives the reader almost no clue for interpretation."[37]

Von Rad goes on, however, to describe Jacob as "the guilty one" and ends with a statement of "how God, in pursuit of his plans which had to remain concealed from all relevant persons, broke into a family, and how he seems to pass beyond its ruins." The story "awakens in the reader a feeling of sympathetic suffering for those who are caught up mysteriously in such a monstrous act of God and are almost destroyed in it."[38] Rather than grapple with the problem of Jacob's ethical ambiguity, von Rad, it seems, is content to sermonize on it.

Moses' youthful deed of slaying an Egyptian has also prompted questions concerning moral culpability. Brevard Childs has

---

[34]Gunkel, *Genesis*, 286; see also Buber, "Leitwortstil," 1139-1141.

[35]Gunkel, *Genesis,*, 282.

[36]von Rad, *Genesis*, 279-280, cf. 267.

[37]Ibid., 267, cf. 280.

[38]Ibid., 280-281.

written sensitively on the problem:

> The Old Testament does not moralize on Moses' act of
> violence. Nowhere is there an explicit evaluation that
> either praises or condemns it. Rather, a situation is painted
> with great realism and sensitivity, and the reader is left to
> ponder on the anomalies of the deed.[39]

Without either praising or condemning Moses, Childs places the
task of moral reflection in the lap of the reader. Yet the story
ought not to be regarded as if it were merely a test of the reader's
theological attitudes toward justice; rather we should try to
understand it in its context as an extraordinary event in the life of
an extraordinary traditional figure.

Perhaps the most appropriate approach toward an
understanding of Jacob's and Moses' youthful deeds would be to
consider them together, under the same aspect. As is clear from
the common pattern in which these two story cycles are enmeshed,
the youthful deed, along with its ethical ambiguity, is a common
link of both cycles. Both deeds, Jacob's acquisition of the
birthright/blessing[40] and Moses' slaying of the Egyptian, have a
problematic character to them, and yet both are tailored to the
nature of the hero involved.

Jacob's twin deeds occur after a notice is given of his growing up:
"And the boys grew up . . ." (וַיִּגְדְּלוּ הַנְּעָרִים; Gen 25:27). Jacob's
trickery of Esau is, as Gunkel noted, an earthy, burlesque scene, yet
there is a dark air about it. We read at its end: "Esau spurned (lit.
'despised': וַיִּבֶז) the birthright" (Gen 25:34), an emotion that
presages Esau's attitude at the end of the other episode, the
deception of Isaac, in which we read that: "Esau hated (וַיִּשְׂטֹם)
Jacob because of the blessing with which his father had blessed
him" (Gen 27:41). Isaac's great trembling, Esau's wild cry, and the
threat of death at the end of the episode combine to highlight the
disturbing, dangerous aspect of Jacob's deed; indeed, we may regard

---

[39]B. S. Childs, *The Book of Exodus: A Critical, Theological Commentary* (OTL;
Philadelphia: Westminster, 1974) 44.

[40]Since, following Gunkel, I regard these two episodes as variations on a
theme, I will discuss them as essentially the same "deed." I am of course not
proposing to ignore the individual characteristics of each story.

the deception and trickery as a transgression of the moral code implicit in the story. Jacob himself admits that his act might bring a curse, not a blessing (27:12). The ethical ambiguity is inherent in the tale and cannot simply be explained away.

Moses' murder of the Egyptian is similarly depicted after a notice of his growing up: "when Moses had grown up (וַיִּגְדַּל מֹשֶׁה) he went out to his kinsfolk and observed their toil" (Exod 2:11). Emphasis is given here to Moses' initial contact with his kin, as we can see from the repetition of word אֶחָיו, "his kin," twice in v. 11. Interestingly, the term for "kin" is juxtaposed with the word "Hebrew" (עִבְרִי) a designation for the Israelites that tends to be used in biblical narrative primarily from the perspective of a non-Israelite, or to distinguish an Israelite from a non-Israelite.[41] This emphasis on difference is highlighted explicitly in the contexts of the occurrence of the word עִבְרִי. In v. 11 Moses "saw (וַיַּרְא) an Egyptian striking a Hebrew man, one of his kinsmen." In v. 13 we find the usage of the particle הִנֵּה to mark a shift in perspective from the narrator's point of view to the character's:[42] "He went out the next day and (וְהִנֵּה) two Hebrews were fighting" (Exod 2:13). The juxtaposition of the terms "Hebrew" and "kin," both presented from Moses' point of view, present in miniature the nature of Moses' dilemma: he has been raised an Egyptian, yet the Israelites are his kin. His struggle is to reconcile his paradoxical state as a foreigner and an Israelite; he is as yet still "betwixt and between."

Moses acts by killing an Egyptian who was oppressing a Hebrew, but when he attempts to intervene in a dispute between two Hebrews he is rebuked. One of the Hebrews replies to him: "Who has appointed you ruler and judge over us? Do you mean to kill me as you killed the Egyptian?" (Exod 2:14). The rebuke emphasizes Moses' lack of status among the Israelites; just as he looks at them and sees Hebrews, so they look at him and see an Egyptian. Moses has not yet assumed his role as leader of the Israelites.

---

[41]See the discussion of the term in Weippert, *Settlement of the Israelite Tribes*, 84-101, esp. 84-85; see also the studies cited above, p. 22 n. 92.

[42]See F. I. Andersen, *The Sentence in Biblical Hebrew* (The Hague: Mouton, 1974) 94-95.

Moses' murder of the Egyptian is the subject of a taunt by the Israelite, thus its moral problematics are made plain, yet it is appropriate for Moses to be in conflict with the Egyptians in his youthful deed: this is his future role as the deliverer of his people. The Israelites are not yet fully his people, or rather he is not yet wholly theirs, as the diction of the episode reveals to us. The ambiguities of Moses' act are a function of his ambiguous state in the early part of his career, just as Jacob's acts are functions of his ambiguous state as the younger son destined for the blessing. In their illicit, subversive deeds, the youthful heroes, Jacob and Moses, display key aspects of their heroic identities and play out the paradoxes inherent in their nature. The hero is in his very essence an extreme character; while not beyond good and evil, the hero is enmeshed in the incessant play of the extremes of good and evil, self and other, human and divine.

FLIGHT, AS RESULT OF YOUTHFUL DEED

As a result of their illicit youthful deeds, Jacob and Moses are each forced to flee; their adversaries, having discovered the deed, are seeking to kill them. In the Jacob story we read of Esau's response:

> Esau hated Jacob because of the blessing with which his father had blessed him, and he thought to himself, "When the days of my father's mourning arrive, then I will kill my brother Jacob" (Gen 27:41).

Rebekah learns of Esau's plot, and she instructs Jacob to "rise and flee" (וְקוּם בְּרַח-לְךָ) to the home of Laban, her brother, in Haran. She instructs him to remain there until Esau's anger subsides, and then she will send for him (Gen 27:42-45).

There follows in the text a variant account of the motive for Jacob's flight from the P source. In characteristic P diction, the text recounts that the reason for Jacob's flight is Rebekah's fear that he will marry a Canaanite woman, so Isaac sends Jacob to Laban's house to marry one of Laban's daughters. Esau, when he discovers his parents displeasure at his Canaanite wives, goes off to Ishmael to marry a proper wife there (Gen 27:46-28:9). The P variant fits well into the general plot sequence, but the motivations of the characters are at some odds with the situation at the end of the scene of Isaac's deception. It seems probable that this motive for Jacob's journey stems from a multiform of the episode (compare Genesis 24) conforming to P's interest in the purity of Israelite kinship.

In the Moses story, the account of Moses' flight is less elaborate: "Pharaoh heard of the matter and he sought to kill Moses, but Moses fled from Pharaoh, and he arrived in the land of Midian, and he sat down by a well" (Exod 2:15). The movement flows smoothly from Pharaoh's knowledge of Moses' offense to Moses' flight to his arrival at the well in Midian. No one, it seems, has informed Moses of Pharaoh's wrath as Rebekah had told Jacob of Esau's wrath; he decides to flee himself. This note is appropriate for the two stories: Rebekah is Jacob's accomplice and advisor, she loves him rather than Esau (Gen 25:27), and she mediates between the two. Moses is directly Pharaoh's adversary, without an intervening figure until he later acquires the service of Aaron. We can see even in this brief narration of the sequence of events a bit of the characterization of Moses and of his adversarial relationship with Pharaoh.

PROMISE/COMMISSIONING BY DEITY AT SACRED PLACE

The multiformity of the common episodic pattern that we have discerned becomes clear when we consider the next scene in the Jacob cycle and contrast it with the corresponding scene in the Moses cycle. The scene of Jacob at Bethel constitutes Jacob's investiture as a patriarch of Israel, complete with the promise of descendents and land (in J), and the promise of the protection and guidance of the deity (J and E).[43] Here Jacob discovers his divine benefactor and acquires knowlege of his sacred destiny. Bethel is a sacred place that Jacob has stumbled across unknowingly, and he leaves it with a new purpose and identity. The events at Bethel constitute a rite of passage for Jacob: as he crosses over geographically toward Haran on his journey he crosses over

[43]See above, pp. 61-67.

spiritually to a new state: he is now the chosen one, blessed with the new role of religious founder and patriarch.

The scene of Moses' commissioning by the deity occurs in a different position in the episodic pattern, after the incident at the well and after marriage and offspring. The different placement of the episode is, however, not an argument against the existence of a common episodic pattern, rather it gives us a clearer insight into the nature and formation of the common pattern. As Lord notes, it is in the nature of oral narrative patterns that the pattern itself is changeable and multiform, guided by the inclinations of the performer in the moment of performance:

> While recognizing the fact that the singer knows the whole song before he starts to sing (not textually, of course, but thematically), nevertheless, at some time when he reaches key points in the performance of the song he finds that he is drawn in one direction or another by the similarities with related groups at those points. The intensity of that pull may differ from performance to performance, but it is always there. . . . Even though the pattern of the song he intends to sing is set early in the performance, forces moving in other directions will still be felt at critical junctures, simply because the theme involved can lead in more than one path.[44]

The multiformity of the story pattern, based on the different directions that a performance can take, results in such instances as the different sequences of episodes in the Jacob and Moses cycles. While I am not contending that the Jacob and Moses cycles are, in the form in which we have them, the direct utterances of oral singers of tales, nonetheless the type of multiformity that we see in the two story cycles is best explained by a derivation from the oral narrative tradition of early Israel.

The story of the commissioning of Moses at the burning bush (J) or Mount Horeb (E) is, in its context in the overall pattern, a multiform of Jacob's encounter with the deity at Bethel. The commissioning occurs on sacred space onto which Moses has trodden unknowingly, he encounters the deity for the first time, and he

[44]Lord, *Singer of Tales*, 123.

learns of his new task as religious leader and deliverer of the Israelites. This episode constitutes Moses' rite of passage into his new identity. He becomes the future deliverer of Israel just as Jacob had become the future patriarch. In this encounter, Moses discovers his divine patron and discovers his own heroic destiny.

There are episodes in the careers of other figures in the biblical text that are related to the scene of Moses' commissioning. Some scholars have even defined a "Call Narrative" *Gattung* in which the scene of Moses' commissioning finds its place.[45] Examples of this *Gattung* are found in the calls of Moses and Gideon in narrative sources, and in the calls of Isaiah, Jeremiah, Ezekiel, and Second Isaiah in the prophetic sources. While I would not dispute the many lines of continuity in these various scenes, I would dispute the fixity that many scholars attribute to this *Gattung*. Traditional stories do not exist as elaborations on a fixed, immutable narrative form. Genres cannot be determined by drawing up a list of required features.[46] Traditional stories are multiform: elements can be added, deleted, or altered at will. Within the bounds of the body of traditional lore, a story can take on different forms on different occasions. The belief in a fixity of narrative forms prevalent among practitioners of *Formgeschichte* is an illusion: stories are related according to the terms of tradition, not according to our modern literary notions of fixed texts. As Lord comments: "Our real difficulty arises from the fact that, unlike the oral poet, we are not accustomed to thinking in terms of fluidity. We find it difficult to grasp something that is multiform."[47]

The scenes of Jacob at Bethel and Moses at the burning bush/Mount Horeb are essentially multiforms of each other - stories of revelations to heroes at sacred places, elaborated as cult legends - while still being specific to each individual story cycle. The scene of Moses' call may also be related to other episodes on

[45]See, e.g., N. Habel, "The Form and Significance of the Call Narratives" *ZAW* 77 (1965) 297-323; W. Zimmerli, *Ezekiel 1*, trans. R. E. Clements (Hermeneia; Philadelphia: Fortress, 1979) 97-100; Childs, *Exodus*, 53-56.

[46]For some of the problems involved in determining the genres of oral literature, see especially D. Ben-Amos, "Analytical Categories and Ethnic Genres," in *Folklore Genres*, ed. Ben-Amos (Austin: University of Texas, 1976) 215-242.

[47]Lord, *Singer of Tales*, 100.

the basis of the essential multiformity of oral tradition, as well as by means of the later modeling of literary accounts on the already established Exodus text.

INCIDENT AT WELL WITH FUTURE WIFE

As mentioned above, Moses' flight from Pharaoh leads directly into the episode of the meeting of his future wife at the well, while Jacob's story leads first to his encounter with the deity at Bethel and then to the well episode. The location of the cult site of Bethel necessitates this sequence of episodes in the Jacob cycle, while the Moses cycle follows a slightly varied order of events. Once again, though the well episodes are clearly multiforms, there is a specificity to each episode that highlights important aspects of each hero's identity. I might add that, while I will be treating only the well episodes in the Jacob and Moses cycles, these episodes along with the related story of Isaac's betrothal (Gen 24:10-33) have been treated in recent years by commentators.[48]

On his arrival at the well near Haran, Jacob sees three flocks of sheep lying down by the well and a large stone over the mouth of the well. He learns that the shepherds there know Laban, and they announce to him that Laban's daughter Rachel is arriving with his flocks. The action then quickens:

> When Jacob saw Rachel, the daughter of Laban his mother's brother, with the sheep of Laban his mother's brother, Jacob went up and rolled off the stone from the mouth of the well and he watered the sheep of Laban his mother's brother. Then Jacob kissed Rachel, and he lifted up his voice and he wept (Gen 29:10-11).

The repetition of the kinship relations of Jacob, Rachel, Rebekah, and Laban in these and the following verses emphasizes the importance of the themes of kinship and family that are central in Jacob's career; he is after all to become the patriarch *par excellence*. The patriarch can only marry the proper wife, and

---

[48]See especially Culley, *Structure of Hebrew Narrative*, 41-43; and Alter, *Art of Biblical Narrative*, 51-58.

this scene represents Rachel in that light. He only sees her once and immediately is inspired to action; he rolls off the stone, he waters the flocks, he kisses her, and he weeps.

Robert Alter has pointed astutely to the symbolism of the well in this and the other multiforms of this scene. He states: "The well at an oasis is obviously a symbol of fertility and, in all likelihood, also a female symbol."[49]   While Alter's conjecture that the well is at an oasis is unwarranted (the text describes the setting as a שָׂדֶה [Gen 29:2], an "open field," perhaps best translated here as "pasture-land"),[50] his remark about the female symbolism of the well is intriguing. Jacob's immediate effort in rolling the rock off of the mouth of the well at the moment that he sees his future wife is suggestive of sexual symbolism.

Freudian interpretations of biblical narrative often seem forced, but in this case I suspect that the interpretation is essentially correct. As in the *Odyssey* when the returning Odysseus in his begger's disguise shoots the arrow through the rings in order to win the hand of Penelope, we have here a sexually symbolic marriage test for Jacob, a task that the others have not the strength or the will to attain. Jacob removes the stone from the mouth of the well and waters the sheep, then his own waters flow in his tears after kissing Rachel. It is appropriate to note in this scene that Rachel's name literally means "ewe," so Jacob's opening the well and watering the sheep carries at least a double meaning in its context.

The story of Moses meeting his future wife at the well is also narrated to emphasize themes central to the hero's identity. While he is sitting at the well in the land of Midian, the seven daughters of the priest of Midian arrive to water their flock, but the shepherds drive them away. The text then tells us: "Moses rose and saved them, and he watered their flock" (Exod 2:17). As commentators have noted,[51] the verb used here, וַיּוֹשִׁעָן, "and he saved them," is appropriate for Moses' later role as the savior of Israel. When the daughters report the event to their father, they

---

[49] Alter, *Art of Biblical Narrative*, 52.

[50] See the lexical data collected in *BDB*, 961.

[51] E.g., U. Cassuto, *A Commentary on the Book of Exodus*, trans. I. Abrahams (Jerusalem: Magnes, 1967) 27; Alter, *Art of Biblical Narrative*, 57.

tell him that "an Egyptian saved us (הִצִּילָנוּ) from the hand of the shepherds, and he drew water for us, and he watered the sheep" (Exod 2:19). The theme of Moses, outwardly an Egyptian, saving helpless victims from the hand of the oppressor is sounded here as it was in the previous scene of his slaying the Egyptian. This time, however, Moses is welcomed by the ones saved, and he is given one of the priest's daughters to wed.

I might add that there may be an additional play on words in the daughters' report of Moses' deeds. They say that he "saved us from the hand of the shepherds" (הִצִּילָנוּ מִיַּד הָרֹעִים), a phrasing that alludes to Moses' future role in saving the Israelites from the hand of Pharaoh. I would note that the word "shepherd" is often used as a title for the Egyptian king and other royalty in the ancient Near East, suggesting a thematic resemblence that may be a part of the resonance of this verse.[52] If so, it would then highlight even more emphatically the multiple reference of Moses' saving activity.

MARRIAGE AND OFFSPRING

The narration of the marriages and the birth of offspring in the Jacob and Moses cycles are quite different. Indeed, the variation in the traits and careers of the two heroes are nowhere more evident. Jacob, as the patriarch and forebear of Israel, is distinguished by his numerous offspring, while Moses, the deliverer, is distinguished by events that occur later in his career. The stories of the rivalries of Jacob's wives and the circumstances attending the birth of each of the children are narrated in detail, while Moses' marriage and the birth of his child are told in a brief, almost perfunctory manner.

As R. A. Oden, Jr., has emphasized in a recent article, the position of Jacob and his offspring in the genealogical traditions of

---

[52]On the Egyptian king as a "shepherd" of the people, see the texts cited by J. A. Wilson in *The Intellectual Adventure of Ancient Man*, eds. H. Frankfort, et al. (Chicago: University of Chicago, 1946) 78-79. See Exod 18:10 for similar diction (spoken by the priest Jethro): בָּרוּךְ יהוה אֲשֶׁר הִצִּיל אֶתְכֶם מִיַּד מִצְרַיִם וּמִיַּד פַּרְעֹה.

Israel is a pivotal one.[53]   Until the birth of Jacob's sons, the genealogy of Israel is linear, from Adam all the way to Jacob. Branching off from this linear genealogy are the ancestors of the other nations; thus by means of the early linear genealogy Israel saw herself defined in contrast to the other nations of the world. Beginning with the birth of Jacob's sons, the genealogy becomes segmented; this represents a shift in the type of self-definition provided by the genealogy. By means of the post-Jacob segmented genealogy, Israel saw herself divided into various tribes and lineages. The difference between the two types of genealogy, linear vs. segmented, corresponds to two types of self-definition, external vs. internal. As Oden writes: "Therefore, *externally* Israel is the particular line descended solely from Abraham and from Isaac, but *internally* the Israelites are the various descendants of the various sons of Jacob."[54] By recognizing the importance of this shift in the genealogical system we can appreciate more readily the significance of the narratives of the births of Jacob's offspring.

Jacob's marriages and the birth of his offspring are the central episodes of his life story, and we find, appropriately enough, other moments and relationships in his life story embellished and reflected here. The relationship between Jacob and Laban picks up where the Jacob-Esau conflict left off. As has been often remarked, Laban's substitution of Leah for Rachel on the night of the wedding is a classic example of the theme of "the trickster tricked."[55] Later in the relationship between Jacob and Laban we find Jacob getting the last laugh, as he tricks Laban out of most of his flocks by practicing some herdsmen's folk-medicine on the sheep's reproductive tendencies. Jacob leaves Haran with both of Laban's daughters and with the bulk of Laban's wealth. All that Laban gets in return is a promise that Jacob will be good to his

[53]R. A. Oden, Jr., "Jacob as Father, Husband, and Nephew: Kinship Studies and the Patriarchal Narratives" *JBL* 102 (1983) 189-205.

[54]Oden, "Jacob as Father," 196. Oden's discussion of other kinship matters in the Jacob cycle (the avunculate, cross-cousin marriage) is to be qualified by J. Pitt-Rivers's more precise description of Israelite endogamy: *The Fate of Shechem or The Politics of Sex: Essays in the Anthropology of the Mediterranean* (Cambridge: Cambridge University, 1977) 151-168.

[55]See above, p. 101.

daughters and that Jacob will stay on his side of the border between them (Gen 31:48-52; J+E).

The relationship between Rachel and Leah also mirrors the early relationship between Jacob and Esau.[56] Rachel is the younger daughter and Leah is the older. Not suprisingly, they are bitter rivals. Rachel wins Jacob's love, but Leah marries him first because of her father's ruse. The trickery of the father on behalf of the elder child is ironic in light of Jacob's trickery of *his* father in gaining the blessing of the firstborn. The trickery occurs in the darkness of night when Jacob could not see, just as Jacob had tricked his own father who was blind and could not see.[57] Laban's response the following morning is deadpan: "It is not done in our place to give the younger before the first-born" (Gen 29:26).

After Jacob finally marries Rachel, the rivalry between the two sisters increases. Leah bears the first son and Rachel becomes jealous (Gen 30:1). She gives Jacob her handmaid to bear surrogate children for her, and finally schemes to acquire some of the mandrakes that Leah's son Reuben had found as a means to become fertile (Gen 30:14-20). Rachel trades Jacob's sexual services that night to Leah for the mandrakes, and that night Leah conceives. We are not told of Rachel's response, but we can be sure she was not pleased with the outcome of the trade. The rueful humor of this scene is notable. Finally, we are told that God remembered Rachel and she bore a son, Joseph (Gen 30:22-24).

With the birth of Joseph, the rivalry between the two wives ends and the list of Jacob's children is nearly complete (but for the birth of Benjamin in Gen 35:16-20). The time is ripe for Jacob's return to his homeland, but one more final touch awaits: Jacob is not ready to return until he has both offspring and wealth. He acquires wealth by tricking Laban out of the flocks by means of his manipulation of the fertility of the flocks (Gen 30:25-43). It has not been pointed out, I believe, that it is appropriate for the patriarch who had engendered twelve children to be able to coax numerous offspring from the sheep and goats. For a man with many offspring, whose two principle wives are named רָחֵל, "ewe," and

לְאָה, "cow," it is surely fitting for his powers of fertility to extend to the animal kingdom. In the episode of the fertility of the flocks we see Jacob's character as a trickster and as a progenitor neatly combined.

The story of Moses' marriage and offspring is insignificant in comparison to the comparable events in the Jacob cycle. We are told simply:

> Moses was content to stay with the man, and he gave Zipporah his daughter to Moses. She bore a son and he named him Gershom, for he said, "I have been a stranger in a foreign land" (Exod 2:21-22).

The thematic appropriateness of the name of the son is evident as a reflection on Moses' state, for he is both a גֵּר, "a stranger, sojourner," and one who has been driven out (גֹּרְשׁ).[58] The folk etymology and the real etymology of the son's name are both significant here, both reflecting on the father. We notice also that, while in many birth stories the name of the child is given by the mother, here it is given by Moses, the father. We may infer that, even in this brief passage, a significant nuance is being conveyed: even at the most passive moment for a father, Moses is the center of the story, not the mother, or the son.

RETURN TO LAND OF BIRTH (AT COMMAND OF DEITY)

After their marriages and the birth of their offspring, both Jacob and Moses are commanded to return to the land of their birth by the deity. In the Jacob story the command is contained in both the J and E versions; in the Moses story the command is given in the J text, while in the E text Moses asks to return on his own initiative. The consistency of the divine command to return indicates that it is a part of the pattern of events common to the two story cycles.

[58]See the comments of J. S. Ackerman, "The Literary Context of the Moses Birth Story (Exodus 1-2)," in *Literary Interpretations of Biblical Narratives*, eds. K. R. R. Gros Louis, et al. (New York: Abingdon, 1974) 105-106.

In Gen 31:3 we are told that: "Yahweh said to Jacob, 'Return to the land of your fathers, to the land where you were born, and I will be with you,'" repeating the diction of Yahweh's promise to Jacob at Bethel: "I am with you, and I will protect you wherever you go, and I will bring you back to this land" (Gen 28:15; J). Similarly, in the E version of the command to return, the text relates: "I am the god of Bethel, where you anointed the massebah and where you made a vow to me. Now, rise and leave this land and return to the land of your birth" (Gen 31:13). This command echoes the terms of the E version of the episode at Bethel, forming a thematic closure to the events of Jacob's journey to Haran. On the command of the deity, Jacob returns to his homeland, though his return is interspersed with further adventures.

In the Moses story, the direct command from the deity is contained in Exod 4:19 (J): "Yahweh said to Moses in Midian, 'Go back to Egypt, for all the men who sought your life are dead.'" In the E version, Moses simply requests of Jethro, his father-in-law, that he be allowed to return to his "kinsmen in Egypt" to see if they are still alive. Jethro , a kinder in-law than Laban, gives his permission and says to Moses: "Go in peace" (Exod 4:18).[59] The variation in these descriptions of the decision to return is once again indicative of oral multiforms in the tradition, in which the agent is variable but the essential action is consistent.

DANGEROUS ENCOUNTER WITH DEITY

The next episode in the pattern common to both story cycles is the puzzling event of the dangerous encounter with the deity. The episode of Jacob's wrestling with the deity at Penuel has been discussed earlier;[60] what I will point out are some of the elements that this event shares with the odd event of the divine encounter in Exod 4:24-26.

The episode in Exod 4:24-26 is one of the most problematic of all biblical narratives, and I cannot pretend to solve its many

---

[59]Note Gen 30:25 in which Jacob asks Laban for permission to return to his homeland, and Laban refuses.

[60]Pp. 103-109.

puzzles.[61] Yet an understanding of the placement and function of the episode in the context of the pattern that we have discerned may help to shed light on some of the difficulties. V. 24, an intelligible verse, presents the main features of the episode: "At a night encampment on the way, Yahweh met him and sought to kill him." The following verses are more difficult: Moses' wife Zipporah takes a flint knife, circumcises "her son" and touches the foreskin to "his feet," and says, "you are a חֲתַן־דָּמִים to me," whereupon Yahweh leaves "him" alone (Exod 4:25-26). The uncertainty of the references of the pronouns (whose feet? who is the חֲתַן־דָּמִים?) and the uncertainty of the meaning of some of the words (does רֶגֶל here literally mean "feet" or is it a euphemism for the male genitalia?[62] what is the meaning of חֲתַן־דָּמִים?) renders a clear unravelling of the significance of the episode impossible. In the context of the episodic pattern common to the Jacob cycle and the Moses cycle, however, some observations can be made.

The dangerous encounter with the deity in both the Jacob and Moses cycles occurs during the homeward journey of the heroes. The encounter also occurs in both stories at night. In the Jacob cycle, there is a relationship between the divine encounter at Penuel and the initial encounter at Bethel in that both are points of passage for Jacob on his journey to and from the land of Israel. Both encounters are, for Jacob, rites of passage, geographically and spiritually: at his exit from his homeland Jacob acquires his divine benefactor and his promise, while at his re-entry into the land he acquires his new name, Israel, signalling his new identity as the patriarch of Israel. The dangerous encounter with Yahweh in the Moses cycle contains fewer clues concerning its function in the formation of Moses' heroic identity, but it may be that here too something important is occuring in the development of Moses' identity as the deliverer of Israel.

Thematically there are some elements in this episode that link it to other events in Moses' career, but it is difficult to evaluate

[61]For discussions of the problems of the passage, see especially Childs, *Exodus*, 95-101, 103-104, and references; H. Kosmala, "The 'Bloody Husband'" *VT* 12 (1962) 14-28; and W. Dumbrell, "Exodus 4:24-26: A Textual Re-examination" *HTR* 65 (1972) 285-290.

[62]See *BDB*, 920, for citations of the use of רֶגֶל as a sexual euphemism.

these elements. As H. Kosmala has pointed out in a valuable article,[63] the hint of danger to the first-born son and the act of applying blood to ward off death link these verses to episodes elsewhere in the narrative of the exodus. While I would dispute Kosmala's reading of the attack in Exod 4:24 as directed towards the son, there is a repeated theme in the Exodus story of danger to the first-born son. The verses that precede the passage in question make this theme explicit. Yahweh instructs Moses to say to Pharaoh: "Thus says Yahweh: Israel is my son, my first-born. I say to you: Let my son go, that he may serve me. If you refuse to let him go, I will kill your son, your first-born" (Exod 4:21-22). The theme of the saving power of blood is sounded again later in the Exodus story when the Israelites apply lamb's blood to their doorposts to ward off the final plague of the death of the first-born son (Exod 12:1-7,21-23).

The themes here of danger and of the power of blood to ward off danger are central to Exod 4:24-26, yet the associations of these themes are puzzling. The danger in this episode is to Moses, and the application of blood to ward off the attack of Yahweh is connected with the rite of circumcision, which somehow also connects with the obscure term חֲתַן־דָּמִים, "bridegroom of blood" (perhaps better translated "affine of blood," following the general Semitic meaning of the nominal form חתן as "relation by marriage").[64] According to the least problematic reading of the passage, it seems that Yahweh attacks Moses because he has neglected to circumcise his firstborn son. Zipporah saves Moses by circumcising the son and by applying the blood of the foreskin to Moses, whom she then calls her חֲתַן־דָּמִים. As a result of these acts, Yahweh withdraws his attack.

The peculiarities of this episode are undeniable, yet the general sense of the encounter is apparent. Yahweh, who had formerly been Moses' benefactor, suddenly becomes his adversary. The attack occurs at night on Moses' journey home. The features that link this episode with Jacob's mysterious night encounter with his divine adversary at Penuel indicate a common pattern

[63]Kosmala, "Bloody Husband," 22-24.

[64]See T. C. Mitchell, "The Meaning of the Noun ḤTN in the Old Testament" *VT* 19 (1969) 93-112; E. Kutsch, "חתן" *TDOT* Vol. V, 270-277.

behind the episodes. It seems that the dangerous encounter with the deity is a necessary element in this pattern of the life of the hero. The hero has a bond with the deity, yet the bond is fraught with danger. The god-hero relationship is extreme both in promise and in threat.[65] It seems that the final test, the test of death, is determinant for the hero: if he survives this rite of passage, his stature is certain, whether as patriarch or as deliverer. The mysterious nature of the test is fitting, for it indicates a most problematic aspect of the power of the divine and of the stature of the hero.

MEETING WITH BROTHER, ARRIVAL HOME

The final element - we might call it a transitional element - in the common pattern of the Jacob and Moses cycles is the meeting of the hero with his brother and the return of the hero to the land of his birth. Jacob meets with his brother Esau after he leaves the sacred site of Penuel; Moses meets with Aaron after he leaves the site of his dangerous encounter with Yahweh. After the meeting with his brother, Jacob returns to Sukkot and then to Shechem (J), or directly to Shechem (E and P); Moses returns to the land of Egypt (J).

Jacob's meeting with Esau has been discussed earlier;[66] suffice it to say that in the reunion of the brothers, Jacob and Esau are reconciled. The story of Jacob's life then continues with a series of loosely connected episodes: the story of the rape of Dinah (Genesis 34), the return to the cult site of Bethel (Gen 35:1-15), the birth of Benjamin and the death of Rachel (Gen 35:16-21), the sin of Reuben (Gen 35:22), and the final note by P of the death of Isaac and of his burial by Jacob and Esau (Gen 35:27-29).

It is appropriate that P should frame the Jacob cycle with the passing of generations: the Jacob cycle begins after an account of the death of Abraham and his burial by his sons Isaac and Ishmael (Gen 25:7-11). The structural framework of P is evident; these story cycles are genuine "generations" (תּוֹלְדוֹת). The JE cycle also

---

[65]Note Yahweh's final condemnation of Moses in Deut 32:48-52 (P).
[66]Pp. 130-131.

seems to begin and end on a similar note: at the beginning of the cycle Rebekah endures a difficult pregnancy and gives birth to Jacob and Esau, while at the end of the cycle Rachel succumbs during her painful delivery of Benjamin. Although the former scene is J and the latter is E, we may surmise that the narrative traditions drawn upon by both sources contained similar versions of the two events. The theme of the continuity of the generations is central to this plan of narration, for these are stories of the patriarchs and ancestors from whom the nation of Israel traced its lineage. Birth, in these stories, means survival.

The return of Moses and the meeting with his brother Aaron in Exod 4:27-31 signifies not the beginning of the end of the Moses cycle but rather the end of the beginning. It is after this point that Moses and Aaron together confront Pharaoh and demand that he let the people of Israel go.[67]   Moses has established his credentials as the emissary of Yahweh, and with Aaron as his mouthpiece he convinces the elders of Israel that he is their leader (Exod 4:29-31). Here is the authority that Moses was lacking in his first attempt to adjudicate the problems of the "Hebrews" in Exod 2:13-14. At that point Moses was rebuffed; now he is recognized, not by the "Hebrews" but by the "Israelites." The shift in diction is significant: Moses is now one of them, and they are his. The question that the "Hebrew" posed him can now be answered: "Who has appointed you ruler and judge over us?" (Exod 2:14). The answer is now clear: Yahweh.

PRELIMINARY CONCLUSIONS

The obvious question at this point is: why does the Moses story essentially begin at the end of this episodic pattern while the Jacob story essentially ends? The answer is not clear, but it perhaps lies in a consideration of the reason for the existence of the common pattern. First of all, it seems evident that the origin of the common pattern cannot be attributed to the hand of an

[67]The relationship between Moses and Aaron in the biblical text is, I should note, extremely complex. For a discussion of the stories of conflict between Moses and Aaron and their respective clans, see Cross, *Canaanite Myth and Hebrew Epic*, 195-206.

individual literary composer, for the differences between the two story cycles are so acute, and the relationships of the various episodes to other narratives - Israelite, Canaanite, Mesopotamian, Egyptian - are so diverse that attribution of the whole to a single hand would exceed credibility. If a writer composed the two story cycles out of whole cloth, *ex nihilo*, then we would be forced to surmise that he/she had a library of ancient Near Eastern texts that would rival those of Ashurbanipal, the British Museum, and the Louvre.

If, on the other hand, the composer(s) wrote the stories drawing on bits and pieces of Israelite oral tradition, then we would have to assume that the overall shape of the two story cycles was *de novo*, and the pattern was supplied as a unifying device. If such was the case, then the manifold interconnections between the various episodes in each cycle would also have to have been composed extemporaneously. Such a scenario is possible, but, as we have seen in the discussion above, the density of the interconnections is so great that individual composition of them is as implausible as individual composition of the whole. The interconnections are integral to the stories; to conceive of the stories without them is to conceive of nothing at all.

The most plausible scenario, and the one that I have advocated in my discussion, places the origin of the stories and the common episodic pattern in the oral narrative traditions of early Israel. The nature of the composition/performance of narrative in an oral traditional setting provides an understandable basis both for the similarity of the episodic pattern and for the diversity and specificity of the individual episodes. The continuities with the narrative traditions of neighboring cultures, both geographical and chronological, are also understandable in the context of a tradition of oral narrative. As Lord notes: "An interweaving of elements in this way is the normal method of formation and of continued re-formation of 'songs' in oral traditional narrative."[68] The Jacob story and the Moses story, it seems, were both performed in the oral tradition of early Israel, subject to the multiformity and conservatism of oral traditional narrative art.

[68]Lord, "Tradition and the Oral Poet," 22.

The sacredness of the two story cycles perhaps contributed to the elaboration of the two stories in similar ways. If narrative can be regarded as an elevated form of normal speech, then perhaps we can say that the common episodic pattern of the two story cycles communicates part of the special meaning of the two heroes: a way of communicating greatness in one instance can be fruitfully used to communicate greatness in another.

In an archaic reference in Judg 5:11, we are told:

> To the sound of cymbals,[69]
>   between the watering holes,
> There they recite the righteous deeds of Yahweh,
>   the righteous deeds of his heroes[70] in Israel.

This is the oldest reference in the Hebrew Bible to the performance of oral narrative in early Israel. The stories, it seems, are chanted to the accompaniment of percussion instruments. Figurines of women holding tambourines are known from ancient Israelite sites; perhaps we can imagine them playing while the songs of the heroes of Israel were recited.[71]

In Josh 24:1-13 we find a depiction of a summary recital of the narrative traditions of early Israel.[72] At the covenant renewal ceremony at Shechem, Joshua recounts in schematic form the traditions of Israel from the patriarchs to the entry into the Promised Land. It seems likely that the festivals of Israel provided a regular setting for the recitation of Israelite narrative

---

[69]For the translation of מחצצים as "cymbals," see W. F. Albright ("The Earliest Forms of Hebrew Verse" *JPOS* 2 [1922] 81 n.4) who relates the word to Arabic *ḥḍḍ*, "to shake".

[70]For the translation of פרזנו as "his heroes," cf. Hab 3:14, פרזו, translated by the Greek as δυναστῶν, "mighty ones," and by the Targum as ניברי, "warriors, heroes." For additional lexical data, see Albright, *Yahweh and the Gods of Canaan*, 49 n. 101; and P. C. Craigie, "Some Further Notes on the Song of Deborah" *VT* 22 (1972) 350.

[71]Cf. Exod 15:20, Ps 68:26.

[72]Among the many discussions of Joshua 24, see especially D. J. McCarthy, *Treaty and Covenant* (2nd ed.; AnBib 21A; Rome: Pontifical Biblical Institute, 1978) 221-242, 279-284, with references to earlier literature; for an alternate view, see J. Van Seters, "Joshua 24 and the Problem of Tradition in the Old Testament," in *In the Shelter of Elyon*, eds. W. B. Barrick and J. R. Spencer (JSOTSup 31; Sheffield: JSOT, 1984) 139-158. See also the remarks of Cross, "Epic Traditions," 25.

traditions,[73] and it is perhaps in this setting that the Jacob and Moses stories were elaborated at greatest length.

The narration of the Jacob and Moses cycles in these settings evolved to the point of the essential stability of story and of pattern, and it is this form that was adapted into the written sources that became the Pentateuch. A writer does not materially alter traditional stories that have become sacred to his/her culture; to do so would be to court unintelligibility or worse. The composers of the Pentateuchal sources may have abridged or expanded certain themes, motifs, or details, but it is unlikely that they would have invented new characters or episodes. The writers would have drawn on the narrative performances that they had heard (as well as any written texts at their disposal) and would have retold the stories in the new medium, with such skill and insight as they had, drawing upon the sacred body of tradition. In this way the richness of tradition was preserved, and the glory of the ancestors recaptured in a new setting: the written text.

[73]See Gunkel, *Genesis* (3rd ed.) lxiii; Cross, "Epic Traditions," 19.

Conclusions

The dictionary on my desk defines Jacob as follows:

> Hebrew patriarch; son of Isaac and grandson of Abraham; father of 12 sons, ancestors of the 12 tribes of Israel. See *Israel*.[1]

A clear, concise definition, as far as it goes. In this study I have sought to define some of the more elusive aspects of Jacob's character and destiny in the biblical text: Jacob as a child, a trickster, a smooth man, a hero, a founder of cult, an exponent of culture, a patriarch, an ethically ambiguous figure, a man shaped by his encounters with human and divine adversaries, a man of blessing and promise. Each of these aspects of Jacob contributes to his image, an image which is perhaps inexhaustible.

Along the way I have tried to point to various kinds of relationships that link Jacob to other stories and to other heroes in Israel and the ancient Near East. The basis for these relationships is the practice of storytelling that existed in the ancient world: stories of renowned figures that were passed along, in ever-changing form, from generation to generation, from village to village, from mouth to mouth. These stories preserved the beliefs and dreams of a people, joined to the figures and events of a distant past. The pastness of these events lent them an authority and an immediacy that went beyond the life of the present. The stories of tradition provided an orientation for their audience; they supplied the lenses through which a culture perceived its world. Jacob, Rachel, Aqhat, Gilgamesh, and the others are heroes of ancient epic traditions; as such they are also expressions of ancient worlds.

Can we in any significant sense reach an understanding of these heroes or these worlds? Can we join the present to the past? Perhaps not. But we can read the stories, and we can try to grasp

---

[1] *The American Heritage Dictionary of the English Language,* ed. W. Morris (Boston: Houghton Mifflin, 1976) 699.

their meaning, even across the millennia. It seems that the heroes, their worlds, and their stories are still with us, maintaining a presence in our world. Like aging and distant relations, we may not fully understand them, but they are still ours.

Bibliography

Abusch, T. "Ishtar's Proposal and Gilgamesh's Refusal: An Interpretation of *The Gilgamesh Epic*, Tablet 6, Lines 1-79" *HR* 26 (1986) 143-187.

Ackerman, J. S. "The Literary Context of the Moses Birth Story (Exodus 1-2)," in *Literary Interpretations of Biblical Narratives*, eds. K. R. R. Gros Louis, et al. New York: Abingdon, 1974, 74-119.

Ackroyd, P. "Hosea and Jacob" *VT* 13 (1963) 245-259.

Aharoni, Y. *The Archaeology of the Land of Israel*, trans. A. F. Rainey. Philadelphia: Westminster, 1982.

Alain. *The Gods*, trans. R. Pevear. New York: New Directions, 1974.

Albertz, R. *Persönliche Frömmigkeit und offizielle Religion: Religionsinterner Pluralismus in Israel und Babylon.* Stuttgart: Calwer, 1978.

Albright, W. F. "The Earliest Forms of Hebrew Verse" *JPOS* 2 (1922) 69-86.

_____ *The Vocalization of the Egyptian Syllabic Orthography.* New Haven: American Oriental Society, 1934.

_____ "A Vow to Asherah in the Keret Epic" *BASOR* 94 (1944) 30-31.

_____ *From the Stone Age to Christianity: Monotheism and the Historical Process.* Garden City, NY: Doubleday, 1957.

_____ "Abram the Hebrew: A New Archaeological Interpretation" *BASOR* 163 (1961) 36-54.

_____ *The Biblical Period from Abraham to Ezra: An Historical Survey.* New York: Harper & Row, 1963.

_____ *Yahweh and the Gods of Canaan: A Historical Analysis of Two Contrasting Faiths.* Garden City, NY: Doubleday, 1968.

Alt, A. "Der Gott der Väter," in *Kleine Schriften zur Geschichte des Volkes Israel*, vol. I. Munich: Beck, 1953 [1929], 1-78. ET: "The God of the Fathers," in *Essays on Old Testament History and Religion*, trans. R. A. Wilson. Garden City, NY: Doubleday, 1966, 1-100.

_____ "Die Wallfahrt von Sichem nach Bethel," in *Kleine Schriften*, vol. I, [1938], 79-88.

Alter, R. *The Art of Biblical Narrative.* New York: Basic, 1981.

_____ "How Convention Helps Us Read: The Case of the Bible's Annunciation Type-Scene" *Prooftexts* 3 (1983) 115-130.

Amiet, P. "Observations sur les 'Tablettes magiques' d'Arslan Tash" *Aula Orientalis* 1 (1983) 109.

Andersen, F. I. *The Sentence in Biblical Hebrew.* The Hague: Mouton, 1974.

_____ and Freedman, D. N. *Hosea*. AB; Garden City, NY: Doubleday, 1980.

Astour, M. C. *Hellenosemitica*. Leiden: Brill, 1965.

_____ "Yahwe," in *IDBSup*, 971.

Attridge, H. A. and Oden, R. A., Jr. *Philo of Byblos: The Phoenician History. Introduction, Critical Text, Translation, Notes*. CBQMS 9; Washington DC: Catholic Biblical Association, 1981.

Auerbach, E. *Mimesis: The Representation of Reality in Western Literature*, trans. W. R. Trask. Princeton: Princeton University, 1953

Bailey, J. A. "Initiation and the Primal Woman in Gilgamesh and Genesis 2-3" *JBL* 89 (1970) 137-150.

Barnett, R. D. "Lions and Bulls in Assyrian Palaces," in *Le palais et la royauté*, ed. P. Garelli. Paris: Geuthner, 1974, 441-446.

Barthes, R. "The Struggle with the Angel: Textual Analysis of Genesis 32:22-32," in *Image - Music - Text*, trans. S. Heath. New York: Hill and Wang, 1977, 125-141.

Bartlett, J. T. S. "The Land of Seir and the Brotherhood of Edom" *JTS* 20 (1969) 1-20.

Baumgarten, A. I. *The Phoenician History of Philo of Byblos*. Leiden: Brill, 1981.

Ben-Amos, D. "Analytical Categories and Ethnic Genres," in *Folklore Genres*, ed. Ben-Amos. Austin: University of Texas, 1976, 215-242.

Berlin, I. *Vico and Herder: Two Studies in the History of Ideas*. New York: Viking, 1976.

Biebuyck, D. P. "The African Heroic Epic," in *Heroic Epic and Saga: An Introduction to the World's Great Folk Epics*, ed. F. J. Oinas. Bloomington: Indiana University, 1978, 336-367.

Bland, K. P. "The Rabbinic Method and Literary Criticism," in *Literary Interpretations of Biblical Narratives*, eds. K. R. R. Gros Louis, et al. New York: Abingdon, 1974, 16-23.

Bordreuil, P. and Pardee, D. "Le rituel funéraire ougaritique RS 34.126" *Syria* 59 (1982) 121-128.

Bottéro, J. Le problème des Ḫabiru. Paris: Imprimerie Nationale, 1954.

Botterweck, G. J., and Ringgren, H., eds. *Theological Dictionary of the Old Testament*. Grand Rapids, MI: Eerdmans, 1974-.

Bremond, C. *Logique du récit*. Paris: Seuil, 1973.

Brinkman, J. A. "Kudurru," in *Reallexikon der Assyriologie*, Vol. VI. Berlin: de Gruyter, 1983, 267-274.

Brown, F., Driver, S. R., and Briggs, C. A. *A Hebrew and English Lexicon of the Old Testament*. Oxford: Clarendon, 1907.

Buber, M. "Leitwortstil in der Erzählung des Pentateuchs," in *Werke. Band II: Schriften zur Bibel*. Munich: Kösel, 1964 [1936], 1131-1149.

Buccellati, G. *The Amorites of the Ur III Period.* Naples: Istituto Orientale di Napoli, 1966.

Burkert, W. *Griechische Religion der archaischen und klassichen Epoche.* Stuttgart: Kohlhammer, 1977. ET: *Greek Religion,* trans. J. Raffan. Cambridge, MA: Harvard University, 1985.

_____ *Structure and History in Greek Mythology and Ritual.* Berkeley: University of California, 1979.

_____ *Homo Necans: The Anthropology of Ancient Greek Sacrificial Ritual and Myth,* trans. P. Bing. Berkeley: University of California, 1983.

Buttrick, G. A., et al., eds. *The Interpreter's Dictionary of the Bible. with Supplementary Volume.* Nashville: Abingdon, 1962-1976.

Campbell, J. *The Hero with a Thousand Faces.* Princeton: Princeton University, 1949.

Caquot, A. "Les songes et leur interprétation selon Canaan et Israel," in *Les songes et leur interprétation.* Sources orientales II; Paris: Seuil, 1959, 99-124.

_____ "Observations sur la première tablette magique d'Arslan Tash" *JANES* 5 (1973) 45-51.

_____ "La tablette RS 24.252 et la question des rephaim ougaritiques" *Syria* 53 (1976) 295-304.

_____ "Rephaïm," in *Supplément au Dictionnaire de la Bible,* Vol. X, ed. H. Cazelles and A. Feuillet. Paris: Letouzey & Ané, 1985, 344-357.

_____, Sznycer, M., and Herdner, A. *Textes ougaritiques. Tome I: Mythes et légendes.* Paris: Cerf, 1974.

Cassuto, U. *A Commentary on the Book of Exodus,* trans. I. Abrahams. Jerusalem: Magnes, 1967.

_____ "The Israelite Epic," *Biblical and Oriental Studies,* Vol. II, trans. I. Abrahams. Jerusalem: Magnes, 1975, 69-109.

Cauvin, J. *Religions néolithiques de Syro-Palestine.* Paris: Maisonneuve, 1972.

Cazelles, H. "The Hebrews," in *Peoples of Old Testament Times,* ed. D. J. Wiseman. Oxford: Clarendon, 1973, 1-28.

Cheyne, T. K. "The Connection of Esau and Usöos" *ZAW* 17 (1897) 189.

Childs, B. S. "The Birth of Moses" *JBL* 84 (1965) 109-122.

_____ *The Book of Exodus: A Critical, Theological Commentary.* OTL; Philadelphia: Westminster, 1974.

Clark, R. T., Jr. *Herder: His Life and Thought.* Berkeley: University of California, 1955.

Clifford, R. J. *The Cosmic Mountain in Canaan and the Old Testament.* HSM 4; Cambridge, MA: Harvard University, 1972.

_____ "The Word of God in the Ugaritic Epics and in the Patriarchal Narratives," in *The Word in the World,* eds. Clifford and G. W. MacRae. Cambridge, MA: Weston College, 1973, 7-18.

Cohen, C. "The Legend of Sargon and the Birth of Moses" *JANES* 4 (1972) 46-51.

Conroy, C. "Hebrew Epic: Historical Notes and Critical Reflections" *Bib* 61 (1980) 1-30.

Coote, R. "The Meaning of the Name Israel" *HTR* 65 (1972) 137-142.

Cornford, F. M. *From Religion to Philosophy.* London: Arnold, 1912.

Courtois, J.-C. "Ugarit Grid, Strata, and Find-Localizations. A Reassessment" *ZDPV* 90 (1974) 97-114.

Craigie, P. C. "Some Further Notes on the Song of Deborah" *VT* 22 (1972) 349-353.

Cross, F. M. "A New Qumran Biblical Fragment Related to the Original Hebrew Underlying the Septuagint" *BASOR* 132 (1953) 15-26.

_____ *Canaanite Myth and Hebrew Epic: Essays in the History of the Religion of Israel.* Cambridge, MA: Harvard University, 1973.

_____ "אל" *TDOT* Vol. I, 242-261.

_____ "Prose and Poetry in the Mythic and Epic Texts from Ugarit" *HTR* 67 (1974) 1-15.

_____ "The Epic Traditions of Early Israel: Epic Narrative and the Reconstruction of Early Israelite Institutions," in *The Poet and the Historian: Essays in Literary and Historical Biblical Criticism,* ed. R. E. Friedman. Chico, CA: Scholars, 1983, 13-39.

_____ and Freedman, D. N. *Studies in Ancient Yahwistic Poetry.* Missoula, MT: Scholars, 1975.

_____ and Saley, R. J. "Phoenician Incantations on a Plaque of the Seventh Century B.C. from Arslan Tash in Upper Syria" *BASOR* 197 (1970) 42-49.

Culley, R. C. *Oral Formulaic Language in the Biblical Psalms.* Toronto: University of Toronto, 1967.

_____ "Oral Tradition and the OT: Some Recent Discussion" *Semeia* 5 (1976) 1-33.

_____ *Studies in the Structure of Hebrew Narrative.* Philadelphia: Fortress, 1976.

_____ "Exploring New Directions," in *The Hebrew Bible and Its Modern Interpreters,* eds. D. A. Knight and G. M. Tucker. Chico, CA: Scholars, 1985, 167-200.

Day, J. *God's Conflict with the Dragon and the Sea: Echoes of a Canaanite Myth in the Old Testament.* Cambridge: Cambridge University, 1985.

Dever, W. G. "The Beginning of the Middle Bronze Age in Syria-Palestine," in *Magnalia Dei: Essays on the Bible and Archaeology in Memory of G. Ernest Wright*, eds. F. M. Cross, et al. Garden City, NY: Doubleday, 1976, 3-38.

_____ "The Patriarchal Traditions. Palestine in the Second Millennium BCE: The Archaeological Picture," in *Israelite and Judaean History*, eds. J. H. Hayes and J. M. Miller. Philadelphia: Westminster, 1977, 70-120.

_____ "New Vistas on the EB IV (MB I) Horizon in Syria-Palestine" *BASOR* 237 (1980) 35-64.

Diedrich, F. *Die Anspielungen auf die Jakob-Tradition in Hosea 12,1 - 13,3*. Würzburg: Echter, 1977.

Dietrich, M., Loretz, O., and Sanmartin, J. "Die angebliche Ug.- He. Parallelle SPSG // SPS(J)G(JM)" *UF* 8 (1976) 37-40.

Donner, H. and Röllig, W. *Kanaanäische und aramäische Inscriften*. 3 vols. Wiesbaden: Harrassowitz, 1968.

Dorson, R. M. "Introduction," in *Heroic Epic and Saga: An Introduction to the World's Great Folk Epics*, ed. F. J. Oinas. Bloomington: Indiana University, 1978, 1-6.

Dossin, G. "Enkidou dans l'épopée de Gilgameš" *Académie royale de Belgique. Bulletin de la classe des lettres...* 42 (1956) 580-593.

Douglas, M. *Purity and Danger: An Analysis of the Concepts of Pollution and Taboo*. London: Routledge & Kegan Paul, 1966.

_____ *Implicit Meanings: Essays in Anthropology*. London: Routledge & Kegan Paul, 1975.

Dundes, A., ed. *The Study of Folklore*. Englewood Cliffs, NJ: Prentice-Hall, 1965.

Draffkorn, A. E. "Ilāni/Elohim" *JBL* 76 (1957) 216-224.

Dressler, H. H. P. "Is the Bow of Aqhat a Symbol of Virility?" *UF* 7 (1975) 217-220.

Drews, R. "Sargon, Cyrus and Mesopotamian Folk History" *JNES* 33 (1974) 387-393.

Dumbrell, W. J. "The Midianites and their Transjordanian Successors." Dissertation, Harvard University, 1970.

_____ "Exodus 4:24-26: A Textual Re-examination" *HTR* 65 (1972) 285-290.

Dumézil, G. *Loki*. Paris: Maisonneuve, 1948.

Ebach, J. *Weltenstehung und Kulturentwicklung bei Philo von Byblos*. Stuttgart: Kohlhammer, 1979.

Eissfeldt, O. "Schamemrumim 'Hoher Himmel,' ein Stadtteil von Gross-Sidon," *Kleine Schriften*, vol. II. Tubingen: Mohr, 1963 [1938], 123-126.

Eliade, M. *The Myth of the Eternal Return*, trans. W. R. Trask. Princeton: Princeton University, 1954.

Emerton, J. "The Riddle of Genesis XIV" *VT* 21 (1971) 403-439.

Engnell, I. *Studies in Divine Kingship in the Ancient Near East.* Uppsala: Almqvist & Wiksells, 1943.

Evans-Pritchard, E. E. *Theories of Primitive Religion.* Oxford: Clarendon, 1965.

_____ *The Zande Trickster.* Oxford: Clarendon, 1967.

Fauth, W. "SSM BN PDRŠSA" *ZDMG* 120 (1970) 227-256.

Ferrara A. J. and Parker, S. B. "Seating Arrangements at Divine Banquets" *UF* 4 (1972) 37-39.

Finkelstein, J. J. "The Genealogy of the Hammurapi Dynasty" *JCS* 20 (1966) 95-118.

Fishbane, M. *Text and Texture: Close Readings of Selected Biblical Texts.* New York: Schocken, 1979.

Fisher, L. R. "Two Projects at Claremont" *UF* 3 (1971) 27-31.

_____, Rummel, S., et al., eds. *Ras Shamra Parallels: The Texts from Ugarit and the Hebrew Bible, Vols. I-III.* AnOr 49-51; Rome: Pontifical Biblical Institute, 1972-1981.

Fokkelman, J. P. *Narrative Art in Genesis: Specimens of Stylistic and Structural Analysis.* Amsterdam: Van Gorcum, 1975.

Foley, J. M. *Oral-Formulaic Theory and Research: An Introduction and Annotated Bibliography.* New York: Garland, 1984.

Fontenrose, J. *The Ritual Theory of Myth.* Berkeley: University of California, 1966.

_____ *Orion: The Myth of the Hunter and the Huntress.* Berkeley: University of California, 1981.

Frankfort, H. *Kingship and the Gods.* Chicago: University of Chicago, 1948.

_____ *The Problem of Similarity in Ancient Near Eastern Religions.* Oxford: Clarendon, 1951.

_____ *The Art and Architecture of the Ancient Orient.* London: Penguin, 1954.

_____ et al. *The Intellectual Adventure of Ancient Man.* Chicago: University of Chicago, 1946.

Frazer, J. G. *The Golden Bough: A Study in Comparative Religion.* London: Macmillan, 1890.

Freedman, D. N. and Cross, F. M. *Studies in Ancient Yahwistic Poetry.* Missoula, MT: Scholars, 1975.

_____ and Andersen, F. I. *Hosea.* AB; Garden City, NY: Doubleday, 1980.

Frei, H. W. *The Eclipse of Biblical Narrative: A Study in Eighteenth and Nineteenth Century Hermeneutics.* New Haven: Yale University, 1974.

Friedman, R. E. "Deception for Deception" *Bible Review* 2 (Spring, 1986) 22-31, 68.

Friedrich, J. and Röllig, W. *Phönizisch-punische Grammatik.* 2nd ed.; AnOr 46; Rome: Pontifical Biblical Institute, 1970.

Gadamer, H.-G. *Truth and Method,* trans. G. Barden and J. Cumming. New York: Sheed and Ward, 1975.

Gammie, J. G. "Theological Interpretation By Way of Literary and Tradition Analysis: Genesis 25-36," in *Encounter with the Text: Form and History in the Hebrew Bible,* ed. M. J. Buss. Philadelphia: Fortress, 1979, 117-134.

Garelli, P., ed. *Gilgameš et sa légende.* Paris: Klincksieck, 1960.

Gaster, T. H. *Thespis: Ritual, Myth and Drama in the Ancient Near East.* New York: Schuman, 1950.

_____ *Myth, Legend, and Custom in the Old Testament.* New York: Harper & Row, 1969.

Gay, P. *The Enlightenment: An Interpretation.* The Rise of Modern Paganism. New York: Norton, 1977.

van Gennep, A. *The Rites of Passage,* trans. M. B. Vizedom and G. L. Caffee. Chicago: University of Chicago, 1960.

Gibert, P. *Une théorie de la légende: Hermann Gunkel et les légendes de la Bible.* Paris: Flammarion, 1979.

Gibson, J. C. L. "Myth, Legend and Folk-lore in the Ugaritic Keret and Aqhat Texts" VTSup 28 (1975) 60-68.

_____ *Canaanite Myths and Legends.* Edinburgh: Clark, 1978.

Ginsberg, H. L. "The North-Canaanite Myth of Anat and Aqhat" *BASOR* 97 (1945) 3-10.

Giveon, R. *Les bédouins shosou des documents égyptiens.* Leiden: Brill, 1971.

_____ "Yaʿqob-har" *Göttingen Miszellen* 44 (1981) 17-20.

Goetze, A. *Kleinasien.* Munich: Beck, 1957.

Good, E. M. "Two Notes on Aqhat" *JBL* 77 (1958) 72-74.

_____ "Hosea and the Jacob Tradition" *VT* 16 (1966) 137-151.

Gordon, C. H. *The Common Background of Greek and Hebrew Civilizations.* New York: Harper and Row, 1965. Originally published as *Before the Bible,* 1962.

Gottwald, N. K. *The Tribes of Yahweh: A Sociology of the Religion of Liberated Israel, 1250-1050 B.C.E.* Maryknoll, NY: Orbis, 1979.

Graesser, C. F. "Studies in Maṣṣēbôt." Dissertation, Harvard University, 1969.

_____ "Standing Stones in Ancient Palestine" *BA* 35 (1972) 34-63.

Gray, J. *The KRT Text in the Literature of Ras Shamra: A Social Myth of Ancient Canaan.* Leiden: Brill, 1964.

_____ *The Legacy of Canaan.* VTSup 5; Leiden: Brill, 1965.

Greenberg, M. *The Ḫab/piru.* AOS 39; New Haven: American Oriental Society, 1955.

_____ "Another Look at Rachel's Theft of the Teraphim" *JBL* 81 (1962) 239-248.

Greenfield, J. C. "Some Glosses on the Keret Epic" *ErIsr* 9 (1969) 60-65.

_____ "Un rite religieux araméen et ses parallèles" *RB* 80 (1973) 46-52.

Greimas, A. J. *Sémantique structurale.* Paris: Larousse, 1966. ET: *Structural Semantics,* trans. D. McDowell, et al. Lincoln: University of Nebraska, 1983.

Gressmann, H. "Sage und Geschichte in den Patriarchenerzählungen" *ZAW* 30 (1910) 1-34.

Griffiths, J. G. *The Conflict of Horus and Seth from Egyptian and Classical Sources.* Liverpool: Liverpool University, 1960.

Gunkel, H. *Genesis übersetzt und erklärt.* HKAT; Göttingen: Vandenhoeck & Ruprecht, 1901; 3rd ed. 1910. ET of introduction: *The Legends of Genesis,* trans. W. H. Carruth. New York: Schocken, 1964.

_____ "Die Grundprobleme der israelitischen Literaturgeschichte," in *Reden und Aufsätze.* Göttingen: Vandenhoeck & Ruprecht, 1913, 29-38. ET: "Fundamental Problems of Hebrew Literary History," in *What Remains of the Old Testament and Other Essays,* trans. A. K. Dallas. London: Allen & Unwin, 1928.

_____ "Ziele und Methoden der Erklärung des Alten Testamentes," in *Reden und Aufsätze,* 11-29.

_____ "Jakob" *Preussische Jahrbücher* 176 (1919) 339-362. ET: "Jacob," in *What Remains of the Old Testament,* 151-186.

Gurney, O. R. "The Sultantepe Tablets. VII: The Myth of Nergal and Ereshkigal" *Anatolian Studies* 10 (1960) 105-131.

Guthrie, W. K. C. *A History of Greek Philosophy. Vol. I: The Earlier Presocratics and the Pythagoreans.* Cambridge: Cambridge University, 1962.

Habel, N. "The Form and Significance of the Call Narratives" *ZAW* 77 (1965) 297-323.

von Hahn, J. G. *Sagwissenschaftliche Studien.* Jena, 1876.

Hallpike, C. R. "Social Hair" *Man* 4 (1969) 256-264, reprinted in *Reader in Comparative Religion: An Anthropological Approach,* eds. W. A. Lessa and E. Z. Vogt. 4th ed.; New York: Harper & Row, 1979, 99-105.

Harrison, J. *Prolegomena to the Study of Greek Religion.* Cambridge: Cambridge University, 1903.

_____ *Themis: A Study of the Social Origins of Greek Religion.* Cambridge: Cambridge University, 1912.

Helck, W. "Die Mythologie der alten Ägypter," in *Wörterbuch der Mythologie,* Vol. I, ed. H. W. Haussig. Stuttgart: Klett, 1965.

_____ "Ṭkw und die Ramses-Stadt" *VT* 15 (1965)

Herder, J. G. *Vom Geist der ebräischen Poesie.* Leipzig: Barth, 1825. ET: *The Spirit of Hebrew Poetry*, trans. J. March. Burlington: Smith, 1833.

_____ *Sämmtliche Werke*, ed. B. Suphan. Berlin: Weidmann, 1877-1913.

Herdner, A. *Corpus des tablettes en cunéiformes alphabétiques.* 2 vols. Paris: Geuthner, 1963.

Hillers, D. R. "The Bow of Aqhat: The Meaning of a Mythological Theme," in *Orient and Occident. Essays Presented to C. H. Gordon*, ed. H. A. Hoffner, Jr. AOAT 22; Neukirchen-Vluyn: Neukirchener, 1973, 71-80.

_____ and McCall, M. H., Jr. "Homeric Dictated Texts: A Reexamination of Some Near Eastern Evidence" *Harvard Studies in Classical Philology* 80 (1976) 19-23.

Hirsch, E. D., Jr. *The Aims of Interpretation.* Chicago: University of Chicago, 1976.

Hoffner, H. A., Jr. "Ugaritic pwt: A Term from the Early Canaanite Dyeing Industry" *JAOS* 87 (1967) 300-303.

_____ "בַּיִת" *TDOT* Vol. II, 107-116.

Hooke, S. H., ed. *Myth and Ritual.* Oxford: Clarendon, 1933.

_____, ed. *Myth, Ritual and Kingship.* Oxford: Clarendon, 1958.

Hornung, E. "Seth. Geschichte und Bedeutung eines ägyptischen Gottes" *Symbolon* 2 (1975) 49-63.

Huehnergard, J. "Biblical Notes on Some New Akkadian Texts from Emar (Syria)" *CBQ* 47 (1985) 428-434.

Irvin, D. "The Joseph and Moses Stories as Narrative in the Light of Ancient Near Eastern Narrative," in *Israelite and Judaean History*, ed. J. H. Hayes and J. M. Miller. Philadelphia: Westminster, 1977, 167-209.

_____ *Mytharion: The Comparison of Tales from the Old Testament and the Ancient Near East.* AOAT 32; Neukirchen-Vluyn: Neukirchener, 1978.

Jacobsen, T. *The Treasures of Darkness: A History of Mesopotamian Religion.* New Haven: Yale University, 1976.

Jaroš, K. *Die Stellung des Elohisten zur kanaanäischen Religion.* OBO 4; Göttingen: Vandenhoeck & Ruprecht, 1982.

Katzenstein, H. J. *The History of Tyre.* Jerusalem: Schocken Institute, 1973.

Kempinski, A. *Syrien und Palastina (Kanaan) in der letzten Phase der Mittelbronze IIB-Zeit (1650-1570 v. Chr.).* Wiesbaden: Harrassowitz, 1983.

Kirk, G. S. *Myth: Its Meaning and Functions in Ancient and Other Cultures.* Berkeley: University of California, 1970.

_____ and Raven, J. E. *The Presocratic Philosophers.* Cambridge: Cambridge University, 1957.

Kitchen, K. A. "The King List of Ugarit" *UF* 9 (1977) 131-142.

Klatt, W. *Hermann Gunkel, zu seiner Theologie der Religionsgeschichte und zur Entstehung der formgeschichtlichen Methode.* Göttingen: Vandenhoeck & Ruprecht, 1969.

Knight, D. A. *Rediscovering the Traditions of Israel.* Missoula, MT: Scholars, 1975.

_____ "The Pentateuch," in *The Hebrew Bible and Its Modern Interpreters,* eds. D. A. Knight and G. M. Tucker. Chico, CA: Scholars, 1985, 263-296.

Koehler, L. and Baumgartner, W. *Hebräisches und aramäisches Lexikon zum Alten Testament.* Leiden: Brill, 1951-53.

Kosmala, H. "The 'Bloody Husband'" *VT* 12 (1962) 14-28.

Kraus, H.-J. *Geschichte der historisch-kritischen Erforschung des Alten Testaments.* 3rd ed.; Neukirchen-Vluyn: Neukirchener, 1982.

Kroeber, K., ed. *Traditional Literatures of the American Indian.* Lincoln: University of Nebraska, 1981.

Kugel, J. "On the Bible and Literary Criticism" *Prooftexts* 1 (1981) 217-236.

Kutsch, E. "חתן" *TDOT* Vol. V, 270-277.

Lambert, W. G. "Gilgameš in Religious, Historical and Omen Texts and the Historicity of Gilgameš," in *Gilgameš et sa légende,* ed. P. Garelli. Paris: Klincksieck, 1960, 39-52.

Levine, B. A. and de Tarragon, J.-M. "Dead Kings and Rephaim: The Patrons of the Ugaritic Dynasty" *JAOS* 104 (1984) 649-659.

Lévi-Strauss, C. *Structural Anthropology,* trans. C. Jacobson and B. G. Schoepf. New York: Basic, 1963.

_____ *Totemism,* trans. R. Needham. Boston: Beacon, 1963.

_____ *The Savage Mind.* Chicago: University of Chicago, 1966.

_____ *The Raw and the Cooked,* trans. J. and D. Weightman. New York: Harper and Row, 1975.

Lewis, B. *The Sargon Legend.* Cambridge, MA: ASOR, 1980.

L'Heureux, C. E. *Rank Among the Canaanite Gods: El, Baʿal, and the Rephaʾim.* HSM 21; Missoula, MT: Scholars, 1979.

Lichtheim, M. *Ancient Egyptian Literature. Volume II: The New Kingdom.* Berkeley: University of California, 1976.

Liddell, H. G., Scott, R., and Jones, H. S. *A Greek-English Lexicon.* Oxford: Clarendon, 1968.

Lipinski, E. "Ditanu," in *Studies in Bible and the Ancient Near East Presented to S. E. Loewenstamm,* eds. Y. Avishur and J. Blau. Jerusalem: Rubinstein, 1978, 91-110.

Loewenstamm, S. E. "The Seven-Day Unit in Ugaritic Literature" *IEJ* 15 (1965) 121-133.

Lord, A. B. *The Singer of Tales.* Cambridge, MA: Harvard University, 1960.

_____ "Tradition and the Oral Poet: Homer, Huso and Avdo Medjedović," in *La poesia epica é la sua formazione.* Rome: Accademia Nazionale dei Lincei, 1970, 13-30.

_____ "Perspectives on Recent Work on Oral Literature" *Forum for Modern Language Studies* 10 (1974) 187-210.

_____ "The Gospels as Oral Traditional Literature," in *The Relationships Among the Gospels: An Interdisciplinary Dialogue,* ed. W. O. Walker, Jr. San Antonio: Trinity University, 1978, 33-91.

Loretz, O. *Habiru-Hebräer.* BZAW 160; Berlin: de Gruyter, 1984.

Margalit, B. "Interpreting the Story of Aqhat" *VT* 30 (1980) 361-365.

Mazar, B. "Yahweh Came Out from Sinai," in *Temples and High Places in Biblical Times,* ed. A. Biran. Jerusalem: Hebrew Union College, 1981, 5-9.

McCarter, P. K., Jr. *I Samuel.* AB; Garden City, NY: Doubleday, 1980.

McCarthy, D. J. *Treaty and Covenant.* 2nd ed.; AnBib 21A; Rome: Pontifical Biblical Institute, 1978.

McKane, W. *Studies in the Patriarchal Narratives.* Edinburgh: Handsel, 1979.

McKenzie, S. "The Jacob Tradition in Hosea XII 4-5" *VT* 36 (1986) 311-322.

Millard, A. R. "The Celestial Ladder and the Gate of Heaven (Gen 28.12,17)" *ExpTim* 78 (1966) 86-87.

_____ and Wiseman, D. J., eds. *Essays on the Patriarchal Narratives.* Leicester: Inter-Varsity, 1980.

Miller, P. D., Jr. "Animal Names as Designations in Ugaritic and Hebrew" *UF* 2 (1971) 177-186.

Mitchell, T. C. "The Meaning of the Noun ḤTN in the Old Testament" *VT* 19 (1969) 93-112.

de Moor, J. C. *The Seasonal Pattern in the Ugaritic Myth of Baʿlu.* AOAT 16; Kevelaer: Butzon & Bercker, 1971.

Morrison, M. A. "The Jacob and Laban Narrative in Light of Near Eastern Sources" *BA* 46 (1983) 155-164.

Moscati, S., et al. *An Introduction to the Comparative Grammar of the Semitic Languages.* Wiesbaden: Harrassowitz, 1969.

Mullen, E. T., Jr. *The Divine Council in Canaanite and Early Hebrew Literature.* HSM 24; Chico, CA: Scholars, 1980.

Murray, G. *Four Stages of Greek Religion.* New York: Columbia University, 1912.

Nagy, G. *The Best of the Achaeans: Concepts of the Hero in Archaic Greek Poetry.* Baltimore: Johns Hopkins University, 1979.

Nilsson, M. P. *The Mycenaean Origin of Greek Mythology.* Berkeley: University of California, 1932.

North, R. "Ugarit Grid, Strata, and Find-Localizations" *ZDPV* 89 (1973) 113-160.

Noth, M. *Überlieferungsgeschichte des Pentateuch.* Stuttgart: Kohlhammer, 1948. ET: *A History of Pentateuchal Traditions*, trans. B. W. Anderson. Englewood Cliffs, NJ: Prentice-Hall, 1972.

_____ "Noah, Daniel und Hiob in Ezekiel XIV" *VT* 1 (1951) 251-260.

Obermann, J. *How Daniel was Blessed with a Son: An Incubation Scene in Ugaritic.* New Haven: American Oriental Society, 1946.

Oden, R. A., Jr. "Jacob as Father, Husband, and Nephew: Kinship Studies and the Patriarchal Narratives" *JBL* 102 (1983) 189-205.

_____ and Attridge, H. W. *Philo of Byblos: The Phoenician History. Introduction, Critical Text, Translation, Notes.* CBQMS 9; Washington DC: Catholic Biblical Association, 1981.

Oinas, F. J., ed. *Heroic Epic and Saga.* Bloomington: Indiana University, 1978.

del Olmo Lete, G. *Mitos y leyendas de Canaan.* Madrid: Cristiandad, 1981.

Oppenheim, A. L. *Ancient Mesopotamia: Portrait of a Dead Civilization.* Chicago: University of Chicago, 1964.

Pardee, D. and Bordreuil, P. "Le rituel funéraire ougaritique RS 34.126" *Syria* 59 (1982) 121-128.

Parker, S. B. "The Historical Composition of KRT and the Cult of El" *ZAW* 89 (1977) 161-175.

_____ "The Vow in Ugaritic and Israelite Narrative Literature" *UF* 11 (1979)

_____ "Toward an Interpretation of AQHT." Delivered at the Annual Meeting of the Society of Biblical Literature, 1980.

_____ and Ferrara, A. J. "Seating Arrangements at Divine Banquets" *UF* 4 (1972) 37-39.

Parry, A., ed. *The Making of Homeric Verse. The Collected Papers of Milman Parry.* Oxford: Clarendon, 1971.

Pelton, R. D. *The Trickster in West Africa.* Berkeley: University of California, 1980.

Perlitt, L. *Vatke und Wellhausen.* BZAW 94; Berlin: Töpelmann, 1965.

Pitard, W. T. "The Ugaritic Funerary Text RS 34.126" *BASOR* 232 (1978) 65-75.

_____ "RS 34.126: Notes on the Text" (forthcoming).

Pitt-Rivers, J. *The Fate of Shechem or The Politics of Sex: Essays in the Anthropology of the Mediterranean.* Cambridge: Cambridge University, 1977.

Polzin, R. "Martin Noth's A History of Pentateuchal Traditions" *BASOR* 221 (1976) 113-120.

Pope, M. H. *Job*. AB; Garden City, NY: Doubleday, 1973.

_____ *Song of Songs*. AB; Garden City, NY: Doubleday, 1977.

_____ "Notes on the Rephaim Texts from Ugarit," in *Essays on the Ancient Near East in Memory of Jacob Joel Finkelstein*. Memoirs of the Connecticut Academy of Arts & Sciences 19; Hamden, CT: Archon, 1977, 163-182.

_____ "The Cult of the Dead at Ugarit," in *Ugarit in Retrospect*, ed. G. D. Young. Winona Lake, IN: Eisenbrauns, 1981, 159-179.

_____ and Röllig, W. "Die Mythologie der Ugariter und Phönizier," in *Wörterbuch der Mythologie*, vol. I, ed. H. W. Haussig. Stuttgart: Klett, 1965.

Pritchard, J. B., ed. *Ancient Near Eastern Texts Related to the Old Testament*. 3rd ed.; Princeton: Princeton University, 1969.

_____ *The Ancient Near East in Pictures*. 2nd ed.; Princeton: Princeton University, 1974.

Propp, V. *Morphology of the Folktale*, trans. L. Scott. 2nd ed.; Austin: University of Texas, 1968 [1928].

de Pury, A. *Promesse divine et légende cultuelle dans le cycle de Jacob. Genèse 28 et les traditions patriarcales*, 2 vols. Paris: Gabalda, 1975.

von Rad, G. *Genesis: A Commentary*, trans. J. H. Marks. Rev. ed.; OTL; Philadelphia: Westminster, 1972.

Raglan, F. R. S. "The Hero of Tradition," in *The Study of Folklore*, ed. A. Dundes. Englewood Cliffs, NJ: Prentice-Hall, 1965 [1934], 144-157.

_____ *The Hero: A Study in Tradition, Myth, and Drama*. London: Watts, 1936.

Radin, P. *The Trickster: A Study in American Indian Mythology*. New York: Schocken, 1972 [1956].

Rainey, A. F. "Toponymic Problems" *Tel Aviv* 9 (1982) 130-136.

Rank, O. *The Myth of the Birth of the Hero*, trans. F. Robbins and S. E. Jelliffe. New York: Knopf, 1959 [1909].

Redford, D. B. "The Literary Motif of the Exposed Child" *Numen* 14 (1967) 209-228.

Riemann, P. A. "Desert and Return to Desert in the Pre-exilic Prophets." Dissertation, Harvard University, 1964.

Robertson, D. A. *Linguistic Evidence in Dating Early Hebrew Poetry*. Missoula, MT: Scholars, 1972.

Rogerson, J. W. *Myth in Old Testament Interpretation*. BZAW 134; Berlin: de Gruyter, 1974.

_____ *Anthropology and the Old Testament*. Oxford: Blackwell, 1978.

_____ *Old Testament Criticism in the Nineteenth Century: England and Germany*. Philadelphia: Fortress, 1985.

Saley, R. J. and Cross, F. M. "Phoenician Incantations on a Plaque of the Seventh Century B.C. from Arslan Tash in Upper Syria" *BASOR* 197 (1970) 42-49.

Sarna, N. M. "The Anticipatory Use of Information as a Literary Feature of the Genesis Narratives," in *The Creation of Sacred Literature*, ed. R. E. Friedman. Berkeley: University of California, 1981, 76-82.

Schaeffer, C. F. A. *The Cuneiform Texts of Ras Shamra-Ugarit*. London: Oxford University, 1939.

Selman, M. J. "Comparative Customs and the Patriarchal Age," in *Essays on the Patriarchal Narratives*, eds. A. R. Millard and D. J. Wiseman. Leicester: Inter-Varsity, 1980.

Simpson, W. K., ed. *The Literature of Ancient Egypt*. New Haven: Yale University, 1973.

Skinner, J. *A Critical and Exegetical Commentary on Genesis*. 2nd ed.; ICC; Edinburgh: Clark, 1930.

Smith, W. R. *Lectures on the Religion of the Semites*. London: Black, 1889.

von Soden, W. "Beiträge zum Verständnis des babylonischen Gilgameš-Epos" *ZA* 53 (1959) 209-235.

_____ *Akkadisches Handwörterbuch*. 3 volumes. Wiesbaden: Harrassowitz, 1965-1981.

Speiser, E. A. *Genesis*. AB; Garden City, NY: Doubleday, 1964.

Sperber, D. "Is Symbolic Thought Prerational?" in *Between Belief and Transgression: Structuralist Essays in Religion, History, and Myth*, eds. M. Izard and P. Smith, trans. J. Leavitt. Chicago: University of Chicago, 1982, 245-264.

Spiegel, S. "Noah, Daniel, and Job," in *Louis Ginzberg Jubilee Volume*. New York: American Academy for Jewish Research, 1945, 305-355.

Sternberg, M. *The Poetics of Biblical Narrative: Ideological Literature and the Drama of Reading*. Bloomington: Indian University, 1985.

Talmon, S. "The 'Desert Motif' in the Bible and in Qumran Literature," in *Biblical Motifs: Origins and Transformations*, ed. A. Altmann. Cambridge, MA: Harvard University, 1966, 31-63.

_____ "Did There Exist a Biblical National Epic?" in *Proceedings of the Seventh World Congress of Jewish Studies. Studies in the Bible and the Ancient Near East*. Jerusalem: Magnes, 1981, 41-61.

de Tarragon, J.-M. and Levine, B. A. "Dead Kings and Rephaim: The Patrons of the Ugaritic Dynasty" *JAOS* 104 (1984) 649-659.

Taylor, A. "The Biographical Pattern in Traditional Narrative" *Journal of the Folklore Institute* 1 (1964) 114-129.

Teixidor, J. "Les tablettes d'Arslan Tash au Musée d'Alep" *Aula Orientalis* 1 (1983) 105-108.

Thompson, R. C. *The Epic of Gilgamesh: Text, Transliteration, and Notes*. Oxford: Clarendon, 1930.

Thompson, S. "Myths and Folktales," in *Myth: A Symposium*, ed. T. A. Sebeok. Bloomington: Indiana University, 1958, 169-180.

Thompson, T. L. *The Historicity of the Patriarchal Narratives: The Quest for the Historical Abraham*. New York: de Gruyter, 1974.

Tigay, J. H. *The Evolution of the Gilgamesh Epic*. Philadelphia: University of Pennsylvania, 1982.

van Trigt, F. "La signification de la lutte de Jacob près du Yabboq," in *Studies on the Book of Genesis*, eds. B. Gemser et al. OTS 12; Leiden: Brill, 1958, 280-309.

Turner, V. "Betwixt and Between: The Liminal Period in *Rites de Passage*," in *The Forest of Symbols: Aspects of Ndembu Ritual*. Ithaca: Cornell University, 1967, 93-111.

Van Seters, J. *Abraham in History and Tradition*. New Haven: Yale University, 1975.

_____ "Joshua 24 and the Problem of Tradition in the Old Testament," in *In the Shadow of Elyon*, eds. W. B. Barrick and J. R. Spencer. Sheffield: JSOTSup 31, 1984, 139-158.

de Vaux, R. *Ancient Israel*. New York: McGraw-Hill, 1961.

_____ *The Early History of Israel*, trans. D. Smith. Philadelphia: Westminster, 1977.

te Velde, H. *Seth, God of Confusion*. Leiden: Brill, 1967.

_____ "The Egyptian God Seth as a Trickster" *Journal of the American Research Center in Egypt* 7 (1968) 37-40.

Vorlander, H. *Mein Gott: Die Vorstellungen vom persönlichen Gott im Alten Orient und im Alten Testament*. AOAT 23; Neukirchener-Vluyn: Neukirchener, 1975.

Wagner, S. "דָּרַשׁ" *TDOT* Vol. III, 293-307.

Wallace, H. N. *The Eden Narrative*. HSM 32; Atlanta: Scholars, 1985.

Wallace, R. A. *Animal Behavior: Its Development, Ecology, and Evolution*. Santa Monica: Goodyear, 1979.

Warner, S. M. "Primitive Saga Men" *VT* 29 (1979) 325-335.

Weber, M. *Ancient Judaism*, trans. H. H. Gerth and D. Martindale. New York: Macmillan, 1952.

Weidmann, H. *Die Patriarchen und ihre Religion im Licht der Forschung seit Julius Wellhausen*. Göttingen: Vandenhoeck & Ruprecht, 1968.

Weippert, M. *The Settlement of the Israelite Tribes in Palestine*, trans. J. D. Martin. London: SCM, 1971.

_____ "Abraham der Hebräer? Bemerkungen zu W. F. Albrights Deutung der Vater Israels" *Bib* 52 (1971) 407-432.

Wellhausen, J. *Prolegomena zur Geschichte Israels*. Berlin: Reimer, 1883. ET: *Prolegomena to the History of Ancient Israel*, trans. J. S. Black and A. Menzies. Edinburgh: Black, 1885.

_____ *Israelitische und Jüdische Geschichte.* 5th ed.; Berlin: Reimer, 1904.

Westenholz, J. G. "Heroes of Akkad" *JAOS* 103 (1983) 327-336.

_____ Review of B. Lewis, *The Sargon Legend. J NES* 43 (1984) 73-79.

Westermann, C. "Die Bedeutung der ugaritischen Texte für die Vätergeschichte," in *Die Verheissungen an die Väter. Studien zur Vätergeschichte.* Göttingen: Vandenhoeck & Ruprecht, 1976, 151-168. ET: "The Significance of the Ugaritic Texts for the Patriarchal Narratives," in *The Promises to the Fathers*, trans. D. E. Green. Philadelphia: Fortress, 1980, 165-186.

_____ *Genesis 12-36.* BKAT I/2; Neukirchen-Vluyn: Neukirchener, 1981. ET: *Genesis 12-36*, trans. J. J. Scullion. Minneapolis: Augsburg, 1985.

Whitaker, R. E. "A Formulaic Analysis of Ugaritic Poetry." Dissertation, Harvard University, 1970.

_____ "Ugaritic Formulae," in *Ras Shamra Parallels*, Vol. III, 207-219.

Wilcoxen, J. A. "Narrative," in *Old Testament Form Criticism*, ed. J. H. Hayes. San Antonio: Trinity University, 1974, 57-98.

Willi, T. *Herders Beitrag zum Verstehen des Alten Testaments.* Tübingen: Mohr, 1971.

Williams, J. "The Beautiful and the Barren: Conventions in Biblical Type-Scenes" *JSOT* 17 (1980) 107-119.

Wilson, R. R. *Genealogy and History in the Biblical World.* New Haven: Yale University, 1977.

Xella, P. "Una 'rilettura' del poema di Aqhat," in *Problemi del mito nel vicino oriente antico.* Naples: Istituto Orientale di Napoli, 1976, 61-91.

_____ *I testi rituali di Ugarit.* Rome: Consiglio Nazionale delle Ricerche, 1981.

Yoder, P. B. "A-B Pairs and Oral Composition in Hebrew Poetry" *VT* 21 (1971) 470-489.

Zimmerli, W. *Ezekiel 1*, trans. R. E. Clements. Hermeneia; Philadelphia: Fortress, 1979.

Index of Citations

Hebrew

Index of Authors

Abusch, T., 74n, 80n
Ackerman, J. S., 157n
Ackroyd, P., 103n
Aharoni, Y., 64n
Alain, 101
Albertz, R., 58n
Albright, W. F., 19-23, 24, 30n, 46n, 63n, 126n, 164n
Alt, A., 14, 15
Alter, R., 29n, 36n, 40n, 42n, 87, 112n, 152n, 153
Amiet, P., 105n
Andersen, F. I., 103n, 147n
Anderson, B. W., 13n
Astour, M. C., 74n, 114n
Attridge, H. A., 85n, 125n, 126n
Auerbach, E., 39

Bailey, J. A., 120n
Barnett, R. D., 85n
Barthes, R., 105n
Bartlett, J. T. S., 114n
Baumgarten, A. I., 125n, 126n, 127n
Ben-Amos, D., 7n, 151n
Berlin, I., 2n, 3n
Biebuyck, D. P., 27n
Bland, K. P., 97n
Bordreuil, P., 78n, 79n
Bottéro, J., 22n
Bremond, C., 38n
Bright, J., 24
Brinkman, J. A., 66n
Buber, M., 94n, 130n, 145n
Buccellati, G., 119n
Burkert, W., 66n, 67n, 69n, 74, 80n, 85n, 86n, 99n

Campbell, J., 133, 134
Caquot, A., 46n, 48n, 50n, 58n, 77n, 78n, 79n, 90n, 92n, 104n, 105n
Cassuto, U., 104n, 153n
Cauvin, J., 80n
Cazelles, H., 22n, 25n
Cheyne, T. K., 126n
Childs, B. S., 4n, 142n, 145-146, 151n, 159n
Clark, R. T., 2n
Clements, R. E., 5n
Clifford, R. J., 46n, 47, 62n, 64n
Coats, G. E., 5n
Cohen, C., 142n, 143n
Conroy, C., 31n
Coote, R., 103n
Cornford, F. M., 69n
Courtois, J.-C., 47n
Craigie, P. C., 164n
Cross, F. M., 14n, 23, 24, 28-31, 35, 36n, 44n, 46n, 47n, 50n, 58, 64n, 70n, 104n, 114n, 162n, 164n, 165n
Culley, R. C., 13n, 26n, 28n, 29n, 35, 36n, 152n

Day, J., 104n
Dever, W. G., 21n, 22n
Diedrich, F., 103n
Dietrich, M., 80n
Dorson, R. M., 31n
Dossin, G., 117n
Douglas, M., 4n, 118n
Dundes, A., 133n
Draffkorn, A. E., 96n
Dressler, H. H. P., 73n, 91n

191